Macromedia Flash MX *Express*

Leon Cych
Glen Rhodes
Benjamin J. Mace

Macromedia Flash MX *Express*

© 2002 friends of ED

First Printed June 2002

Trademark Acknowledgements

friends of ED has endeavored to provide trademark information about all the companies and products mentioned in this book by the appropriate use of capitals. However, friends of ED cannot guarantee the accuracy of this information.

Published by friends of ED

30 - 32 Lincoln Road, Olton, Birmingham.
B27 6PA. UK.
Printed in USA

ISBN 1-903450-95-0

Macromedia Flash MX *Express*

Credits

Authors
Leon Cych
Benjamin J. Mace
Glen Rhodes

Consultant
Josh Levine

Reviewers
Adam Dutton
Victoria Idiens

Proofers
Jon Bounds
Victoria Idiens
Simon Collins
Philip Jackson
Fiona Murray

Managing Editor
Ben Huczek

Illustrations
Pete Aylward
Chris Matterface

Commissioning Editor
Andy Corsham

Editors
Dan Britton
Andy Corsham
Steve Rycroft

Author Agent
Gaynor Riopedre

Project Manager
Victoria Idiens

Layout
Ty Bhogal
Rob Sharp

Index
Simon Collins

Design
Matt Clark

Cover Design
Katy Freer

Thanks to Rod Cleasby and RCAD Multimedia for the Apollo images. –
www.bizlink-uk.com/rod

10 Essential ActionScript   203

11 Working with Bitmaps   229

12 Using Sound in Flash   255

13 Publishing Flash Movies   275

14 The Next Steps   305

エクスプレス

Chapter 1
gotoAndPlay...

Why Flash?

Web site front-ends, interactive games, animated cartoons, movie trailers, PDA interfaces, business presentations, Intranets...

This sounds like a list of applications a web designer might consider an essential part of their skill set — a group of topics requiring various design, animation and development packages. While it's true that you can build all these things using multiple software packages, they can actually all be built with just one tool: **Macromedia Flash MX**.

Flash is *the* leading software for producing dynamic web pages. Originally seen as just an animation tool, it's established a position as the principal motion graphics platform, and evolved into a package that can create entire *applications*. Video, sound, and interactivity are now core aspects of the Flash MX make-up, along with the ever-popular animation features.

In the past, a web site was seen as a luxury — a neat bonus to print on your business card, but not essential for running a successful business. Those days are now long gone; today, a corporate web site is a necessity, and consequently the need for an eye-catching, informative, dynamic web site is at a premium. HTML alone cannot provide such a site, but Flash most certainly can!

Flash in action

Before we delve into using Flash and describing its main components, let's check out a few finished designs that are out there in action on the web. First, as a really practical example, take a look at the reservation page for the Broadmoor Hotel (`reservations.broadmoor.com`) to see how a Flash front-end can be used to create a single-screen booking application. You no longer need to click through numerous pages and forms to complete one transaction — Flash can do it all on one page:

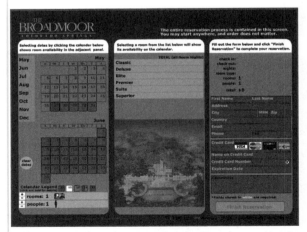

All-in-one registration page for the Broadmoor Hotel, designed with Flash

Another major use of Flash is for creating cartoons and short movies. For example, *I Want My Flash TV* (www.iwantmyflashtv.com) is a community site dedicated to the support and development of Flash-generated films and animations. Check out some of the cartoons there:

You'll find amazing Flash animations all over the web

Finally, Flash is also a popular tool for producing art and carrying out creative experiments. For instance, check out the Flash Math Creativity pages at the friends of ED site (www.friendsofed.com/fmc/). Here, you'll find a whole new universe of Flash designs and interactive experiments.

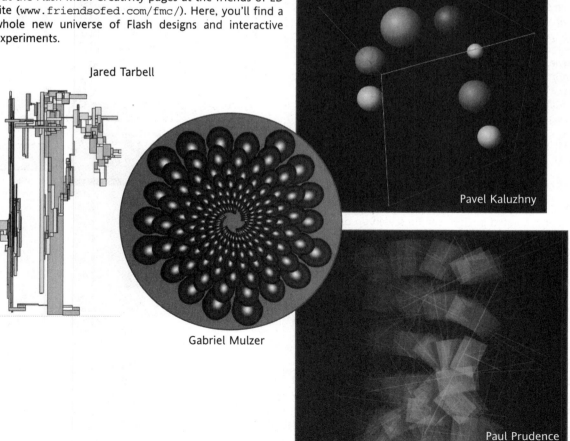

Jared Tarbell

Gabriel Mulzer

Pavel Kaluzhny

Paul Prudence

Inside Flash

Before we get into the meat of the book, let's just sketch out a few vital concepts that you just *have* to know now.

Timeline

Flash started out as an animation package, so clearly it must have some internal concept of time. The timeline consists of a series of frames, just as a traditional cartoon consists of individual frames or cells that are placed one after the other in sequence. In Flash, you can click on a frame in the timeline and see what content exists at that point in the movie. Because the timeline is fundamental to working with Flash, we'll be using it throughout this book. We'll also examine it in detail in **Chapter 5**.

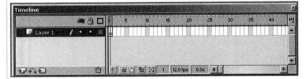

The Flash timeline

File formats

There are two main elements to Flash: the **authoring environment** and the **Flash Player**. The authoring environment is where you actually create your movies, and you save your work in progress in the **FLA file format**. When you've finished creating your Flash movie, you *publish* it – this compresses the content and exports it in a second format: the **SWF file format**. It's the SWF file that you place on the Internet, and which is read by the Flash Player plugin that sits on the viewer's machine:

We'll be looking at these different file types in more detail in the next chapter.

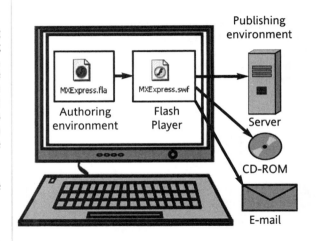

Resolution-independent quality

Flash is a **vector-based** program, which means that elements created in Flash can be scaled up or down to any size in the Flash Player with **no loss of quality**. As a designer, you'll probably have come across the various bitmap image formats (BMP, GIF, JPEG, etc.); bitmaps are the antithesis of vector graphics. In **Chapter 2** you'll try scaling a bitmap and immediately see why vector graphics are so beneficial. We'll also take a deeper look at importing and using bitmaps with our Flash designs in **Chapter 11.**

ActionScript

Flash has its own programming language called **ActionScript**. Code strikes fear into the hearts of many designers, but ActionScript can be remarkably simple. It's perfectly possible to create a Flash movie without *any* scripting, but to create a truly rich interactive site, some basic knowledge of ActionScript is necessary – this book will teach you what you need to know to start 'scripting'. In fact, ActionScript is full of highly intuitive tags – you can probably guess what a `stop()` action does, for example. The **Actions panel** in Flash allows you to simply click on an action in a selection list, and Flash will create the correctly formatted ActionScript code for you:

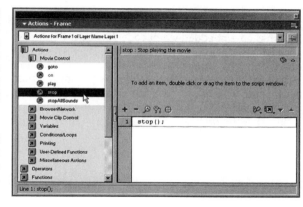

We'll cover plenty of ActionScript techniques in passing as we progress through this book, and we'll fully explain those specific uses in the detail that's needed to understand them in context. We'll also deal with ActionScript more systematically in **Chapters 10** and **14**.

Context-sensitive Property inspector

Each bit of content that's included in a Flash movie has its own set of properties, such as color, size, position, type, and so on. In the authoring environment, the Flash MX **Property inspector** gives you a single place where you can edit all the main properties:

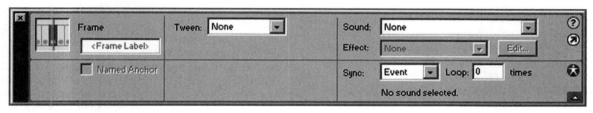

The Property inspector

Whenever you select a movie content element in the FLA, whether it's an object like a drawn rectangle, a frame on the timeline, or whatever, the Property inspector changes to show you the properties associated with the selection. This is probably the most important tool in Flash, so get to know it, and use it wisely! (We'll be seeing the Property inspector frequently throughout this book, and using it plenty.)

Dynamic links

Like HTML documents, Flash can link to external image and sound files in our movies without having to import them into Flash MX at the FLA stage. Linking to external JPEG and MP3 files dynamically cuts down the SWF file size dramatically in comparison with embedding these files in the FLA. Reading the relevant sections in **Chapter 14** will make all of this become clear.

Video

Flash has an embedded video coder/decoder (known as a 'codec') that resides within the Flash player. There's no need for any other plug-in such as QuickTime (although, of course, QuickTime does bring other advantages with it). In addition to supporting video pictures, Flash MX can even synchronize any audio track included in the original video source.

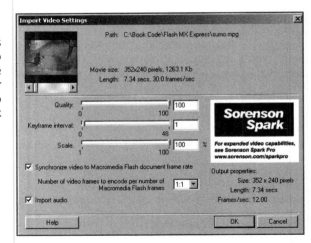

How to use this book

The aim of this book is to teach you core Flash MX knowledge in a concise, visually-oriented fashion. To get you up and running with Flash MX as quickly as possible, this book is rich in images and practical examples, and it's designed for the reader who prefers to learn by example and play rather than by following a fixed tutorial route: it'll give you a fast – but thorough and structured – introduction. The content is completely modular, so you can read it in any order you like – if you're itching to get your hands dirty and start creating animations in Flash, head for **Chapter 6**; if you want to jump right in at the deep end and figure out what ActionScript is all about, open up **Chapter 10.** Use the Table of Contents and the Index, and come back to specific modules for reference purposes later.

In order to achieve this modular nature, we've used a three-pronged attack: **What**, **How**, and **When**. These headings are designed to help you zoom in on what you need to know about a specific Flash MX feature, be it a Flash tool, a design technique, or a key piece of ActionScript.

 The **What** sections describe the content and purpose of each feature.

 The **How** sections explain how to use each feature, demonstrating its use through practical examples.

 The **When** sections explain when you might want to use the feature in your projects.

To use this book, all you'll need is a copy of Macromedia Flash MX and a computer to run it on. If you want to publish your Flash movies onto the Internet, you'll also need a connection and some web space to publish them to. Your Internet Service Provider (ISP) will be able to sort this out for you if you have any problems. You can, of course, send your SWFs to your friends on CD or in e-mail, too.

Layout conventions

We've tried to keep this book as clear and easy to follow as possible, so we've only used a few layout styles to avoid confusion. Here they are:

- New or important terms will be in **bold**.

- `This font` is used to emphasize `code` and `file names`.

- Menu commands are written in the form **Menu > Sub-menu > Sub-menu**.

- Keyboard shortcuts are in the following format: SHIFT+F3/⌘+F3. This means pressing down the SHIFT (PC)/⌘ (Mac) and F3 keys at the same time.

Windows and Macintosh systems

In order to make the stuff in this book as universally applicable as possible, we've included both PC and Mac commands and shortcut keys, wherever necessary, throughout this book. When demonstrating mouse actions, if we just say 'click' we mean *left-click* on the PC or simply *click* on the Mac. We've also included a mix of PC- and Mac-based screenshots, and pointed out where menus and keystrokes differ across the different platforms.

Downloads

Throughout this book you'll see practical examples on how to use the Flash MX features, and we've provided worked-through versions of the examples in the download files to help you with your learning. Although they're not critical to the use and enjoyment of this book, the download files will enhance your learning no end – we've supplied support files containing the sounds and images that we've used to allow you to recreate the worked examples exactly as they are in the book. These files, and all support material, can be found in the **Downloads** section of our web site at `www.friendsofed.com`. We'll point you to the relevant files in the chapters as necessary.

Support

This book, like all friends of ED books, is fully supported at www.friendsofed.com. In addition to the source code you'll find our support forums where you can find help, inspiration, or just chat with other members of the Flash community.

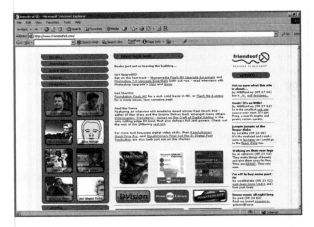

You'll find a dedicated page for this book on the site, providing you with author information, code links, errata and any other information we think you should know. The friends of ED site also has interviews with top designers, information and sample chapters from other books, and much more. This book is just the first part of the friends of ED experience.

If you run into trouble – perhaps you have a problem with a certain file or tutorial, or you've just got plain confused, we're right here for you! Leave a message on our forums, use the online feedback form, or drop a mail to our dedicated support team at support@friendsofed.com. *We'll get you back on track in no time.*

Feedback on our books, whether positive or negative, is always welcome. Mail feedback@friendsofed.com or use the reply card at the back of the book. We'd love to hear from you.

OK, that's the introduction over with – now let's dive head first into the world of Macromedia Flash MX!

Chapter 2
Flash Fundamentals

What's in this chapter:

- Working with Flash files and using the **Flash Player**:
  - O **FLA** source files
  - O **SWF** movie files

- The authoring environment:
  - O Navigating around the **stage** via scrollbars, the **Zoom** tool, and the **Hand** tool
  - O Movie properties

- The **timeline** – using **frames** and **keyframes** for simple animations

- The **bandwidth profiler**

- An Introduction to **ActionScript**

- **Shortcut Keys**

Flash files and the Flash Player

 When developing Flash movies, you'll mainly be working with two file formats. The first is the **FLA** file, which is the source file for a movie's content. This file would not usually go on the web, except for the purpose of file transfer. Only computers with the Macromedia Flash program installed can view FLA files; these are the files you work with at authoring time and then export to create the finished Flash movie that people watch on their monitor screens.

The other file format is **SWF** – the actual Flash movie file. Compiled from the FLA file, this is the file that is placed on the web for all to see (or used as a stand-alone Flash movie file).

Rest assured that every Flash movie you've ever seen on the web will have been a SWF file. Here's how the FLA and SWF files inter-relate via the authoring environment, which we'll look at more closely later in this chapter. Note that it is always the SWF file that is viewed over the Internet:

What happens inside the FLA at authoring time is like what happens in a film production company. When you open up the FLA in Flash and work on it, you can direct its cast and crew to do your bidding and create something. When you're done creating, the production phase is over, and you're ready to distribute your work of art. The SWF file is like the finished movie produced by the company – you can only stick it in your video player and watch it. You can't rework the source material in the SWF; that's all done in the FLA.

MXExpress.fla

The FLA is the
authoring file

MXExpress.swf

The SWF is the
file you publish for
people to view

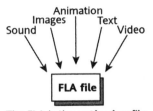

The FLA is the **authoring** file

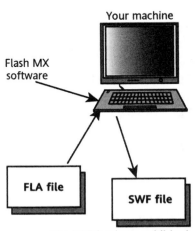

The SWF is what's published,
and viewed by the world

The Flash plug-in

SWF files are viewed on a computer with the Flash Player installed, and on the web through a web browser with the Flash Player plug-in installed. The Flash Player is a separate application included with Flash, used only for viewing Flash movie files (SWFs). If you've installed the Macromedia Flash MX application on your computer, it's likely you've already installed the necessary players and plug-ins. Otherwise they'll always be available for download at www.macromedia.com/downloads.

This is also the URL to give your friends, family, and associates if they don't have the correct version of the Flash Player to view your Flash movies. The current version is Flash Player 6, and this is compatible with all Flash movies, not just those movie files exported from Flash MX. Lower numbered versions of the player are only compatible with movie files of the corresponding (or lower) Flash version.

Flash MX also has the ability to export as Flash 5, Flash 4, or Flash 3 movies, for greater accessibility to the lowest common denominator – a common industry term meaning the "largest possible audience". Though it's still possible, there's no longer a good reason to export as Flash 2 or Flash 1 movies, unless of course you were purposely creating movies for vintage computers!

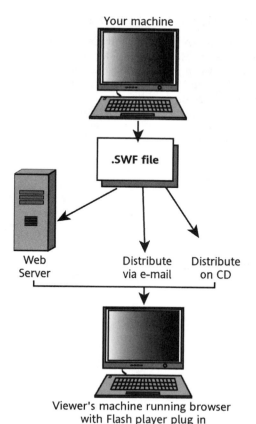

Your machine

.SWF file

Web Server   Distribute via e-mail   Distribute on CD

Viewer's machine running browser with Flash player plug in

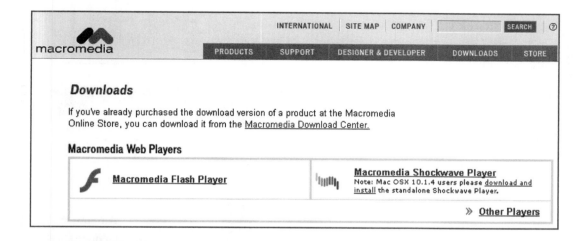

Working with source FLA files

It's common for a FLA file to be considerably larger in file size than the corresponding SWF file it exports. This is especially true when you're including certain types of image files (bitmaps) and sound files (WAVs, for example). Since the compression takes place at export time, when the slimline SWF is extracted from the chunkier FLA, don't be surprised if you find yourself with a 3 MB FLA file that exports a 100 KB SWF file!

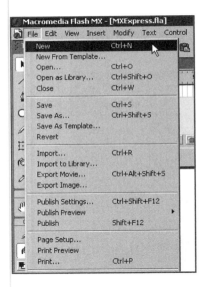

Each time you open Flash, it will default to a new blank FLA source file. To create a new FLA file, choose **File > New**:

To open a pre-existing FLA file, choose **File > Open**, then locate and select the desired file. Note that you might want to select the 'All Files' option to see exactly what files (not just FLAs) are in a particular folder:

To save a FLA file that you've been working on, choose **File > Save**, as usual.

Performance issues

The performance of FLA and SWF files depends on the processor of the machine they're on. Every computer has a processor and, as the name suggests, it processes all data, including the data downloading off the web. Processors differ in the amount of data they can handle during any given period of time. Data passes through the processor like liquid passes through a straw – faster processors essentially use more 'straws' to process the same amount of data.

Make no mistake, when you view a Flash file on the web, it's on your machine in one way or another. You're actually downloading the movie file to your computer while simultaneously viewing it.

There are two separate sets of issues related to the processor, one with each file format (the source FLA on your local machine, and the SWF which is downloaded from the web).

FLA source files

- Source files inherently use quite a bit of RAM. The official word from Macromedia is that you need 64 MB of free available system RAM, although 128 MB would be even better.

- Having multiple source files open at the same time will often slow down the file you're currently working on.

- Very large file sizes will affect the processor and thereby slow down Flash. Files typically become rather bloated when they include lots of bitmap (image) and/or sound files.

- Having multiple applications open at the same time also affects the speed of each application. For instance, if you intend to work with Macromedia Flash at the same time as Adobe Photoshop and Illustrator, *and* you want to use your web browser simultaneously, you'd be much better off with at least 256 MB of RAM.

SWF movie files

- Ideally, Flash movies are light and airy, but often that's not the case. The time a Flash movie takes to download relates exactly to its size, so bear in mind that larger files take up more processing power and time for the user.

- The processor is affected by how many things are happening within the Flash movie at any given time.

- Again, lots of image and/or sound files will certainly impact the processor's ability to cope with what's being thrown at it.

- Having multiple Flash movies open at the same time will negatively affect the performance of all the movies. This includes situations where one movie is open and another is in the web browser. In fact, just having any web browser with the Flash plug-in open at all will affect any other Flash movies that happen to be open.

- Likewise, multiple web browsers containing Flash movies will negatively affect the performance of all your Flash movies.

It's always important to keep these issues in mind during the authoring and publishing stages of our designs. Throughout this book we'll be looking at many ways to keep our Flash movies running more efficiently.

The authoring environment

In Macromedia Flash MX, the authoring environment is more commonly referred to as the **stage** – this is where you actually make the visual content for your Flash movies.

You can draw directly onto the stage using the drawing tools found in the top left corner of the screen. We'll study these tools in detail in the next chapter. You can also import artwork or other content, or dynamically generate it using **ActionScript** at runtime when the movie is being viewed. There's more on basic ActionScripting later in this book.

When you first open up your brand new copy of Flash MX you will see a series of **panels** and **windows** in your workspace similar to the ones shown in the screenshot.

The stage – the white rectangle in the middle – represents the area that'll be visible to the viewer who's looking at your published SWF file. The area around it is known, logically, as 'off stage'. Think of it as the wings to your stage, where your actors are all sat waiting to go on – indeed, you can still place things in this area but they won't be seen until they are moved on to the stage.

 This may seem pretty pointless at first, but imagine you have a car that you wish to drive across the stage. At the beginning of your movie it might sit off to the left of the stage, then move onto the stage slowly coming into partial view, until you can see the complete vehicle drive across the stage, before it disappears off again on the other side:

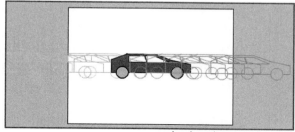

authoring time

Although the car will always be fully visible both on and off stage at author-time, only the parts visible through the 'window' of the stage will be seen at runtime:

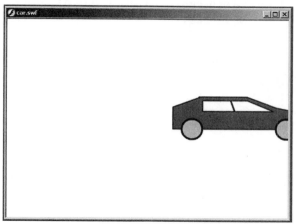

Runtime – when the SWF is viewed

Navigating the stage

Next we'll familiarize ourselves with moving around within the authoring environment.

Scrollbars

Notice the scrollbars at the side and bottom of the work area. Click and pull on them with your mouse to see how to move the stage up and down and left and right, like any windowed application:

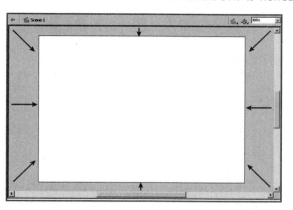

Zoom tool

To make the stage smaller and bigger you can use the **Zoom tool.** Click on it and then the little **zoom icon** with the plus sign on it in the Options box:

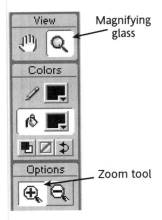

Magnifying glass

Zoom tool

Click and pull a little rectangle with the Zoom tool and then release the mouse. Watch those scrollbars as they get smaller indicating that we've zoomed into the selected area.

These controls will become very important when you find that a lot of your screen's real estate is taken up by a variety of tools and panels and you have some fine details to alter.

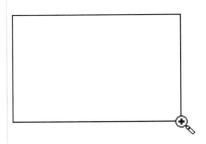

Hand tool

The **Hand tool** provides another method for navigating the stage. When you click on it your cursor changes into a hand.

Click on the stage with your mouse – don't forget to keep holding the mouse button down – and use the hand to pull the stage around. Again, notice the gray scrollbars will move to reflect your position within the authoring environment. Note that the shortcut key to move to the Hand tool and remain with it is H. We'll look at more shortcut keys towards the end of this chapter.

You can toggle between the Hand tool and any other tool whenever you want. For instance, use the **Brush tool** to scrawl something on the stage:

Click on it, or press the letter B on your keyboard, then click-drag the brush around. Then release the mouse button and hold down the SPACEBAR instead – you'll notice the return of the hand, but only for as long as you're holding down the SPACEBAR. This is the only tool in the bag given this honor, so use it wisely! Whatever tool you're using (except the Text tool), pressing and holding down the SPACEBAR will make the hand tool appear, ready to grab and move around the stage. We'll take a look at all the other design/drawing tools in the next chapter.

Movie properties

To look at the movie's dimensions (and therefore the stage's) we need to open the Document Properties box. On the menu, go to **Modify > Document** (or hit CTRL+J) to bring this up:

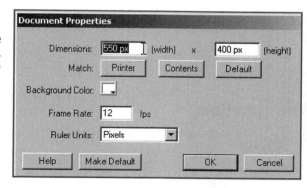

You can also bring up this window by simply clicking on the **Size** button in the Property inspector:

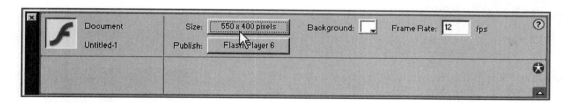

As you can see, the default settings for the movie dimensions are 550 x 400 px (pixels). This fits fairly snugly into your average browser depending on how you export the movie, but you can change the dimensions to suit your needs.

> **Tip**
> If you press the Contents button, the movie size is automatically cropped to match the contents currently on stage, meaning that any blank space is converted into dead space when you display the movie. This can save some file 'weight' on export. Clicking on the Default button returns the movie to the 550 x 400 px dimensions.

> **Tip**
> With Flash MX, the smallest movie you can make is one with dimensions of 1 x 1 pixels. This could be useful if you want to just have a sound load into a web page with no visual content, or you might just have a piece of ActionScript that you want to load in to a pre-existing movie. (For more on ActionScript see later in this chapter and in Chapter 10).

By clicking on the Ruler Units drop-down menu in the Document Properties window you'll see that the units come in quite a few flavors, and that you can use the units that you're most comfortable with. When you alter the units here, the movie remains the same size, but the dimensions at the top of the window are converted into your chosen units of measurement.

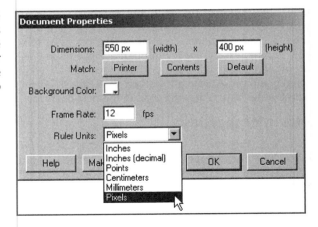

The timeline

Think of the timeline as a set of **frames** in a film.

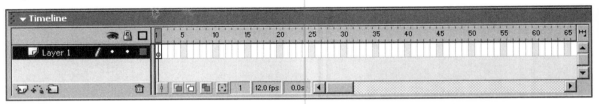

Each of the little boxes that span the timeline represents a frame into which a still image can be placed. When the Flash player reads through these frames at playback time, it gives the impression of movement in the same way as a child's flick book does.

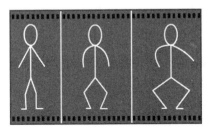

Take a look at this chapter's source code, which you can download from the friends of ED web site. Open up the jump.fla file, in which you'll find a movie with 12 frames. This file is available for download, along with the code for all of the other examples in this book, from the friends of ED website www.friendsofed.com:

There's a little black dot in each frame on the timeline – this signifies that it is a **keyframe**. A keyframe is a frame that contains some new content, or where a major change is happening to the existing content.

Notice that the first frame consists of a stick man standing still. On the second frame he's bracing himself to jump, and so on. It's worth spending a moment becoming familiar with the timeline before we continue – this is probably the single most important feature of Flash! Click through each of the little black dots or, better yet, click on the **playhead** (the red rectangle above the frames) and pull it along. This moves you through the frames, and the stage will display the content at each point.

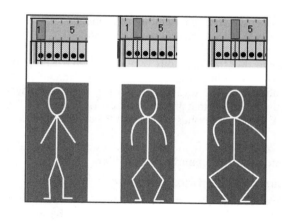

Pressing the ENTER key will make the playhead move across all 12 keyframes and step through the animation on the stage.

To insert a new frame you can right-click on the box in the timeline where you want the frame to appear, then click **Insert>Frame** (or press F5). To insert a keyframe then do the same but click **Insert>Keyframe** (F6).

 You'll soon realize that the timeline forms the foundation of all designs and animations in Flash. Notice that the timeline is made up of frames that sit on different **layers**; you can have several layers, each with their own distinct sets of frames. When traditional animators make cartoons they make separate layers; for instance, a solid painted background might sit beneath a separate transparent layer, onto which the characters are drawn. This is clearly more efficient for animators, and saves them from the need to repaint the background for each frame. As we shall see, layers in Flash have a similar function.

How does time relate to motion?

With old-fashioned celluloid film there is usually a frame rate of 24 **frames per second (fps)**, which is comfortably quick enough to fool the human eye into believing it is seeing movement. When the frame rate is low, then the movement can seem too 'jerky'. On the other hand, lower frame rates are equivalent to less data and therefore smaller files. When moving information over slow connections the loss of quality is often accepted in return for smaller media files.

Low frame rate =
● Jerkier motion
● Smaller file size
● Less processor intensive

High frame rate =
● Smoother motion
● Larger file size
● More processor intensive

The default rate in Flash MX is 12 fps, but you can adjust this figure. Our jumping stick man consisted of 12 frames, so in the default case the movie takes one second to play. If you look at a film in the **movie player** by clicking **Control > Test Movie** on the main menu (or even simpler use the shortcut keys CTRL+ENTER - *more on shortcuts later in this chapter*) you'll see the stick man movie play through continuously. Indeed, each run through of the animation takes 1 second.

We can alter the frame rate of our movie in the Property inspector. For instance, if you change the Frame Rate of a movie from 12 to 24 and then run the Flash player again you'll see that the movie runs twice as fast. The stick man now finishes his jump in 0.5 seconds.

We can study this in finer detail using an incredibly useful tool – the **bandwidth profiler**.

Using the bandwidth profiler

While testing your movie, open up the bandwidth profiler in the player by clicking **View > Bandwidth Profiler**. Stop the movie playing by clicking on the first small bar of the bar graph at the bottom of the profiler:

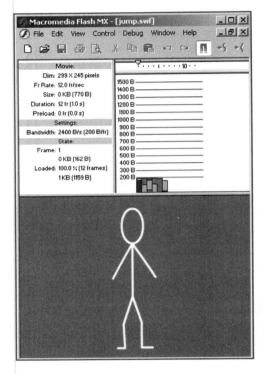

Look on the left hand side of the profiler. This gives you lots of handy information. It shows you that the movie is running at 12 fps, and it tells you how long the movie takes to run, which for our stick man is one second. It also shows you that there's no **preloading** of the movie needed. This means it'll load into the viewer's browser over the web and play instantaneously, without any delay.

Returning our attention to the bar graph at the bottom of the profiler, note that there are seven bars – click on each bar in turn and you will see the corresponding picture in the jump animation. These correspond to the first seven frames on the timeline of our movie.

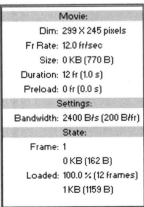

But wait a minute – have you noticed that something 'funny' is going on here? Although frames 8 to 12 are obviously there, they have no corresponding bars on the graph. In fact, they take up no disk space because they're *copies* of frames two to six in reverse order! Flash automatically performs some **optimization** on movies; it can detect duplicate shapes and includes these in the file only once when the movie is exported and run – that's why bars 8 to 12 aren't visible as bandwidth.

 The bandwidth profiler can be useful for ensuring that your movie isn't getting too big to download in a reasonable time. If you *do* find that your movie's getting out of control, you can reduce the number of frames you use, slow the frame rate down, or spread out the content over the duration of your movie so that it streams in more efficiently. But remember, when streaming over the web there is generally a compromise between quality and file size.

We'll be using the timeline constantly throughout this book, and we'll take a look at some of its additional features in **Chapter 5**.

ActionScript

 ActionScript, the brains behind Flash MX, is a powerful **scripting language**. If you acquire a smattering of the ActionScript language you'll soon be able to harness the power of Flash MX to do whatever you want. If this is your first experience with scripting, don't worry – ActionScript is actually very straightforward to get to grips with. ActionScript provides a means to communicate to Flash MX and have things happen in the specific way you want.

If, when you visit another country, you already know some fundamental key words and phrases of that country's language, you can generally make yourself understood and have other people interact and do things for you. You can get away with the odd line and

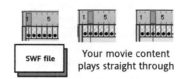

Without Actionscript

SWF file

Your movie content plays straight through

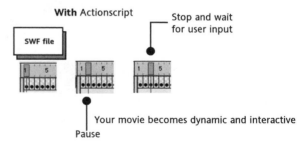

With Actionscript

SWF file

Stop and wait for user input

Your movie becomes dynamic and interactive

Pause

a few gestures, but to get a handle on the way to *really* speak the language you have to work a little harder at learning some of the main ideas and concepts, such as vocabulary, syntax and grammar.

For example, with the basics of any language you can order food and book hotel tickets with minimum effort, but if you want to discuss politics and philosophy then you're going to have to put in a little bit more effort understanding how the more advanced details of the language work. ActionScript is similar, in that the more you put in to learning it, the more you'll get back when you come to use it.

 As a teaser, we'll show a very simple bit of ActionScript that stops the animation on a specific frame. In fact, as you'll soon see, our script is only one word.

Click on a frame in the timeline of our stick man movie, frame 7 for instance, and press F9 to bring up the **Actions panel**:

The Actions panel lets you write or edit actions for objects (distinct pieces of content inside a movie) or frames. The Actions panel is where you create ActionScript; this is where we create the scripts that 'talk' to Flash and tell it what we want it to do, and when. If your Actions panel looks like the one in the picture above, then click on the little black triangle on the left and pull it to the right like a sliding screen door. You'll see a menu like this:

Click on the blue Actions folder on the left, then click on the Movie Control sub-menu, and lastly double-click on the `stop` action to add it to the selected frame:

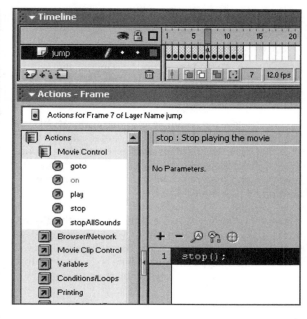

The ActionScript `stop();` action will now appear in your Actions pane. Press F9 again to close the Actions panel and run the movie (CTRL+ENTER) to see what happens. If all goes well the movie will run and the figure will stop on your chosen frame.

 ActionScript can be used to make your movies *interactive* and *dynamic*. Rather than simply showing the same movie each time, the user could select what they wanted to view themselves, or their movie could automatically turn green on St. Patrick's day! ActionScript can be used to make applications, games, interactive learning tools, and a thousand other things.

Normal vs Expert Mode

 It's worth pointing out that there are actually two versions of the Actions panel – the **Normal Mode** and the **Expert Mode**. To see which version you are using click on the little blue arrow pointing diagonally upwards on the bottom right of the Actions panel:

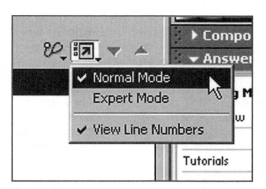

 The Normal Mode is for beginners who want a lot of support when writing, editing, and testing their scripts. As you have already seen, there are a lot of predefined menus and automatic help prompts. The Expert Mode, on the other hand, is intended for Flash users with a little more experience with the ActionScript language. Accordingly, as this is a book about beginning with Flash MX we'll stick with Normal Mode for now.

We'll return to scripting and look at some more basic actions in **Chapter 10** of this book.

Shortcut keys

Like in any software application, shortcut keys are an invaluable aid to working faster in Flash MX. If you discipline yourself to learn most of them it will save a *lot* of time in the long run.

Here's an example of a useful shortcut key – you can hide all the clutter of the open panels, perhaps while completing some intricate design, by hitting the F4 key on your keyboard, and then return all the panels to their original position by pressing F4 again.

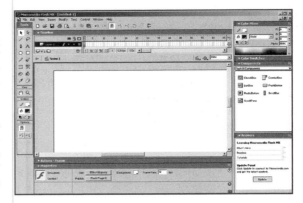

Actually, the TAB key will do exactly the same thing – this is a legacy key press from the previous version of Flash that's still there in the MX version. Both these options will close all the panels except the timeline – you can hide that too, using the CTRL+ALT+T key combination (PC only).

Now hold down CTRL and press 1 for a 100 per cent view (⌘ and 1 on the Mac). CTRL+2 will show the complete stage in the window allotted with a little gray around it; CTRL+3 will do the same but not leave any dead space showing if possible. The best way to see what I'm talking about is to try it out, and all will become clear.

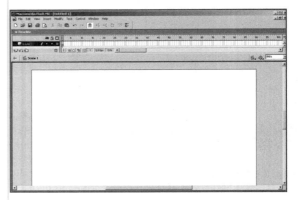

Customizing your shortcuts

To see the shortcuts in MX just click your cursor on the items in the menu bar and see the dropdown lists – the shortcuts are listed (when available) on the right hand side of each menu. This is the **Window** menu list:

As you can see, there are quite a few. But Flash MX makes life even easier – if you have to learn a few different applications you can soon become confused having to learn a whole new set of keyboard shortcuts for each program. Ideally, what you want is a familiar roadmap.

In Flash MX you can either tailor-make your own shortcuts or use the pre-configured ones in line with other major graphics applications that you may use regularly, like Photoshop, Illustrator, or Fireworks.

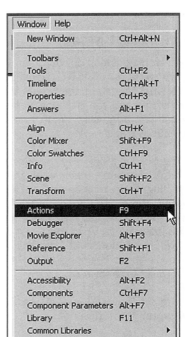

To create a custom keyboard shortcut set on a PC, choose **Edit > Keyboard Shortcuts...** :

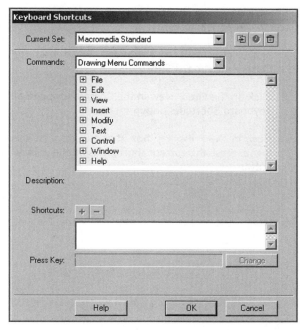

On the Mac, this panel is accessed via the **Flash > Keyboard Shortcuts...** menu:

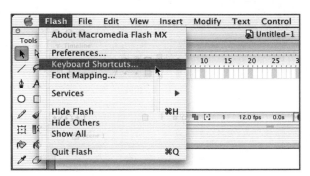

First of all, so that we don't do any damage to the pre-existing sets of keyboard shortcuts, we're going to duplicate a set. But don't worry about *wiping* the default set of Flash keyboard shortcuts – you can't!

To create your clone choose a set of shortcuts from the **Current Set** drop-down menu – grab the Fireworks 4 one for now. Click on the Duplicate Set icon to the right of this menu, then click the OK button. Now try hitting the TAB key we used earlier... nothing happens! That's because we're in the Fireworks shortcut mode now.

What we'll do now is change a key press shortcut in this mode to see what happens:

1. Again, click **Edit > Keyboard Shortcuts...**(or **Flash > Keyboard Shortcuts...**).

2. Click on the **File > New** in the Commands pane of Keyboard Shortcuts popup menu.

3. Now, in the Press Key box at the bottom of the menu, erase the current shortcut using the 'minus' button.

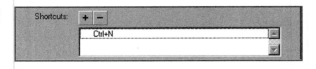

4. Next, click on the plus button, click the TAB key, then click Change.

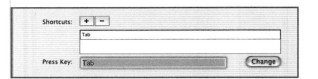

5. Click OK and, back on the main stage, press TAB – it now gives you a new MX file!

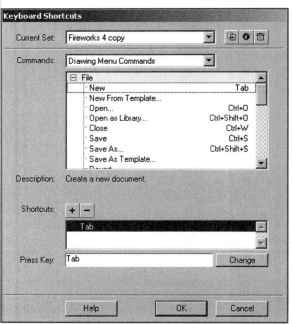

Remember to go back to the Keyboard Shortcuts menu and restore the Macromedia Standard menu (throughout this book we'll be using the Macromedia Standard shortcuts). Press OK and you're back on home ground, having had a taste of the possibilities of customizing your own shortcuts.

Summary

Let's recap on what we've covered in this chapter:

- How Flash files relate to the authoring environment and Flash Player
  - FLA source files and Flash MX
  - SWF movie files and the Flash Player

- The authoring environment
  - Navigating Flash through scrollbars, the Zoom tool, and the Hand tool
  - Movie properties

- The **timeline**
  - Using **frames** and **keyframes** to make a simple animation of a jumping man

- The **bandwidth profiler**

- A basic introduction to scripting with Flash's own ActionScript language

- Shortcut keys
  - The default shortcuts and how to find them
  - Customizing shortcuts

Next

Creating artwork content in Flash MX.

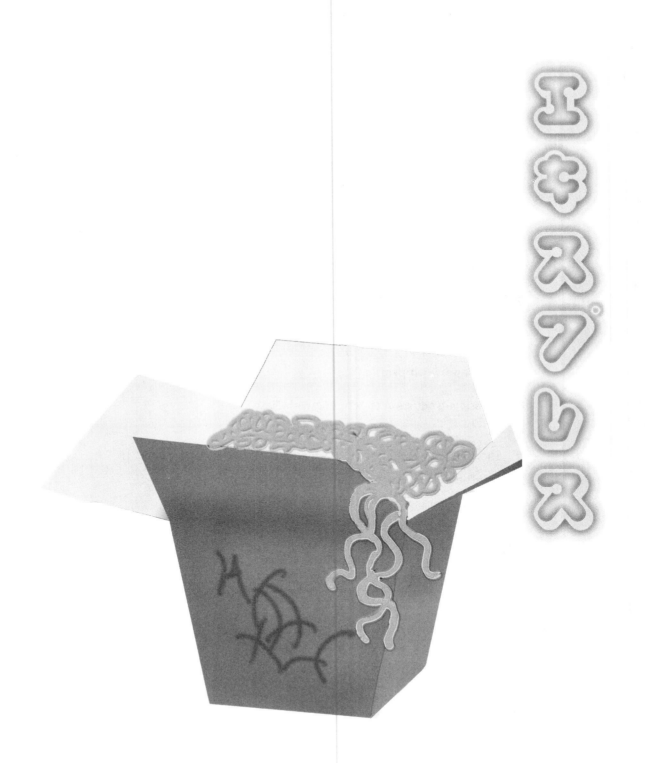

エクスプレス

Chapter 3
Artwork and
Drawing Tools

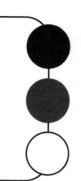

What's in this chapter:

- **Importing artwork**, and the benefits of vector graphics

- The context-sensitive **Property inspector**

- **Drawing** in Flash MX:
  - o   Strokes and Fills
  - o   The drawing tools
  - o   The Color Mixer

- **Selection** tools

- **Grouping** artwork

- **Transformation** tools

There are two main ways of getting artwork into your Flash MX movies – *importing* the artwork from an external source, and *creating* the artwork using Flash's native drawing tools. We'll cover the basics of both methods in this chapter, and look at the tools that you can use to manipulate your artwork, whatever its source.

Importing vector and bitmap artwork into Flash

 One of Flash's great advantages is that it works with **vector** images, and one of the great things about vectors is that, no matter how much you enlarge or reduce them, they don't lose quality as the resolution increases. The limits of vector images are the physical constraints of your computer (or projector). Let's take a look at an example to see just why vector images are so important.

In the source files for this chapter, you'll find two files, `peacock_feather_bmp.fla` and `peacock_feather.fla`. Open up the first of these files in Flash and use the Zoom tool (keyboard shortcut Z) to zoom in on the image as far as you can go. You'll find that the more you zoom in, the lower the quality is:

This graininess is a consequence of the pixelated nature of bitmaps.

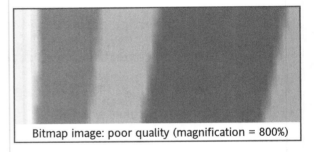

Bitmap image: poor quality (magnification = 800%)

Now do the same on `peacock_feather.fla` – you'll see there that there's no loss of quality, and that the power of vector graphics in Flash is now apparent.

Vector images remain sharp because they are mathematical instructions about lines, shapes and color fills, and they're rendered by the computer's processor in line with those instructions. A bitmap, in contrast, is a fixed series of pixels laid side by side; this is why the image breaks down into blocks of color when it's enlarged – you're just blowing up a fixed number of picture elements that have a fixed level definition.

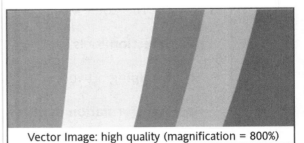

Vector Image: high quality (magnification = 800%)

 Images of almost any type – whether bitmap or vector – can be imported into Flash very easily. Simply go to **File > Import...** and a dialog will appear allowing you to choose which image you want to import into Flash. There's a choice of 28 file formats, including sound and video, which you can import into Flash. Take a look at the Files of type drop-down menu to see the options.

As we've discovered, vectors don't lose their quality with size. This is great for scalable Flash presentations. There's also the added benefit of file sizes: because a vector image is a set of instructions on how to draw the image rather than a definition of each pixel, the file sizes are much smaller.

So, if vectors are so great, why would you use bitmaps at all? Well, the downside to vectors is that they can appear sterile and lifeless if you're trying to represent photorealistic images. Bitmaps are much better for this because the colours aren't so clearly defined when laid side by side – they appear to mix together at a distance, and this fools the eye into seeing subtler gradations of tone and color.

Whenever you work with *any* kind of artwork inside Flash MX, you'll find that the **Property inspector** is an essential aid.

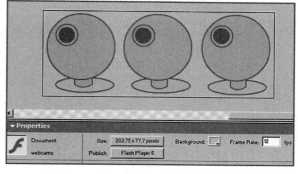

Context Sensitive Property inspector

The Property inspector is one of the most important features of Flash MX. It appears in the default layout of Flash, but if you can't see it make the panel visible using **Window > Properties**, or the Ctrl+F3 /⌘+F3 keyboard shortcut. The information and options available in the Property inspector change in response to what graphical element has been selected on the stage, which tool has been chosen, and so on. In other words, it is **context sensitive**.

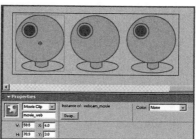

Take a look at the screenshot of what appears to be three identical webcams taken from the file webcams.fla:

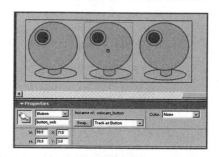

Open this file so you can take a closer look. Click on each webcam in turn with the Arrow tool and you'll see from their details in the Property inspector that they're actually three different types of symbol: a movie clip, a button and a graphic (we'll look at symbols in detail in **Chapter 4**). It's the Property inspector that allows us to spot the difference. Without it we would believe that each of the webcams is identical, with the same set of properties and behaviors. How wrong would we have been!

Not only can we see information on particular elements in the Property inspector, we can also modify the elements *within* the Property inspector.

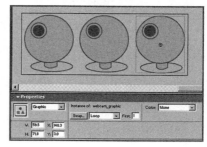

'Live' objects

When we clicked on each of the webcam symbols we made that selected object the current or **live** object. It's when an object is live that we can modify it through the values currently displayed in the Property inspector. It's not just symbols that we can make 'live' in this way; we can do this with any on-stage element in Flash.

Let's suppose we've just opened up a new FLA and drawn a line on the stage. We want to edit this line, but in the Property inspector we only see general movie properties:

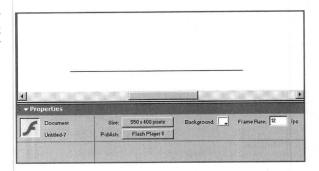

We can make this line 'live' by clicking on it with the Arrow tool. The Property inspector will change to reflect our selection, displaying the live object's editable options that we have full control over – or *will* have control over once we've read the section on drawing lines:

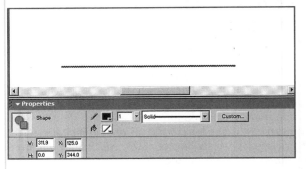

Drawing in Flash

There are two main elements to any drawing in Flash: the **stroke** and the **fill**.

Strokes and fills

A *stroke* is simply a line, whether it is curved or straight, and a *fill* is a block of color. Every shape we draw in Flash is made up of one or both of these elements:

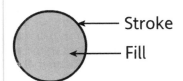

Stroke

Fill

Most Flash drawing tools can combine strokes and fills, but some (such as the Line tool) can only use a stoke, and some (e.g. the Brush tool) can only use a fill. This table illustrates which drawing elements can be used with each tool:

Tool	Stroke	Fill
Line	Yes	No
Pen	Yes	No
Pencil	Yes	No
Ink Bottle	Yes	No
Brush	No	Yes
Paint Bucket	No	Yes
Oval	Yes	Yes
Rectangle	Yes	Yes
Fill Transform Tool	No	Yes
Text	Yes (if broken apart)	Yes
Eraser	Yes	Yes
Eyedropper	Yes	Yes

 There are two places where you can change the color of a stroke or fill; the Property inspector and the Tools panel:

The latter option is always there on the Tools panel, whereas the Property inspector option is content/tool sensitive. Throughout this book we'll use the Property inspector option, since we can modify all the properties here, not just the color. We'll learn how to alter each of these properties as we take a look at the different tools.

To select a stroke or a fill you can simply click on it with the Arrow tool. If you double-click on an object that has both a stroke and a fill, both will be selected. Groups of strokes and fills can be selected by holding down the SHIFT key and clicking on them.

Drawing lines

 As we've just discovered, a line is basically just a stroke. This means that once we've drawn the line we have a full set of stroke properties that we can modify; these properties affect the line's appearance – its width, color, and so on.

Drawing a line can been seen as a three step process. Just follow the steps below:

1. Select the Line tool. As with all the tools, this can be found in – you've guessed it – the Tools panel. Selecting this tool changes the cursor from an arrow to a crosshair when you move it over the stage:

2. Click on the stage where you want to start your line and keep the mouse button held down.

3. Drag the cursor to where you want your line to end and release the mouse.

Now that you can create a basic line, let's take a look at the properties we can alter for the line – its **stroke properties**. A simple line can't have a fill – it's just a solid stroke – but other drawn elements, such as circles and rectangles, can have strokes *and* fills, as we'll see shortly.

Stroke properties

When you want to modify the properties of a stroke, the first thing to do is select the line on the stage using the Arrow tool. This will make the line 'live' and you'll see that the Property inspector changes to give the line's properties:

> **Tip**
> *The shortcut key for selecting the Line tool is N.*

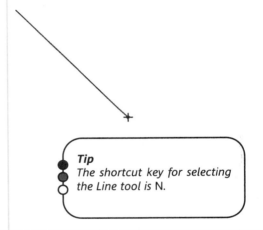

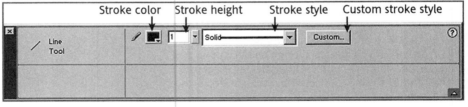

Let's take a look at what each of these options will do to a line.

Changing Color

Clicking on the **Stroke color** box reveals the selection palette of colors that we can apply to our lines. You'll see that, along with the pop-up color box, the Eyedropper tool also appears.

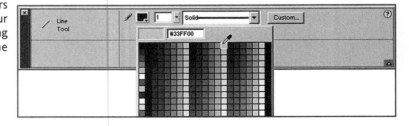

The Eyedropper tool lets us select any of the colors in the pop-up box, or any color within any visible element on the stage. The Eyedropper is an indiscriminate kleptomaniac – it'll pick up *any* color from anywhere on the screen and apply it to the 'live' object immediately, so be careful where you click!

Click on the color you want in the palette, and your selected line will change to that color. When the palette minimizes, the Stroke color box still displays the newly selected color.

> **Tip**
>
> *In the pop-up box you'll see that when you move over the colors their hexadecimal value appears in the value box (e.g. #0000FF for blue). If you know the hexadecimal value of the color you're after you can simply type it into this box. This is useful for matching your Flash movies up with the colors you've used in an HTML page.*

Height

This next option represents the thickness of the stroke. On a horizontal line, this would equate to the line's vertical height:

There are two ways to alter the thickness of the stroke; both are based on a numerical value that's displayed in the Property inspector's Stroke height box:

The numerical value of the thickness can be typed straight into the value box, or you can use the value slider to change the value instead:

Thickness   Thickness

Style

The Style property determines the essential characteristics of the line – solid, dotted, wavy, and so on.

A quick look at the drop-down menu for this option will reveal what it's all about:

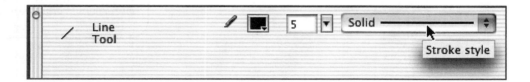

We're provided with a choice of seven styles that we can apply to our line.

We simply choose the one we want from the drop-down menu. Easy!

> **Tip**
> *Be aware that the hairline option overrides any thickness you've previously set for the stroke. The two options can't co-exist: choose one or the other.*

Custom

The Custom options let you change the default settings for the Line tool; if you change these, they'll be used next time you choose the Line tool from the Toolbox. Any changes you make here will be lost when you close down Flash.

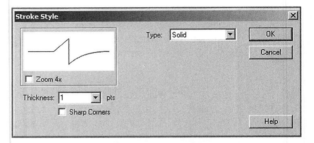

If we click on the Custom... button we get our final options for the stroke. We could spend days covering all the options available here, but you'll be glad to learn that we're *not* going to do that. Have a play around with these different options and see their effects on your stroke. The **Hatched** type of stroke provides the greatest number of configurable attributes for you to play with.

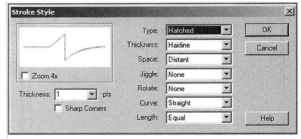

Make sure you change all these modifiers back to their defaults before moving on to the next section.

> **Tip**
> *Be careful about applying too many of these line property modifiers in your movies for drawing lines – they may take up a lot of file space, since the computer has to render more instructions to draw the vectors.*

Before or after?

We can set the stroke and fill options before we draw the shape or after – this goes for most of the tools in the Tools panel. If you set the options before you draw, the Property inspector will display the attributes for the tool you're about to draw with:

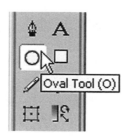

If you set the attributes after you've drawn the shape, the Property inspector will be display the **Shape** attributes when you select the object to edit it:

Drawing objects

Now let's move beyond the simple stroke and look at drawing some slightly more complex shapes.

Ovals

You can probably guess the first thing we need to do to draw an oval shape – select the **Oval** tool. I'm sure that you'll have also worked out that, like all the other tools, it lives in the Tools panel:

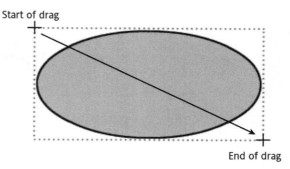

Like the Line tool, the cursor for drawing an oval shows up as a cross-hair on the stage. With the Line tool, the cross-hair marked the start of our line when we clicked down – this time, things are slightly different; imagine that the oval we're going to draw has a bounding rectangle that touches the top, bottom, left, and right extremes of the oval.

> **Tip**
> *The Oval tool's keyboard shortcut is* O.

Click down to start drawing the oval – you're marking out the top left corner of the bounding rectangle. Now drag the mouse to what will be the bottom right corner of the bounding rectangle and release it to complete the oval:

Start of drag

End of drag

> **Tip**
> *If you hold down the* SHIFT *key while you draw your oval shape you'll get a perfect circle.*

Rectangles

If you've managed to draw an oval you'll have no problems with the rectangle. It's exactly the same principle, except that the imaginary bounding rectangle is also the actual shape you're drawing! Let's recap on what we should be doing:

1. Select the Rectangle tool (shortcut key R).

2. Click the mouse down where you want the top left corner of the rectangle to be.

3. Hold the mouse down and drag the mouse to where you want the bottom right corner of the rectangle.

4. Release the mouse and admire your rectangle:

The oval and rectangle shapes have exactly the same options available for the stroke as the Line tool, so we won't cover them again here.

By default, ovals and rectangles have both strokes and fills. However, you don't *have* to have a stroke on your shapes if you don't want one, and there are two ways to make sure you don't end up with one. First, you can choose the 'no color' (for the stroke) option in the Tool panel *before* you draw the object (ensuring that you've got the Stroke Color icon selected first:

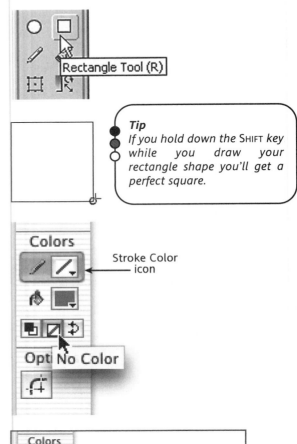

Tip
If you hold down the SHIFT *key while you draw your rectangle shape you'll get a perfect square.*

Stroke Color icon

This option is also available in the drop-down color palette for the Stroke Color:

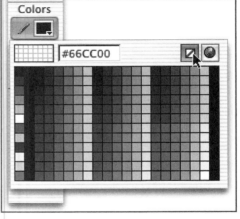

The second 'no stroke' method involves selecting the object's stroke (by clicking on it) *after* you've drawn it, and then pressing DELETE.

Equally, we don't have to have a fill for the object and we can make sure we don't end up with a fill in exactly the same way:

Speaking of fills...

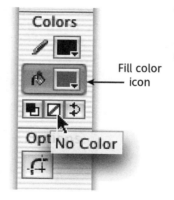

Fill color icon

Fill properties

Modifying a fill color is similar to changing a stroke color. You simply select the fill you want to change with the Arrow tool, and then click on the **Fill color** box. You'll see the same selection of basic colors, and have the same ability to use the Eyedropper tool to select whatever color you want:

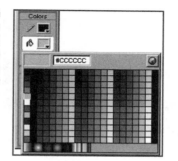

However, if you look at the bottom of the pop-up box, you'll see that you have some extra options this time:

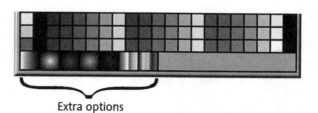

Extra options

Open up the **Color Mixer** panel (**Window > Color Mixer** or SHIFT+F9). If you look at the mixer before clicking on any of these extra options, you'll see that your chosen color is **solid**:

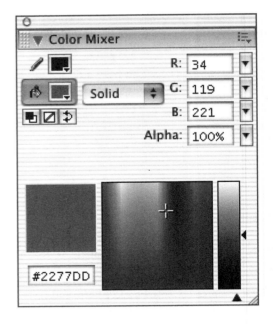

If you now click through a few of the additional options in the Fill color box and look at the Color Mixer, you'll see that these extra options are preset **radial** and **linear** gradients:

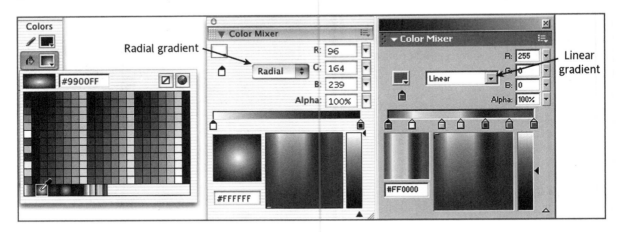

These predefined gradients are pretty cool, but we can also use the Color Mixer to create our own gradients and fills. Let's look at those options now.

Tip
The Color Mixer has a broader range of colors than the Tool panel pop-up boxes do, and you can set the stroke color here as well as the fill – which will save you mouse clicks!

Using the Color mixer

 As we've just discovered, the Color Mixer provides us with a vast range of color options, and the ability to use different types of fills rather than the standard solid fill.

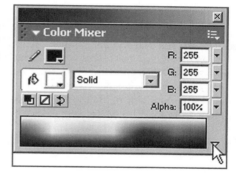

Draw yourself an oval on the stage and select the fill so that you can see what each of the fills does when you select them. Make sure the Color Mixer panel is visible and click on the little downward-pointing arrow at the bottom to ensure the panel is fully expanded:

The **Fill style** drop-down menu reveals that there are four types of fill that we can use:

The **Solid** fill is the default. It's what we've used on every shape we've drawn so far with a fill. It's the other three types of fill we're interested in here: Linear, Radial and Bitmap. Let's look at each in turn.

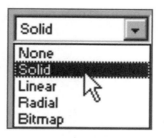

> **Tip**
> *You can only use the **None** option, which means 'no fill', if you're using the Color Mixer in conjunction with a tool before you draw a shape; you can't use it when you're changing a fill after drawing the shape.*

Linear fills

Select the Linear option from the drop-down menu. You'll see that the appearance of the Color Mixer alters to reveal a Gradient Definition bar. Note that the fill for the oval selected on the stage has changed to reflect the gradient specified in the gradient definition bar; in this case, one that fades from black to white:

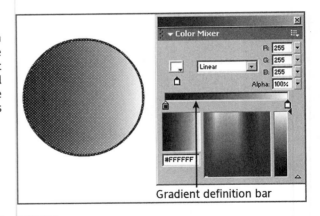

Gradient definition bar

There's a little symbol that looks like a house at either end of the Gradient Definition bar:

Tip
Always choose the type of fill before choosing the color. If you choose the color first, followed by the fill, the default gradient is always reset to black and white.

Each 'house' defines the specific color at that point of the spectrum. You can do a simple click and drag on one of the houses and move it along the bar to change the gradient's characteristics. Click on one of the houses at the end of the definition bar and drag it towards the other one:

This has given the gradient a much narrower range, as you can see in the oval's fill.

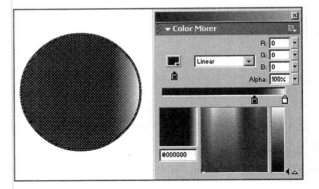

We can build more houses into our gradient – and thereby make the gradient more complex – by moving the mouse cursor under the Gradient Definition bar until the + symbol appears:

Click now, and another house – or paint pot – will appear:

If you look at these paint pots, you'll see that one of them has a black 'roof'. This is the 'currently selected' paint pot; when a paint pot is selected, you can edit its color, gaining finer control over the gradient. You edit the color for a paint pot with the Color Mixer in exactly the same way you'd alter the color of a solid fill. To edit the color of a specific paint pot, just click on it so that it's selected, then go wild with the Color Mixer:

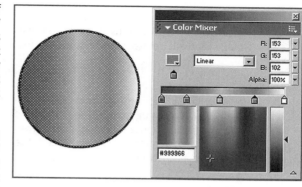

If you find that you've ended up with too many paint pots – colors – and that your gradient's got out of control, you can remove paint pots by clicking on them and dragging the mouse down, away from the Gradient Definition bar. When you release the mouse button the paint pot will disappear, simplifying the gradient by reducing its number of colors.

Radial fills

Radial fills are made in exactly the same way as Linear fills – with the Color Mixer panel. The only difference is that the end effect radiates out from the center in a circular pattern, rather than from left to right in a linear fashion:

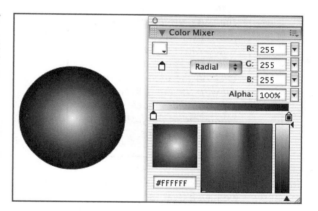

Radial gradients can be very useful for creating a sphere effect. Draw a circle with a solid fill, and then select the **Paint Bucket** tool (keyboard shortcut K – don't worry if you're not yet familiar with this tool, as we'll be looking at it shortly). Now set up a Radial gradient in the Color Mixer. The final step is to click with the Paint Bucket on the circle's fill at the point where you want the gradient to radiate out from:

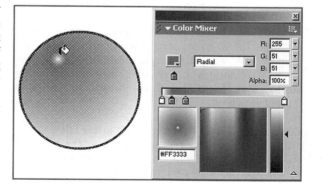

An instant sphere!

Bitmap fills

The final fill type lets us import a bitmap image that will be repeated to form the fill.

Select the Bitmap option from the drop-down menu; a dialog box will open up from which you can choose a bitmap image from your hard drive. Once you've chosen the image, it will be tiled across the fill:

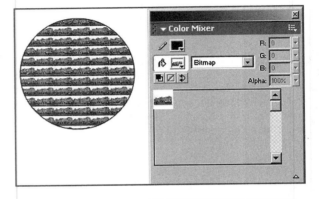

> **Tip**
> *You can also import a bitmap image onto the stage (**File > Import**), break it apart (**Modify > Break Apart**), and then use the Eyedropper tool from the Tools panel (not the Color Mixer's Eyedropper) to select the image as a fill. Then click on the area you want to fill with the Paint Bucket tool. This will fill shapes with the whole image, not just an array of smaller versions.*

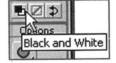

> **Tip**
> *To change your stroke and fill colors quickly back to the default black and white setting, click on the Black and White tool in the Tools panel or Color Mixer.*

To finish off our tour of the Color Mixer, let's consider the options we haven't yet looked at.

More Options

For a start, you can change the **alpha** setting of a color using the Alpha control. This allows you to add *transparency* to your colors, which is useful if you want other movie elements to be visible through a screen of translucent color:

Here, there's a solid light gray circle in the background, with a solid dark gray rectangle laid over the top on a separate layer (see **Chapter 7** for in-depth coverage of layers). The rectangle's fill has an Alpha setting of 75%.

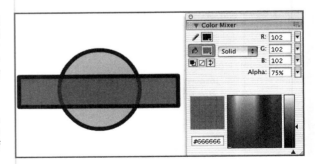

Each color in the Mixer has specific red, green and blue values; you can use the **R**, **G** and **B** controls to modify these color values, either by keying in the numbers or using the slider. Play around with these values and see the effect that this has, both on the color and on its hexadecimal value.

Finally, there's the **brightness control**. This lets you lighten and darken any color you choose. Once again, note that this changes the hexadecimal value:

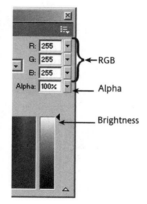

The Pencil tool

The Pencil tool is one of the two main tools for making 'raw' strokes on the stage:

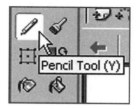

We've already looked at the other drawing instrument – the Line tool; the Pencil tool is more flexible, in that it lets us draw *freehand*.

When you select the Pencil tool, you will see that three options are available from the **Options** section of the Tools panel:

These options act upon the freehand drawings you make:

The first two options are pretty self-explanatory; respectively, they automatically **straighten** up your lines for you, and **smooth** out some of the clunkier curves. The **Ink** option is essentially a 'totally freehand' drawing option – it doesn't enhance your lines at all, but leaves them as they are, however rough and ready they might be.

Stroke optimization

Some complicated shapes in Flash are made up of hundreds of strokes. This can be a problem, in that it often leads to increased file sizes for your movie, and consequently a longer load time. Fortunately, Flash lets you optimize your strokes to help minimize the problem.

Let's look at a quick example to illustrate how Optimization works. Choose the Ink option of the Pencil tool and scribble all over the stage. Neatness isn't important here, so don't worry if you go off the edge of the stage.

> **Tip**
> *You can also draw straight lines with the Pencil tool by holding down the* SHIFT *key as you move your mouse up, down, or across. Note that this is limited strictly to vertical or horizontal lines.*

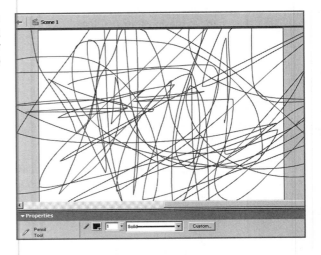

Now grab hold of everything on the stage using the select all (CTRL+A/⌘+A) shortcut. Now choose the Optimize option (**Modify > Optimize...**) – the Optimize Curves box will appear:

Now use the slider bar to define the level of smoothing. Bear in mind that the more you smooth, the less the end result will look like the scribble/drawing that you started with.

Once you've selected the smoothing level, press OK and you'll get a dialog box advising you of the optimization statistics for the operation:

If you want to see the difference that optimization makes publish the SWF before and after optimization and look at the file sizes. This file size reduction can be particularly useful in large, complex movies.

Pixel-precision

Flash allows you to place your lines – and indeed any other elements – with pixel precision. Pixel-level alignment can actually cut file sizes – and subsequently download time – and can also help with the clarity of display, particularly for text.

Make sure that the Snap to Pixels option is checked via the **View > Snap to Pixels** menu option. Now zoom into a movie by 400% or more – the pixel grid automatically appears:

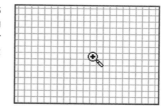

The grid lets you place content with great precision.

The Brush tool

The Brush tool is the Pencil tool's bulkier sibling; it lets you paint thick lines in a variety of styles.

Like the Pencil tool, the Brush tool comes with its own set of options. Click on the Brush tool in the Tools panel and the options will appear:

The Brush Size and Brush Shape options are self-explanatory; just click on the icons and the variations will appear in the drop-down menus.

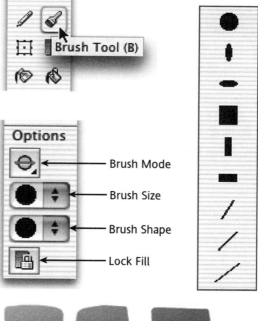

The Lock Fill modifier lets you create an effect where a single gradient or bitmap fill is applied across multiple, separate elements on the stage; for example, a linear gradient that's visible across a number of drawn boxes:

This image was achieved by drawing each box separately using the Brush tool, with a linear gradient as the fill, and the Lock Fill modifier selected.

The Lock Fill Effect

The Brush Mode option is of the greatest interest to us here. This controls how our brush acts, and how it affects the objects we apply it to.

Paint Normal

This mode is the default mode and lets the brush paint freely over strokes, fills, and blank areas of the stage.

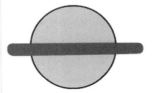

Paint Fills

With this mode selected we can paint over fills and blank areas of the stage, but not over strokes; the strokes remain visible despite our best attempts to obliterate them.

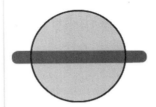

Paint Behind

With this choice we can paint over the *blank* areas of the stage, but not over any strokes or fills.

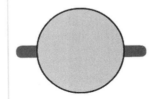

Paint Selection

This mode will only paint over selected (or 'live') fills. It doesn't work on the blank stage, or strokes (regardless of whether they're selected or not).

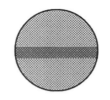

Paint Inside

This final mode will ignore any marks you paint when you cross over a boundary line defined by a stroke. For example, let's suppose we've drawn a circle with a stroke but no fill. We now select the Brush tool with this option and start coloring in the middle. It doesn't matter if we go over the circle's stroke and onto the blank stage, as it won't be painted – Flash ignores any painting we do *outside* the boundary line:

The Eraser tool

The Eraser tool is very similar to the Brush tool.

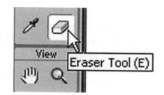

We all know what an eraser does, and the options provided are virtually identical to the Brush tool's; the Eraser Mode options work in the same way, and the Eraser Shape options combine the Brush tool's size and shape options:

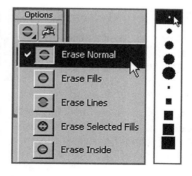

There's one additional option here: the Faucet option, Applying the tip of this tool will erase either a whole stroke or a whole fill in one click. This behavior leads nicely into our next two tools...

The Ink Bottle and Paint Bucket tools

These two tools work hand in hand to help you change the colors of existing objects; the Ink Bottle works with *strokes*, and the Paint Bucket with *fills*:

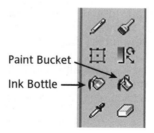

The Ink Bottle can add a stroke to a fill that's currently strokeless, and modify a stroke that already exists. The Paint Bucket can add a fill inside an area bounded by strokes, and can also modify existing fills.

We've already looked at how the Paint Bucket worked when we dealt with fills earlier. It's really as simple as selecting the tool, setting the color you want in the Property inspector or Color Mixer, and then clicking on the area that you want to fill. The Ink Bottle is very similar. Click on the tool in the Tools panel and you'll see all the configurable stroke properties that we looked at earlier reappear in the Property inspector. Once you've set these properties to your required stroke type, click on the fill you want to add a stroke to, or click on the stroke you want to replace.

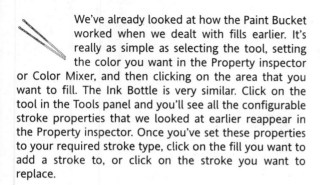

Unstroked   Stroke added   Stroke replaced

The Paint Bucket tool has additional **Gap Size** options; in some circumstances, the strokes in a picture don't join together to make an enclosed area (sometimes by accident, and sometimes by design). You can define the criteria that Flash uses to decide whether to fill an area when it finds that the area's boundaries aren't *quite* closed.

Some of us are better at freehand drawing than others; it's a matter of personal taste and experiement to get these settings right for your particular drawing style and needs.

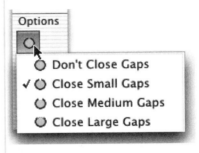

The Lasso tool

The Lasso tool is used for selecting and cutting out objects, a bit like a smart cookie cutter. It's more complex than the Arrow tool we've been using for selection previously, in that it can deal with irregular shapes – and it's also quite an intuitive tool.

Create a picture on your stage. Whether this is a group of shapes drawn together or an imported bitmap doesn't matter – we just need some content to play with. Select the Lasso from the Tools panel, or hit the L key to bring the Lasso to life. Click on the stage and then drag the Lasso around a shape on your picture to cut it out, finishing the drag back at the start point. Your irregular selection will now be 'captured', and you can do what you want with it; delete it, move it, modify it, copy it... whatever you want.

Selected area

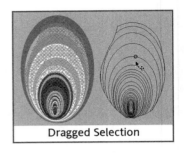

Dragged Selection

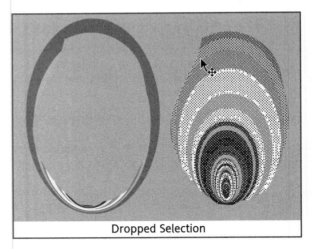

Dropped Selection

That's the basic use of the tool, but there are some additional options we can use:

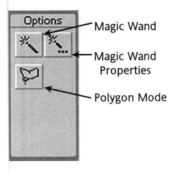

Magic Wand

Magic Wand Properties

Polygon Mode

Polygon mode

This mode lets you make a polygon shaped selection rather than the freehand selection you've just seen in action.

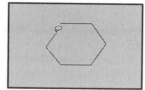

Click where you want to start the selection and release the mouse. A line will follow from where you just clicked to where you move the mouse next. Click again; the first line will become fixed, and another will start at the end of it – it's a bit like a little spider laying its web as it goes along. To finish the polygon selection, simply double-click and the area will be selected.

Magic Wand

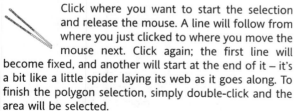

The Magic Wand option is great for harmonizing colors or removing unwanted area. Its best use is touching up photographs.

Import a bitmap photograph into Flash (**File > Import...**). If you haven't got any suitable images on your hard drive, you can find the image in the screenshots, London.jpg, in the download files for this chapter. To make the effect work, select the bitmap with the Arrow tool and then break it apart (**Modify > Break Apart**):

> **Tip**
>
> *You can achieve a mixture of freehand and polygon selections by turning the polygon option on and off as necessary. Draw your freehand area of the selection and release the mouse button, then hold down the ALT key to click your straight lines – holding down the ALT key invokes the Polygon mode.*

The image will still be selected as this point, so click on a blank part of the stage to deselect it. Now choose the Lasso tool and check the Magic Wand option. We want to modify the properties of the Magic Wand before we use it, so open the Magic Wand Properties dialog box by clicking on the icon in the Options panel:

Change the Threshold to 50, and the Smoothing to pixels:

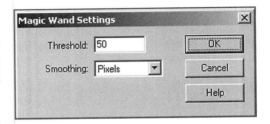

The threshold value (it can be between 1 and 200) specifies how close (in color terms) adjacent pixels must be to the *selected* color in order to be selected by the Magic Wand. Smoothing defines how much the edges of the selection are rounded off.

You're now ready to make your selection. My photograph of London was taken on a gray winter's day, so the sky looks very bleak – let's add some color to it.

Tip
The higher the threshold setting, the greater the number of colors the Magic Wand will select.

Single-click on the sky area of the photo – it will (magically) become selected. If we were removing an unwanted area of the photo we would just press DELETE now, but we're going to change the color to a sky blue to make it appear as if the photo was taken in high summer. There's a tiny copy of the photograph in the Fill Color box of the Property inspector – click on that, and you can choose a nice blue color from the color pop-up to represent the sky:

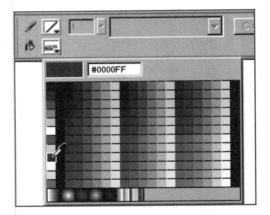

 That's just a quick example of how we use this tool; there are many practical uses for it. Imagine you've found a really old photograph that's been crumpled and creased. You could scan it, import the bitmap into Flash, use this tool to remove the crease marks, and then publish a SWF with the photo looking as good as new.

Grouping artwork

 A **Group** is a set of objects that have been selected on the stage and then 'clipped together'. Grouping provides an easy way of organizing and manipulating multiple objects. You can also *ungroup* these grouped objects and return them to their separate existences.

 To group objects, you first have to select them. There are three ways you can do this, and the option you choose often depends on the type of objects you want to group.

For most of our previous selections we've used the Arrow tool, and that's what we're going to use here, in three variants.

The first method is the SHIFT-click method. Hold down the SHIFT key and click on every object you want to be included in the group.

The second method is for when you want to select everything on the stage. You could still do this with the SHIFT-click method, but it's nowhere near as fast. Select everything using **Edit > Select All**, or using the keyboard shortcut CTRL+A/⌘+A.

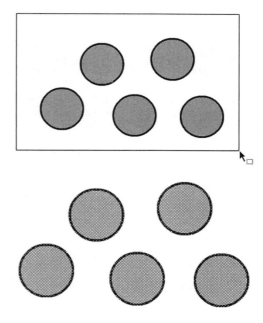

The third method is to drag a box around the objects, which will select everything within the box. With the Arrow tool, click at the top left most point of the objects you're selecting and drag out a box around the objects, releasing the mouse button once you're finished.

Now you've made your selection, you can group the objects together. This is a simple as **Modify > Group** or CTRL+G/⌘+G. (Note that the ungrouping option is also on the same menu.) A blue border will appear around the selected objects to signify the group. This border makes a group look like a symbol; indeed you can move a group around the stage in exactly the same way you would a symbol, as we'll see in the next chapter.

Editing grouped artwork

 To edit an object with a group you simply double-click on the group – this takes you inside the group's 'container'. Once inside, you can edit any of the individual elements just as if they were still sitting individually on the main stage. You can still select more than one element to edit them together.

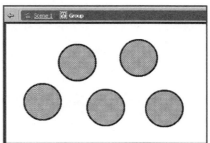

When you're inside a group, the status bar above the stage indicates that to you – so you can always be clear about where you are.

Groups within Groups

It's also possible to group a collection of groups.

 To do this, select all the groups you want to join together, and group them again (**Modify > Group**/CTRL+G/⌘+G).

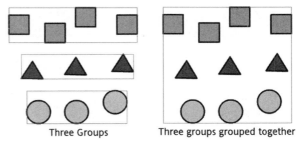

Three Groups   Three groups grouped together

Arranging Groups

 One of the main advantages of groups is easing the placement and alignment of objects on the stage. Take a look at `toy1a.fla` in the download files. Each of the little toys represents a group:

 We want to use the Align panel to distribute the toys across the center of the stage. Start by selecting all the toys on the stage (CTRL+A), and then open the Align panel (**Window > Align** or CTRL+K/⌘+K). In the Align panel, check the To stage button; remember that we want the toys aligned *in relation to the stage* and not to the selected group of objects itself. Next, click on the Align vertical center button to align the toys across the center of the stage:

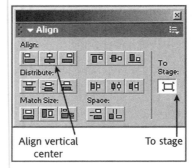

We can now distribute the lines evenly across the stage with the Distribute horizontal center button:

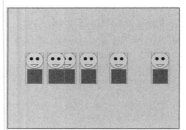

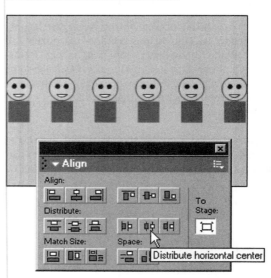

Just to see how important the grouping of each toy is, try doing the same alignment with `toy1b.fla`. Everything looks the same to start with, but the one difference is that the each toy hasn't been grouped this time, and the resulting alignment is not very pretty:

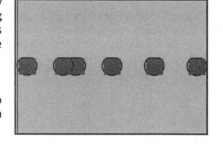

Play around with the other options in the Align panel to see what each of them does. If you hover over a button the tool tips will give you a clue.

Ungroup Vs. Break Apart

These two options sound pretty much the same, but shouldn't be confused with each other. **Ungroup** is the opposite of group; it simply ungroups any 'clipped together' objects we've previously grouped together using the Group function. **Break Apart**, on the other hand, lets us break apart individual elements so that we can edit their internal components. When you break an object apart, you're actually going into its *fabric*. When we broke the bitmap image apart earlier in the chapter, for example, we were decomposing it into its individual pixels.

There are three different types of element that can be broken apart:

- Bitmaps
- Text
- Instances of symbols

You'll remember that we've already used the Break Apart function earlier in this chapter when we looked at the Magic Wand, and it's a useful feature that will recur throughout this book.

Modifying artwork

Next, let's look at some of the remaining tools that you can use to manipulate Flash artwork.

The Subselection tool

The Subselection tool allows you to re-adjust lines or **anchor points**; anchor points define sections of lines or shapes, allowing you to change specific sections of a shape with a high degree of control. Like all the other tools we've looked at, the Subselection tool is found in the Tools panel:

Let's make a quick example to see exactly how the Subselect tool works. Draw a circle with no fill. Now move the Subselection tool towards the circle until you see a little black square next to the cursor arrow:

Click the circle with the Subselection Tool; anchor points appear around the circle:

> **Tip**
> The keyboard shortcut for this tool is A.

When you move the Subselect tool near an anchor point you'll see the small black square appear to the bottom right of the cursor. When the square is colored black you can click and drag the shape around the stage, just as you can move any selected object with the Arrow tool:

> **Tip**
> You can add more anchor points by clicking on the circle's stroke with the Pen tool (Keyboard shortcut P).

When the square has a *white* fill, you can manipulate the shape by click-dragging on the anchor point:

Notice that the anchor points spawn little 'bow ties' when you select/drag them. You can click on the ends of these bow ties and manipulate the curves attached to the anchor points. These bow ties indicate that the shapes we draw are made up of Bezier curves.

> **Tip**
> Bezier curves are special; they give you great control over the shape of each element in a vector drawing.

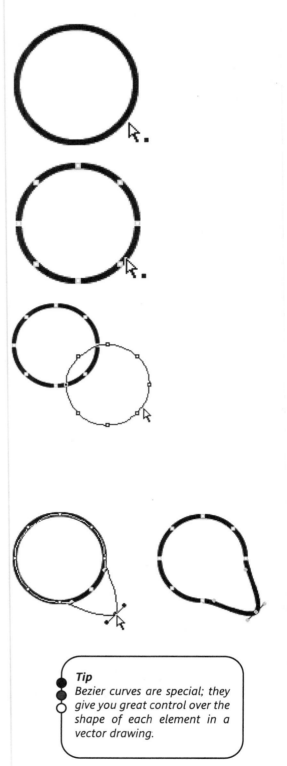

The Free Transform tool

The Free Transform tool can change individual objects, groups, or text fills on the stage. Once again, you'll find this tool in the Tools panel (its keyboard shortcut is Q):

It's a tool with many uses, and one that's well worth getting to know intimately; you can use it to rotate, skew, scale, distort, move, and 'envelope' objects. The different modes of the tool are selected from the Options panel:

Draw a rectangle with no stroke on the stage and we'll take a look at each of these uses.

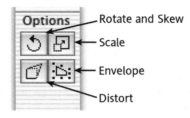

Rotate

Select the Free Transform tool and click on the rectangle you've drawn.

You can rotate the object in either the default mode, or with the **Rotate and Skew** option selected. If you move the cursor over the corners of the rectangle you'll see that the cursor changes to the 'rotate' cursor:

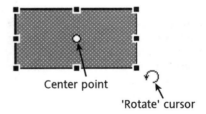

Center point

'Rotate' cursor

When this happens click down and rotate the object by dragging:

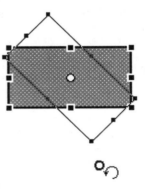

The center point of the rotation is the white circle on the center of the rectangle. This center point can easily by moved by clicking and dragging it:

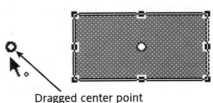

Dragged center point

The rectangle will then rotate rather differently:

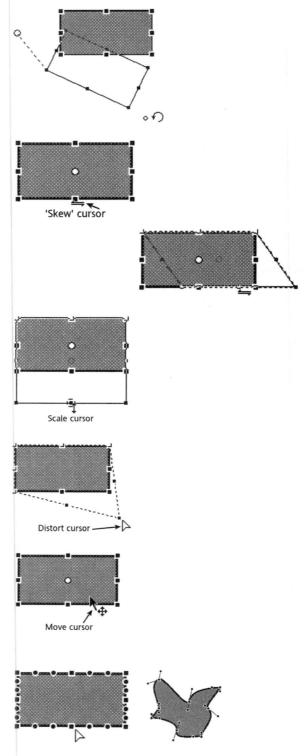

Return your rectangle to its original pre-rotated state.

Skewing

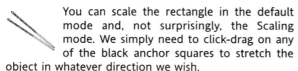

Once again, we can use this function in both the default state and with the Rotate and Skew option – but there's a difference this time; the skew effect works the same with both methods, but where we place the cursor to *enable* the skew is different. In the default mode we place the cursor on the stroke, between the black anchor squares. In the Rotate and Skew mode we actually place it *on* the black anchor squares. Once again it's simply a case of clicking and dragging to achieve the effect.

Scale

You can scale the rectangle in the default mode and, not surprisingly, the Scaling mode. We simply need to click-drag on any of the black anchor squares to stretch the object in whatever direction we wish.

Distort

The distort effect can only be achieved with the Distort option selected. With this tool, click on any of the black anchor points and drag them to any point you like. This option also has its own cursor symbol:

Move

You can move the object around in the default mode, or with any of the options selected, whenever you see the Move cursor – a cross with arrowheads at the end of each arm:

This method is identical to using the Arrow tool to move objects around.

Envelope

This final effect only works with the Envelope option chosen. It works in a similar fashion to the Distort option, but has more anchor points for those lovely Beziers:

To round off this chapter, let's take a brief look at the Text tool.

The Text tool

You'll have no doubt guessed that this tool is used for creating text. It is represented on the Tool panel and has the keyboard shortcut T. Everything we need to create text can be found in the Property inspector when the Text tool is selected:

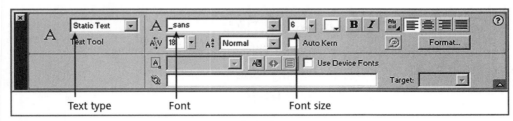

Text type   Font   Font size

Text comes in three varieties: Static, Dynamic and Input. You can choose which type you're going to use in the Text type drop-down menu:

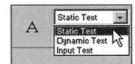

- **Static text** – the mode for text that displays, unchanged, in the finished movie.

- **Dynamic text** – text that can be updated according to ActionScript commands in your movie.

- **Input text** – the type of text field you want for user input, such as data they're keying into a form.

Both dynamic and input fields can be given instance names so that they can be altered and referred to through ActionScript (see **Chapter 10** for more on ActionScript). Since the content in these fields can change during the execution of a movie, you can also specify Line type options:

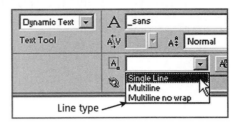

Line type

With each type of text you have the standard type of options that you will find in almost any text editing program: font, color, size and alignment.

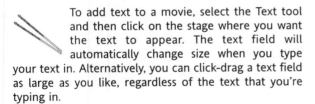

To add text to a movie, select the Text tool and then click on the stage where you want the text to appear. The text field will automatically change size when you type your text in. Alternatively, you can click-drag a text field as large as you like, regardless of the text that you're typing in.

Summary

Let's recap on what we've covered in this chapter:

- **Importing artwork** into Flash

- Understanding of the benefits of vector graphics

- The context sensitive workings of the **Property inspector**

- **Basic drawing** in Flash:
    - Strokes and Fills
    - The drawing tools
    - The Color Mixer

- **Selection tools** – the Lasso and Subselection tools

- **Grouping** artwork

- Object manipulation with the Free Transform tool

- Introduction to the Text tool

Next

Flash Symbols and the Flash Library.

エキスプレス

Chapter 4
Symbols and
the Library

What's in this chapter:

- What **symbols** are, and why they're useful

- Advantages of symbols over groups

- **Creating** and **using** symbols and their instances

- The **Library** and its properties

- The three symbol types:
  - **Movie clip**
  - **Button**
  - **Graphic**

- **Editing** graphics within a symbol efficiently

Using symbols

You can think of a **symbol** as a box holding content that can be used on the stage in Flash MX. This content can be pictures, sounds, video clips, and drawings – anything that can be created within Flash or digitized and imported into the program. Symbols have their own internal timelines and dedicated stage, meaning that you can create symbols that encapsulate animation, ActionScript, and other dynamic, interactive content. And furthermore, a symbol can make 'clones' of itself; you can have many copies of a single symbol on stage, all active simultaneously. This mix of capabilities make symbols powerful tools in the Flash MX world.

There are three types of symbol:

1. Graphic symbols

2. Movie clip symbols

3. Button symbols

We'll be looking at these individually later in the chapter, but for the moment we'll look at symbols more generically.

These boxes of content – symbols – can also hold instances of other boxes within them in order to construct highly complex symbols and graphics.

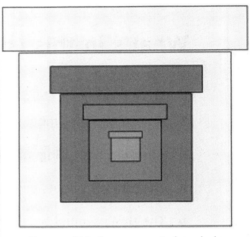

Boxes within boxes – *nested* symbols

Nesting symbols within symbols lets you embed rich and powerful content in discrete little chunks, and makes handling content easier, too. An example of this would be an animation of an 18-wheel rig. You *could* create a single animation of the truck moving along, and animate all the wheels turning at the same time; that would, however, be very difficult to do. Another approach would be to create a *symbol* that contained an animation of a wheel turning, and then embed multiple copies of that inside the truck symbol:

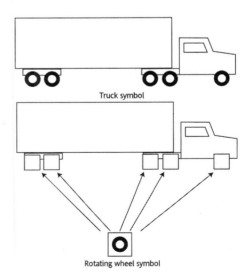

Truck symbol

Rotating wheel symbol

Once the wheels are nested inside the truck symbol, you can animate the truck to move, and the wheels will automatically go with it. The benefits of this approach are that (1) you simplify the construction of the animation, and (2) if you want to change the wheel symbol (add hubcaps, maybe...) you can do that independently of the truck symbol.

Tip
One of the advantages of using symbols in Flash is that you can create a symbol – for example, a piece of artwork – and then use it to create multiple copies of that artwork, without having to redraw it each time, thus saving you time and effort. We'll see this principle in practice later in the chapter.

Here's another way of thinking about symbols: if you're building a house, you're likely to want more than one window, and one door. Chances are that you don't want to handcraft each window and door individually as you come to that part of the construction phase. So what would most of us do? We'd take a trip to our local construction supply yard and buy a set of pre-made doors or windows, which we could use anywhere in the house. If we're going for a consistent look, the windows will all be to the same pattern; each individual window unit would be a mass-produced copy of the original design, or pattern:

Multiple copies
Pre-built, mass produced
components:

The original design is like a template, and the individual window units are based on that. Once a factory is tooled up, it can produce as many copies of the original pattern as it needs.

Another advantage of symbols is that you can change their characteristics **dynamically**; as we'll see later in this book, you can use ActionScript to alter the color, transparency, dimensions, rotation, scale, position, and so on, of a symbol when it's on the stage in the finished movie.

A key benefit of using symbols is that once you have created one, you can **reuse** it many times without bloating the finished SWF's file size. An example should help convince you of this.

Open up the following two FLA files from your downloaded source code folder for this chapter: `iceBmp.fla` and `iceVector.fla`.

The first, `iceBmp.fla`, contains the raw bitmap (BMP) picture files of four different colored icepops. In this case, we've imported four separate picture files to get our different flavors. The important point to note here is the output file size of `iceBmp.swf` – 10 KB.

Now look at the second FLA file, `iceVector.fla`. The is a Flash movie with the icepop image created only *once* in Flash and then turned into a couple of symbols (the head and the stick) – in this version, the size of the output SWF file is only 1 KB!

Test both movies (CTRL+ENTER/⌘+ENTER), right-click with your mouse over each, and zoom in to see the difference in quality. The *smaller* file has the sharper graphics! Indeed, use of symbols and vector graphics can save a great deal of file space.

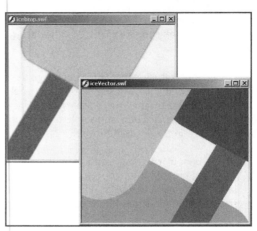

Symbols vs. groups

 To really understand why symbols can be so useful, it's worth reminding ourselves what a 'group' is, and how it differs from a symbol.

A group is simply a collection of graphic images that have been joined together on the stage; there are a limited number of things you can do with a group – you can rotate them, copy them (which increases files size), skew, rotate, or resize them, and change their position. But that's about all; they're useful, but pretty limited in scope. A symbol can do so much more!

 Let's look at another example – open up the `chameleon.fla`. Before you work on this file, save it as `chameleon1.fla` so you can revert back to the original if you move everything about and it gets too messy.

The chameleon and its background rectangle are made up from a series of different objects in Flash. The best way to see how this works here is to click on the different bits and see where the strokes and fills are.

Next, make all the objects into one group, go to **Edit > Select All** (CTRL+A/⌘+A), then select **Modify > Group** (CTRL+G/⌘+G). A border will appear around all of the graphic objects, and they become a group:

> **Tip**
> *The fact that these objects are grouped is indicated by the thin blue line around them, and by the Group identifier in the Property inspector.*

Now for a demonstration of what we can do with a group – choose **Window > Transform** (CTRL+T/⌘+T) to bring up the Transform tool then type 40 in the Rotate entry box. The chameleon group – *all* of the lines and fills – rotates 40°.

Double-click on the group window and you will be returned to the original graphic objects, but notice the **navigation bar** which shows you exactly where you are within your movie. There is a Group symbol highlighted to the right of Scene 1.

This shows that you are inside the group graphic and that the individual objects can be changed. Note also that there's even a little Back arrow facing left that lets you return to Scene 1 – this feature becomes very useful for movies with nesting structures containing many levels.

Continuing with our example, click away from the group (or on an area away from the graphics) and choose a different color from the Color Swatches panel (CTRL+F9/⌘+F9). Use the Paint Bucket tool (press K or click on it to select) to fill in the background behind the chameleon:

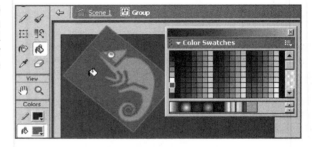

Now click on the blue Back arrow (or even just the Scene 1 link) on the navigation bar to return to the stage and the objects safely grouped together again:

We can also change the size and position of our chameleon group by changing the height/width (H and W) entries and the X and Y coordinates in the Property inspector:

As we mentioned earlier, there are a few other things you can do with a group of objects. Just right-click over the group (CTRL-click on a Mac) to see other options like scaling, skewing, using the Free Transform tool, breaking the group apart, and so on:

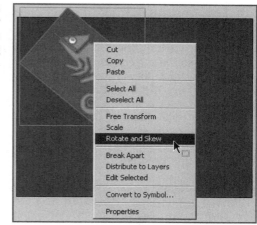

Why symbols?

Let's now look at how much more can be done with a symbol. To speed things along, we've already included a symbol in the `chameleon.fla` file; can you find it? In fact, it's lurking in the **Library**! The Library is a *very* useful part of the Flash MX user interface, and using it can improve your design workflow dramatically – we'll look at it more closely in the next section.

To access the Library panel, go to **Window > Library** or use CTRL+L/⌘+L (or even just F11 - *the Library is so useful it has two shortcut keys!*). The Library window will pop up; this is where the 'master' versions of all this movie's symbols will be located. Click on the word `chameleon` to see the symbol displayed in the Library:

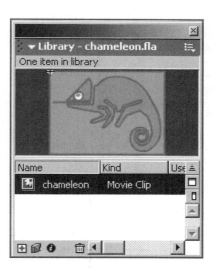

So what have we got here? The chameleon symbol *looks* just the same as the group you've been working with, and in fact this symbol was created by converting that same initial chameleoid group of objects *into* a symbol. However, the symbol version is capable of a whole lot more things than the original group variant.

Note that this symbol is registered as a **Movie Clip** – we'll learn more about the various types of symbols shortly. Right now, we want to learn how to use this symbol. To take the chameleon symbol out from the Library and onto the stage, simply click on it, then drag and drop it onto the stage:

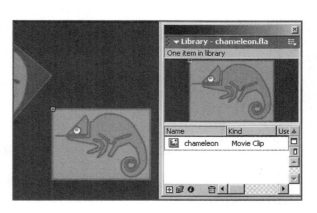

By now you've probably noticed a couple of 'strange' things. Firstly, the chameleon symbol still appears to be sitting happily in the Library – even though you've taken it out and put it on stage! Maybe it has a twin? In fact, the chameleon symbol that you've dragged out of the Library is a 'clone' – or **instance**, in Flash terminology – of the original symbol that sits in the Library.

Attack of the instances!

Instances are duplicates, or clones, of the original symbol in the Library. Instances always reside on stage, whereas the original 'master' symbol they're based on always stays put in the Library. The original symbol in the Library effectively acts like a **shape cutter** producing images of itself – you could drag and drop chameleons from that library all day long ending up with thousands of instances of the chameleon, and the original would sit there in the Library, not moving.

The important point to note is that every instance on the stage is **linked** to the Library version. As we'll see later in this chapter, we can change the individual attributes of each instance, such as size, color, rotation, and shape (using the Free Transform tool) but we cannot change the raw artwork used to create the symbol without affecting *all* of the instances that are based on that symbol. If we try to edit the core graphics within the instance (by double-clicking on an instance on the stage, for example) we automatically link back to the original symbol, and any changes we make will then ripple through to *every* instance.

Library version

Cloning process

Multiple instances on stage

Symbols in the Property inspector

Returning to our `chameleon` symbol, the other thing you'll notice is that the Property inspector is now showing some new information. To get a good impression of the difference between the symbol and the group, click on the group that we were working with earlier and look at the Property inspector, and then click back to an instance of the symbol version on the stage. The symbol's Property inspector will look something like this:

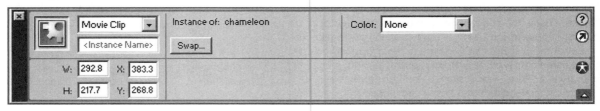

There's a very marked difference in the type and number of attributes of a symbol compared to a group. Our movie clip symbol is sophisticated and debonair unlike its rather clumsier group version.

Now we're going to assign the symbol on the stage a *name*. Groups can't be assigned names, and if you haven't got a name, people can't shout at you to attract your attention to do things! As we shall see, symbols work a lot harder.

Click on the symbol on stage, and look at the Property inspector again. Type the name cham into the Instance Name box left-hand side, under the drop-down box that indicates our symbol is a movie clip:

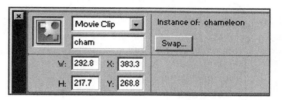

The symbol on stage is now called cham and will happily respond to any ActionScript instructions calling upon it to do something. However, at this early stage we aren't actually going to be calling upon cham to do anything yet – but it's still good practice to give your on-stage instances a name as soon as you create them; this helps avoid any confusion.

Color effects

Let's get back to our group/symbol comparisons. If you want to change the color of a group, you either have to put a semi-transparent screen in front of the graphic, or you can double-click to ungroup and change each individual element. This is way too time-consuming for us, and again symbols score points here.

Click on cham, as he'll affectionately be known as from now on, and return your attention to the ever-useful Property inspector. Click on the Color drop-down menu on the right-hand side:

> **Tip**
> On a PC, you can undock your Property inspector (or indeed any other panel on both PC and Mac) from its default position by dragging it using the little 'knurled' patch on the top-left of the window. To return the Property inspector to its original position just pull the box down to the bottom of the page under the Actions panel and let go – it should snap back into place. Note that the Property inspector on the Mac has different drag and dock behaviors from the PC version.

> **Tip**
> You can use the Swap... button in the Property inspector to switch an instance of a symbol with any other symbol in your Library. Say, for example, you'd created a new version of the animated wheels inside your 18-wheeler rig movie. You could click on the old wheel instances on the stage and swap them for the new version, and they'd retain their same precise position inside the truck movie.

Click one of the options, Brightness for example, and a percentage box with another dropdown arrow appears further to the right. Click on this dropdown arrow and a slider appears. Watch what happens to cham when you slide it up and down; he lightens or darkens accordingly:

The default is 0%, so set cham back to that. Now try the Tint option – click on the little color box to change the color and, again, pull the slider up and down and watch cham turn through the various degrees of dark tint between his true colors and whatever you have selected:

> **Tip**
> *Note that the changes we've been applying here are only being made to this specific instance. This is because we're working at the level of the whole instance on the stage; we haven't drilled down inside the instance here, so we're not rippling changes back to the master symbol.*

Finally, reset the tint to zero and drop down to the Alpha option. Change the percentage to 40% to really camouflage your chameleon:

We'll leave the Advanced control for the moment – it's basically just a combination of the Color/Tint controls, all rolled into one.

As you can see, the symbol is far more versatile than a group, it can be manipulated just like a group, but it has far more attributes that can be changed – either manually or with ActionScript. Don't forget that you could pull out a dozen of cham's brothers and sisters and change them all in different ways. Take a look at the file `chams_clones.fla` to get some ideas.

Although you're probably quite eager to learn how to build your own symbols by now, it's worth our while taking a moment to look at the essential features of the library before we continue. After that, we'll dive right in to creating symbols!

The Library

The Library is the place where you keep your symbols and all the **assets** – the distinct bits of content (wheels and windows, for example) that combine to make up more complicated symbols (such as 18-wheelers or houses). Let's return to the original version of our chameleon movie to study the Library in more detail.

Re-open `chameleon.fla` and go to **Window > Library** (or press F11) to open up the Library panel. You can toggle between opening and closing the Library using those shortcut keys.

Multiple Libraries

Notice that the name of the FLA file the Library's contents belong to is indicated at the top of the Library panel. This is particularly significant if you're working on more than one movie simultaneously, because it means you can link the different Library panels together, and drag and drop symbols between different libraries and stages; your libraries can be shared across different FLAs, which helps make symbols even more reusable.

To link libraries from different movies together open your first movie and bring up its Library, then minimize the first movie, open a second and bring up *that* movie's Library. The first movie's Library attaches itself to the bottom of the second movie's Library, and so on. Using this technique you can drag a symbol from one movie's Library to another's stage quite easily (and from there to *that* movie's Library). Additonally, while you're not using them you can close the content of all the libraries while you're using them, which produces a neat little box that you can tuck away in the corner somewhere:

Background options

OK, returning to our original Library, click on the `chameleon` symbol once, move your cursor over the image that appears, and right-click/CTRL-click:

As well as the original background color of the movie, you'll be offered a couple of background options: a white background and a grid (with or without original background color):

Folders

Another useful trick in the Library is to make use of folders when you have several different symbols. You'll find the New Folder icon in the bottom left of the Library panel:

Use folders as you would to organize the programs, files, and data on your hard-drive. Maintaining a well-structured Library is important for a number of reasons, but primarily it allows you to quickly find what you need when you need it! It's also useful because it allows you to group together the multiple assets that combine to make particular symbols.

Library options

Right-click over the selected symbol to see the plethora of options that are available in the Library:

Rename

Choosing Rename does the same thing as double-clicking on the symbol's name in the Library. A bounding box appears and you can rename the symbol to something new.

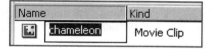

Duplicate

The Duplicate option replicates the symbol in the library. A new Duplicate Symbol dialog box pops up and you can rename it and even make it into a different kind of symbol (we'll look at these more closely shortly) – so you could, for example, change a movie clip to a graphic or a button:

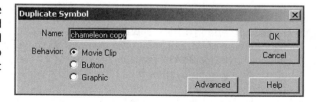

If you click on the Advanced button the box will expand with even more commands relating to Linkage and Source.

These are rather more complex features that needn't detain us here. They relate to optimizing the way that symbols are used in more complicated and performance-critical movies.

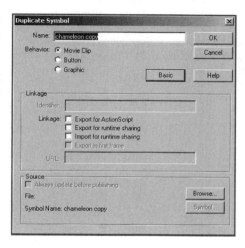

Move to New Folder

Move to New Folder enables you to put the movie clip in a folder.

Delete

Delete is a one-stop-shop – if you delete a symbol that's *it*, it's gone forever! Luckily though, you'll get a warning box before you go through with this irreversible action:

Edit

Selecting Edit offers a way to edit your symbol, as its name suggests! We'll examine in detail the various methods of editing symbols in a short while.

Properties

Similar to Duplicate, Symbol Properties offers you a dialog box in which you can alter your symbol's properties.

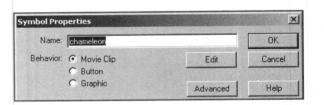

Behavior

The Behavior option offers a quick and easy way to change the type of symbol and how it *behaves* on stage. For instance, you could change a movie clip to act like a button, or a graphic symbol to act like a movie clip.

Additionally, we have the Component Definition and Linkage options within the Library – these are rather more advanced features that allow you to make your own **reusable components** and tailored user interface. We'll return to a discussion of this area in the final chapter of this book.

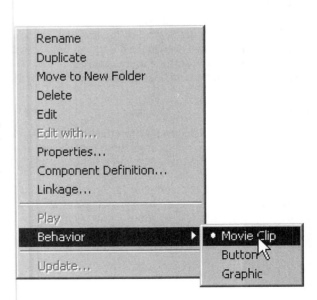

Creating a symbol

The techniques for creating symbols are quick and simple. There are two possible methods:

1. Converting an existing graphic into a symbol

2. Creating a new symbol from scratch

Converting graphics into a symbol

Open up the file `maskCreate.fla` – in it you will find a readymade piece of artwork, in this case a simple mask with a black and white radial fill that makes it look metallic:

Select it by either a quick mouse click or use CTRL+A/⌘+A – this will highlight the mask to show it has been selected. Now imagine you are going to throw an imaginary piece of invisible shrinkwrap around the whole thing and turn it into a symbol. To turn everything currently selected on the stage into a symbol, either select **Insert > Convert to Symbol...** or simply press F8 on the keyboard. You'll see this dialog box appear:

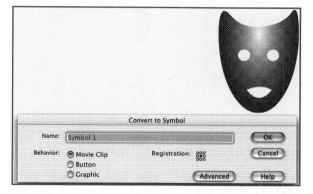

We now have a choice of three types of symbol: a **Movie Clip**, **Button**, or **Graphic** (more on these different types later). Check the Graphic radio button, give your symbol a name, and then hit OK:

When you reselect the image, you'll see the telltale signs that it is now a symbol – it has a **registration point** (indicated by the crosshairs in the center) and a light blue border:

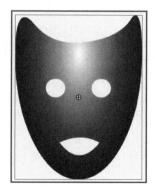

When you create a symbol, its registration point is defined as one of the nine possible points of registration; these nine points are represented by the 3 X 3 array in the Convert to Symbol dialog box:

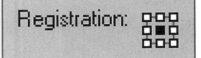

Flash uses a symbol's registration point to determine how to manipulate the symbol on the stage. The position of your registration point is crucial when aligning your symbols and using tools such as Free Transform.

The most common registration point choice is 'center', but you can of course vary this as you wish.

Take a look in your Library (CTRL+L/⌘+L) and you will see that your symbol has indeed been added there:

Now take a look at the Property inspector (are you getting the feeling that this is a pretty useful panel yet?!):

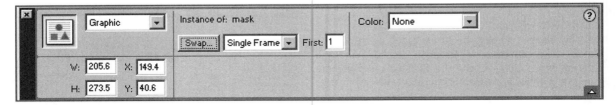

Graphic symbols, like groups, have no instance name. Since repetition of symbols incurs only a small file size increase, designers usually make graphic symbols when they want to use an array of images in a movie – as a background, for example. You can treat a graphic symbol as a **stencil** and use it where the graphic will be repeated many times, in order to save time and memory. An example of this using our symbol might be the background of the entry page to an online video presentation.

As we mentioned earlier, there's another way to make a symbol...

Building a new symbol from scratch

If you want to create a symbol but you don't want it to appear on the stage then select **Insert > New Symbol...** (CTRL+F8/⌘+F8) – this dialog box appears (very similar to the Convert to Symbol box we saw earlier):

If you give the symbol a name here (mask2, for example), click on the radio button next to Graphic again and press OK, you'll be taken to the new symbol's internal timeline. Remember, you can use that navigation bar to see exactly where you are.

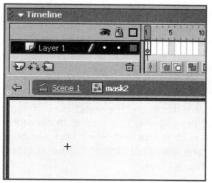

Here you can see that you are inside the timeline for the mask2 symbol. The fact that the symbol has its own timeline is pretty significant: when an instance of this symbol is placed on the stage, its timeline can run *independently* of the main movie's timeline; this means that symbols *have a life of their own*.

If you open up the Library again you'll see a blank space with a crosshair (the center point of the symbol – more on this shortly). This space is blank because we haven't actually created any graphical content for the new symbol yet.

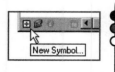

> **Tip**
> There is yet another way of creating a symbol – just click on the little blue cross on the bottom left-hand corner of the Library window.

Let's add some content now – select the Oval tool and draw a simple circle on stage. Look at the Library now and you'll see that the symbol is instantly updated.

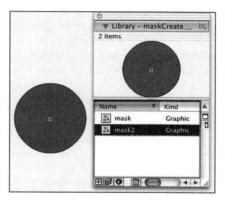

So why would you want to create a symbol in the library but not on stage? Some movie clips are made to appear on stage *dynamically* when the movie is running, and not before – they're downloaded to the user's machine in the Library as part of the SWF file, and make their entrance when called. As we shall see later in this book, ActionScript is used to do this.

Symbol types

Now that we're more familiar with creating and using symbols, and how to store and re-use movie content elements in the Library, we'll take a look at the different types of symbol available to us. In fact, during our introduction to the use of symbols, we've already come across a couple of the different types:

● **Graphics** – contain simple content (animated or otherwise) forming a fundamental building block of cartoon animation in Flash.

● **Movie clips** – independent, self-contained (and often interactive) movie components that free you from the 'linearity' of your movie's root timeline. Movie clips are the most powerful of Flash's symbols, and you'll be seeing much more about these in later chapters, when we'll see how to incorporate animated and dynamic content into movie clip symbols.

● **Buttons** – the easiest method to achieving interactivity in your movies. We'll also be seeing much more about these later in the book.

We've already seen an example of a graphic symbol with the mask we used in the previous example, and we looked briefly at a movie clip symbol with the chameleon example earlier. There's a lot more material on movie clip symbols later in the book. Here, we're going to look a little more closely at the third type of symbol – the **button.**

The button symbol in detail

Button symbols placed in your movies sit waiting to respond to mouse or keyboard events, which, in turn, trigger and control other events on stage. These events often control other movie clip instances. You can make other symbols in the same movie perform actions based on the mouse's interaction with the button symbol; different things can be made to happen when, for example, you click and release the mouse on a button, roll over a button, roll out of a button, or when you drag over or out of a button.

Time for an example – open up `maskbw.fla` and test the movie with CTRL+ENTER/⌘+ENTER.

In this movie, there are four instances of button symbols on the stage. Each button symbol instance controls a mask movie clip instance that sits above it. If

> **Tip**
> *All three types of symbol have their own dedicated timeline, stage, and layers.*

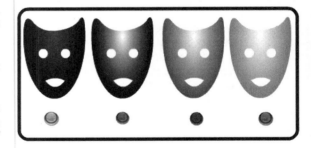

you bring up the Property inspector and click on the buttons in turn, you'll see that all the masks are instances of the single mask symbol in the Library, and that the four button instances are derived from four different button master symbols.

It's worth noting that these buttons were simply dragged and dropped from the **Common Libraries** of Flash MX. If you go to **Window > Common Libraries > Buttons** you'll see the buttons Library panel pop up.

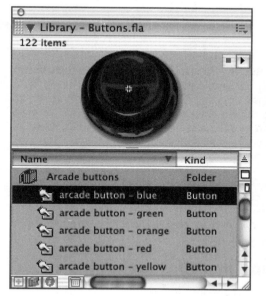

These predefined symbols can be really useful, and they give us plenty of options for different kinds of buttons to use in our designs. You can also make your own buttons in Flash, so you're not just restricted to the ones in the Common Libraries; for example, any *image* can be turned into a button. For more flexibility, you can even make *movie clips* into buttons that respond to mouse events, but for simplicity we'll stick with a basic traditional button for the moment.

 The essence of a button is that it has four 'states', each represented by a key frame in the button symbol's internal timeline; a button is really a small movie with four frames. When you create a button symbol, the four default frames are automatically inserted for you. These frames can be thought of as a generic pizza base; the actual images/content you put in each frame is up to you, a bit like choosing your own custom pizza toppings! The content you add to these frames determines the appearance of the different button states.

 Open up cham_button.fla and double-click on the picture of our old friend the chameleon. You'll see that there is a 4-frame timeline with a different picture on each frame:

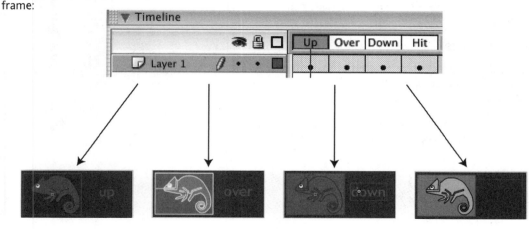

Test the movie. When the SWF opens up, pass your mouse over the button (the chameleon!) and click – you'll see the images change according to whether your mouse is over the button, pressing it down, or off to the side. The content the button displays is determined by the 'state' it's in – inactive, being hovered over, or being pressed.

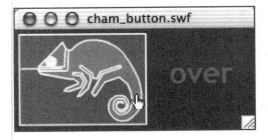

Notice that the Hit state defined in the button's fourth frame is not visible in the finished SWF. The Hit state defines the area that will be sensitive to the presence of the mouse and react to it being clicked. This **hit area** needs to be solid and big enough to sit underneath all the other images so they actually work when you pass your mouse over and click them. If the hit area is smaller than the images then some parts of the Over and Down images won't respond, because there's no area to click or hit on.

Next, we'll look at how to edit the content *inside* symbols effectively.

Tip
There's much more on creating and using buttons in **Chapter 9**.

Editing graphics within a symbol

There are three ways you can edit a symbol in Flash MX:

● Edit in place

● Edit in a new window

● Edit in the Library

We'll examine these techniques in details in the next few subsections.

Edit in place

Editing a symbol in place is pretty straightforward - open up `lollipop_forest.fla` (if your eyes can stand it!).

We're going to play around with it a little, so save it as a new FLA – we've called ours `lollipop_forest1.fla`.

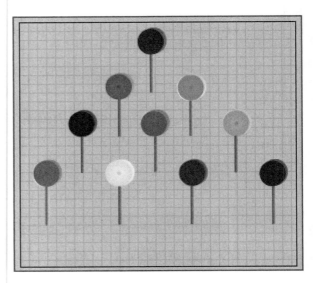

Choose the blue lollipop at the bottom right of the array by double-clicking on it. The first thing you'll notice is that all the other lollipops have grayed out, and that the 'blue' one you're working on has turned *red*. The original symbol in the Library is red (check if you don't believe me – CTRL+L/⌘+L), so it's clear that we've already drilled down to the core artwork for this symbol. This is so significant that it's worth re-emphasizing – we're down to the core graphics of the master symbol this instance is linked to, so any changes you make here will also change **all** the other instances on the stage.

Tip
If you put your arrow cursor a few pixels away from the top of the lollipop you'll see a black curved line appear under it. This indicates that you can click and pull a fill or stroke to resize it, or pull it around like pixilated play dough!

You should also notice that the navigation bar is back, so we can always see where we are:

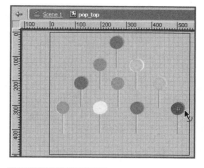

Click and drag a piece of the lollipop off to the left:

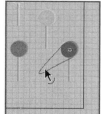

Now let go – *all* the instances change with the symbol! But don't panic – unless you like strangely shaped candy, select **Edit > Undo** (CTRL+Z/⌘+Z) to undo the change.

Tip
CTRL+Z (⌘+Z *on a Mac) is probably the most popular and well-used key combo when working in Flash – Flash is set to 100 levels of undo, more than enough for most corrections.*

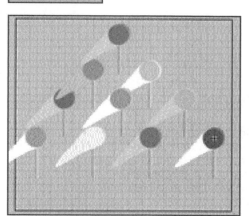

Editing in place allows you to see the whole piece that you're creating *and* the symbol you're currently working on in context. This means that it's easier to see how changing the specific element affects the overall composition.

Edit in a new window

What if you *don't* want to see all of this background clutter while you're editing some masterpiece of a symbol? You'd then choose to edit the symbol in a new window. Use the navigation bar and click on the blue arrow to get back to the stage.

Click once on that blue lollipop again, but this time right-click (Mac, CTRL-click) on it to reveal the options shown here:

Select Edit in New Window. You'll be taken to a nice new clutter-free window where you can work on the symbol in peaceful isolation:

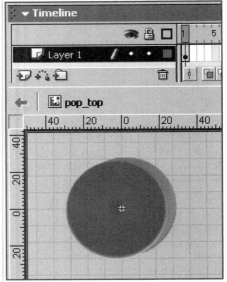

Getting out of this editing mode can be tricky, as there's no Back button to guide you out (note that it is grayed out in New Window mode). Many people recommend clicking on the **X** in the top right-hand corner to close the window – but this might be a bad habit to get in to in this case, because you might shut the entire program down if you *think* you are in editing mode but you actually *aren't*. The best thing to do is to click on the Edit Scene button on the top right of the stage instead – this is a lot safer!

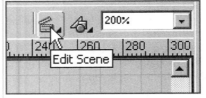

Edit in Library

The last way to edit a symbol is directly from inside the Library. Press F11 with `lollipop_forest.fla` open, and the Library window will pop up – you'll see two symbol logos, along with their names:

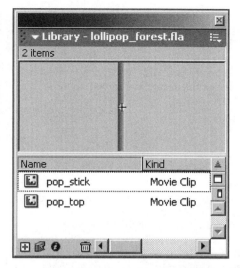

Now double-click on the `pop_top` symbol (or right-click and choose **Edit**). Hey presto, you now have the best of both worlds – a new clutterless window *and* a clear navigation back to the main stage.

Remember when we edited the blue lollipop and all the other instances changed as we dragged out the pixilated play dough? Now is a good time to show an example of **Break Apart** to throw the connection between an instance and a symbol into high relief.

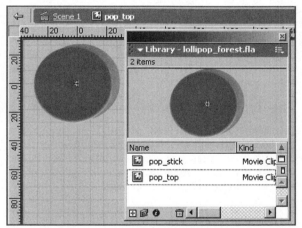

Using Break Apart to edit a symbol instance

So far we've been talking about the benefits of being able to edit your symbol and apply the changes globally to all instances of that symbol. Pretty cool stuff, right? But wait a minute – what if you actually *want* to edit an individual instance of your symbol, and not the whole bunch? Well, with Flash and symbols almost anything's possible!

Go back to the `lollipop_forest.fla` and click once on the blue lollipop in the bottom-right corner again. While it's selected, go to **Modify > Break Apart** (or press CTRL+B/⌘+B), then click away from the lollipop to deselect it. If you put your cursor over the lollipop now and shape it however you wish, you'll see immediately that none of the other instances change!

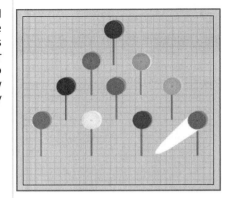

The Break Apart function has effectively disconnected that particular piece of candy from the symbol in the Library. It has been severed from the original master symbol, so it's now perfectly possible to edit the graphic independently from the other instances. You could even make it into a new symbol and start a whole new dynasty!

We'll round off this chapter with a look at the very useful Transform panel and its associated tools, which together make our lives a lot easier when creating and editing symbols.

The Transform panel

The **Transform** panel can be used to change the position, shape, and orientation of a symbol instance on the stage. Although we used it briefly earlier in the chapter, it contains some rather valuable tools, and so deserves a little more attention here.

To see how it works in the symbols context, open up the `frosty.fla` and pull an instance of the Frosty The Snowman symbol out of the Library, and onto the wintry landscape. In the Property inspector, name this instance `frosty`:

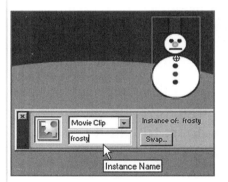

Scale

Scaling an object refers to resizing it in proportion to its original size. Open up the Transform panel – **Window > Transform** or CTRL+T/⌘+T. Check the **Constrain** option, type in 75%, and press ENTER – frosty's height and width reduce by a quarter:

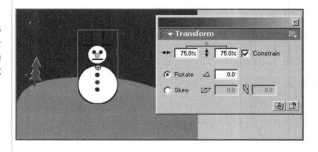

Now let's try some *manual* scaling. Right-click on `frosty` and select Scale – eight scaling handles appear around your snowman:

When we *transformed* `frosty` by resizing him 75% he remained in **proportion**; he was not too fat or too thin – just a scaled down version of his former self. This was because we checked the Constrain option. If we use the Scale option and click and pull on the Transform handles on the *corners* of this bounding box, we can scale him up and down in proportion:

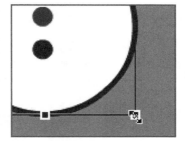

However, if you do the same thing while holding down the SHIFT key you can scale him any which way horizontally or vertically, and make him fat, thin, very tall or very short; this is known as **disproportionate** scaling:

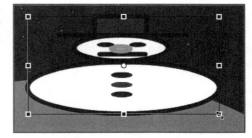

If you now click away from the snowman instance and then back on him, you will find that you're in Free Transform mode (this is also accessible from the tool bar to the left of the stage). You can see this by the fact that your cursor is now *context sensitive* and the possible transformations – scale, skew, and rotate – will change according to where the cursor is:

Rotate

Now try **Rotate** in the Transform panel; make sure it's selected and type in 90: after a 90° rotation, `frosty` doesn't look very well.

The Rotate option allows you to rotate the instance of the symbol around its registration point (also known as **a transformation** point in such cases). In fact, when you apply Free Transform tool (hit Q to select it from the toolbox) you can even move the transformation point to a new position before rotating.

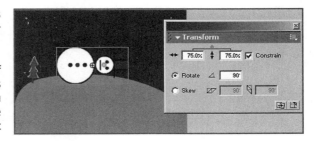

Here we have dragged the transformation point from the center to the side and then applied a rotation transformation:

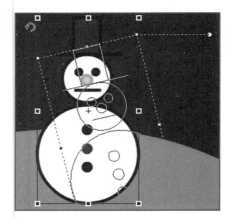

Skew

Back to the Transform panel: click on the skew box on the right and type in 20 – `frosty` levitates!

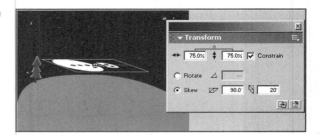

Skewing allows you to shear the image in a certain plane, depending on the angle. We can also skew an object by hand in the Free Transform mode – simply pull in the direction you wish to skew with the twin arrow symbol:

Copy and Reset

Note the two icons in the lower right-hand corner of the Transform panel. **Copy and apply transform** lets you copy an instance of a symbol in its transformed state. **Reset** returns the symbol to its original state.

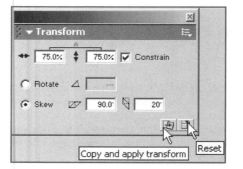

Summary

Here's what we covered in this chapter:

- What **symbols** are, and why they're useful

- Advantages of symbols over groups

- **Creating** and **using** symbols and their instances

- The **Library** and its properties

- The three symbol types:
  - **Movie clip**
  - **Button**
  - **Graphic**

- **Editing** graphics within a symbol efficiently

Next

Getting the most out of the Flash MX timeline.

Chapter 5
The Flash Timeline

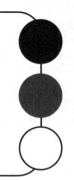

What's in this chapter:

● The **timeline, frames,** and **frame rate**, and how these affect animation

● Types of frames:
  ○ **Keyframes**
  ○ **Blank keyframes**

● Frame references and documentation:
  ○ **Labels** and **comments**

● **Timeline options**

Animation and "the willing suspension of disbelief"

Movement in Flash MX sets up the scenario for us to suspend disbelief and enter into the world of the animated movie. The way to achieve a simulated reality is through animation, movement, and motion graphics. In this chapter we'll be studying the fundamental tool that helps us to achieve this in Flash MX – the humble **timeline**.

Timeline essentials

The best way to demonstrate the basic use of the timeline is by example – open up the file flickBook.fla. This is a brief animated 'bridging' sequence of a cartoon – a spaceship moving across the stage.

Like we did with the jump movie in **Chapter 2**, test this movie (CTRL+ENTER/⌘+ENTER) with the Bandwidth Profiler (CTRL+B/⌘+B), ensuring you have the Frame by Frame graph turned on (**View > Frame by Frame Graph** or CTRL+F/⌘+F), and click on each of the bars to see the movie frame by frame:

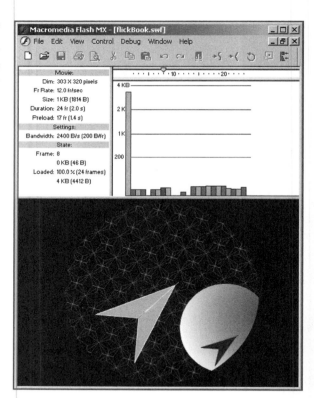

If you were to see this movie in context, between two action scenes, you wouldn't blink twice, accepting the fact that the crew is traveling from one place to another. You wouldn't notice the jerky hand-animated frames, you'd subconsciously suspend disbelief for long enough to take in the fact that a transition or journey was going on. In the old days animators certainly relied on short bursts of animation; next time you watch Disney's *Snow White*, try a little experiment – see if any camera shot in that whole film is anything over 15 seconds long. Very few are!

Now we're going to look in detail at what's happening frame by frame in Flash. Return to the timeline of flickBook.fla:

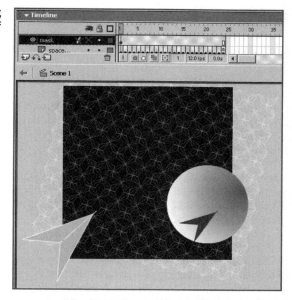

There are a few different **layers** in this timeline – if you can't see all of them put your cursor between the bottom of the timeline and the top of the Scene divider and it'll change into a double arrowed pull-down cursor (highlighted in the screenshot). Click and pull down until you can see all five layers:

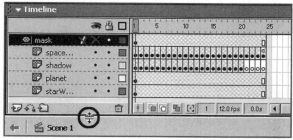

If you press ENTER now the movie will play through once on stage and you'll be able to follow the playhead as it moves over the 24 frames in sequence. You can also click on the top of the playhead and pull it backwards and forwards across the frames to make the spaceship travel back and forth:

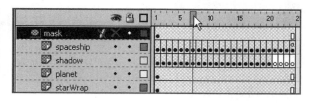

Notice that the timeline itself is made up by a number of layers that contain different types of **frames** – we'll take a look at frames in detail shortly. In the final frame of the spaceship layer you'll see the stop() action that we came across in **Chapter 2**, but don't worry about the finer details of how the animation works for the moment – throughout this chapter we'll be looking at the various aspects of the Flash timeline and exploring its importance for creating animations. Animation is also examined in much greater depth later in the book, particularly in **Chapters 6** and **8**. Let's continue with a brief discussion about the importance of the frame rate to your movies.

Tip
To hide/show the timeline, press CTRL+ALT+T/OPTION+⌘+T.

Frame rate

The frame rate of a Flash movie refers the number of **frames per second** (fps) that your movie will play at, just like a movie at the theater. Keeping in mind that a typical Hollywood movie runs at around 25-30 fps, we'll see in this chapter that Flash MX often has to work with a lot less, meaning that designers and artists have to be a little more savvy when it comes to grabbing people's attention.

In general, the lower the fps you use the more jumpy your movie becomes. Between 8 and 12 is the recommended optimum for the web; 12 fps is the default value when you first start up your copy of Flash MX.

Even if you had a super fast Pentium or the very latest faster-than-light Mac, it would not play your movie any quicker than the number of fps that have been set in the Property inspector or the **Document Properties** box.

Take a look at the Property inspector of the previous example (hit CTRL+F3/⌘+F3 if it's not open already):

> **Tip**
> *So how does the frame rate relate to the length of a movie? It's simple math really; in the previous example,* flickBook.fla, *our movie was 24 frames at 12 fps, and therefore ran for 2 seconds.*

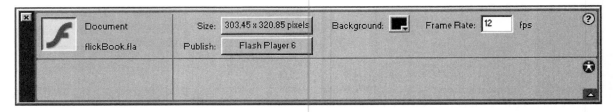

On the right-hand side of this panel you'll see an entry pane for the Frame Rate. Change it to 24, hit ENTER to make the alteration, and then test the movie again. This time you'll see that it runs at twice the speed!

Remember, you can also make changes to the fps from the Document Properties dialog by selecting **Modify > Document** or CTRL+J/⌘+J *(this dialog box also appears if you hit the Size button in the Property inspector).*

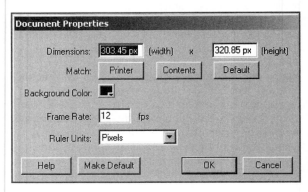

> **Tip**
> *The frame rate can't be varied throughout the movie, so it's a one-stop-shop when setting this value; it applies to the whole movie.*

Processor restrictions

Although you might want to design your movie with a frame rate higher than 12 fps, you should bear in mind the number of people who have older computers connected to the web. Any 'ancient' processors will trudge along and play your artistic *magnum opus* at a much slower rate.

The key word here is **processor** – it takes the older machine much longer to process and render the pixels and any rotations, alpha settings, or complex animations than it would a machine with a faster 'brain'.

When to use a high frame rate

You don't have to be a quantum physicist to work out that if the frame rate is set too high, movies run slower on computers with slower processors. They will stutter and stop and start, then they will play eventually – but it won't be a satisfying experience.

 On the other hand, if you are designing movies for a specific market and a minimum spec of a fast computer with video cards and lightning renders, then go ahead and rack it up! The traditional advice was to test your movie on several machines and browsers of different age and speed to see the effects. However, with the advent of broadband, ASDL, and the new digital video options in Flash MX, you're probably better off flagging up the frame rates of your movies on your website and creating different SWF files with different frame rates for different users.

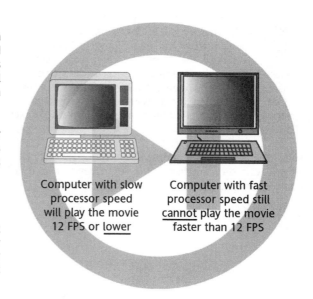

Computer with slow processor speed will play the movie 12 FPS or <u>lower</u>

Computer with fast processor speed still <u>cannot</u> play the movie faster than 12 FPS

Tip
Giving the user options, plus the information they need to make their choices, will help endear you to your audience.

Types of frames in the timeline

When you open up a new FLA in Flash MX (CTRL+N/⌘+N) you'll be presented with a timeline consisting of one layer, called Layer 1, and the first frame of that layer is a **blank keyframe** (the one with the red playhead bisecting it):

You can insert some ordinary frames – denoted by empty white rectangles – after the first frame by clicking on frame 2 so that it darkens, and then either going to **Insert > Frame** or simply hitting F5:

Press F5 right now a few times to insert some new frame.

Notice that the new frames are labeled as Static – we'll come back to this point later in the chapter when we come to look at **frame labels**.

Ordinary frames are fairly inert – they essentially act as padding in a movie, providing the *time* for things to happen. As we shall see, ordinary frames are used as spacers between **keyframes**: they provide space for transformations to happen between keyframes at either end of an animation (or a **tween** in the language of Flash – we'll learn all about tweening in the next chapter).

Let's look at another example – open up planet.fla. As you can see, the first frame of planet.fla is a blank keyframe, and the stage is indeed empty:

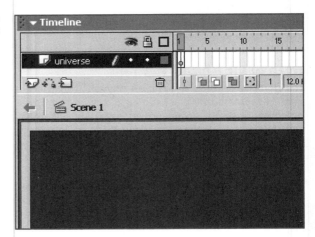

Tip
More frames = longer run time (assuming you're comparing movies with the same frame rate, of course!)

Bring up the Library of planet.fla (F11) and drag an instance of the planet symbol onto the stage in the default frame 1. Notice that the circle in frame 1 is now black indicating that it is now a **keyframe**:

Tip
Whereas keyframes with content show a circle filled with black, blank keyframes, logically enough, show an unfilled circle in the timeline.

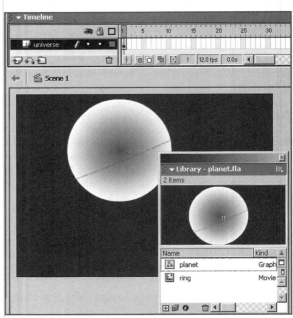

Keyframes are vitally important in Flash, so let's look at them in finer detail.

Keyframes

Keyframes are the frames where key events in a movie occur. Consider the individual panels in a comic book; they represent the *key* pictures that tell us the story – expressions, movement, changes in scene and plot direction, and so on. Likewise, a keyframe in the Flash timeline is where something significant happens to the content of your movie.

As we've just seen, the first frame on a timeline is, by default, a blank keyframe, denoted by the small empty circle. To turn this frame into a keyframe, simply add some content to it – a simple circle, for example:

The first frame is now a keyframe – represented by a rectangle containing a small solid black circle. Note also that this frame is now gray, indicating that it has some content.

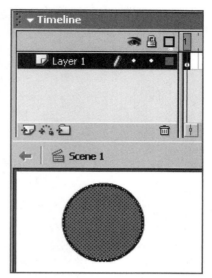

Use a keyframe when you want to make a specific change in your movie or if you want a symbol to remain on stage for a certain time. For instance, if you add a certain amount of frames *after* a keyframe, then your movie would last correspondingly longer.

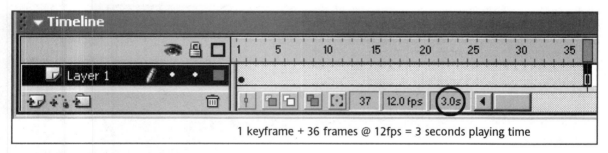

1 keyframe + 36 frames @ 12fps = 3 seconds playing time

If, for instance, you added 36 frames after your keyframe in a movie running at 12 fps, your image would play for 3 seconds.

Notice that although you're inserting ordinary frames, they too are now colored gray to show that they have some content; these frames have 'inherited' the content that's in the previous keyframe. Flash will continue to display that content for as long as the 37 frames last.

So, keyframes form the fundamental moments when animation **begins**, **changes**, or **ends**. Because we'll be coming into contact with frames and keyframes almost

> **Tip**
> *There are many lessons that can be learned from studying comic art, and there are some great books that will help you refine your visual storytelling and design. One example is Scott McCloud's seminal* Understanding Comics *(ISBN 0-06-097625-X).*

constantly, it's worthwhile spending a little time emphasizing the difference between ordinary frames and keyframes.

Take a look at the file `alien.fla` – it's a short animation sequence consisting of 21 frames:

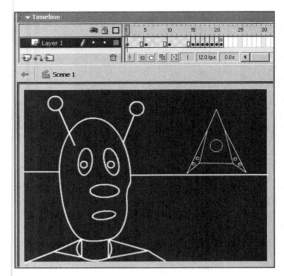

Hit your ENTER key to watch the animation play through, noting the changes that occur at a keyframe (the frames with black circles). As you can see, the keyframes are either points where animation is beginning, in transition, or at an end:

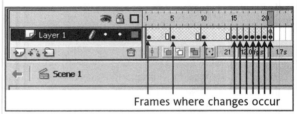

Frames where changes occur

So frame 1 is a keyframe as it introduces all of the content: the alien, the landscape, and his space ship. This is followed by frames 2 through 4 which are ordinary frames in which the content remains the same. Notice that the end of a sequence of non-keyframes that are all the exactly the same is marked by a white rectangle. These gray **spacer** frames are there simply to pad out the time. Spacer frames between keyframes all have the same content; they act like a background picture between frames and are inert – they cannot be animated.

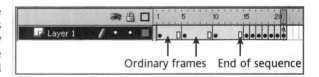

Ordinary frames   End of sequence

In frame 5 we have another keyframe when the alien's eyes move to the right, then frame 9 is another end-of-sequence marker. In frame 10 the alien's eyes move to the right a little bit more so it's a keyframe, with frames 11 to 14 as more time padding. Finally, frames 15 through 21 are all keyframes involving subtle changes; where the rocket lifts off, and where the alien's eyes and mouth move to suggest his surprise. Note also that our final frame contains the ubiquitous `stop()` action, to halt the animation.

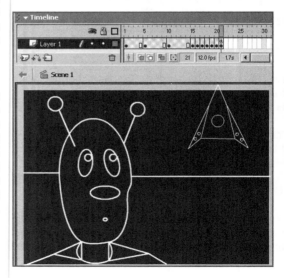

Referencing and documenting frames

It can be very useful to structure the timeline of your movies through generous use of **labels** and **comments**. While frame labels allow you to reference specific frames, comments within frames let you keep track of how and why you designed a movie in a certain way – this can prove to be a real bonus when you come back to update it after a long time. Another advantage, if you're sharing ideas within the Flash community, is that it makes your work easier for other designers to understand.

Labels

Frame labels are markers that you can reference – or *target* – with ActionScript, directing Flash's attention to that precise place in the movie and instigating some action there. A labeled keyframe provides a reference point that you can jump to, send movie clips to, or have certain events occur at, all using ActionScript.

In a new Flash document hold your cursor over the keyframe and you will see a little yellow label appear with the word Static on it (this frame is not labeled and therefore can't be called upon to do anything):

Now select this frame and take a look at the Frame box of the Property inspector:

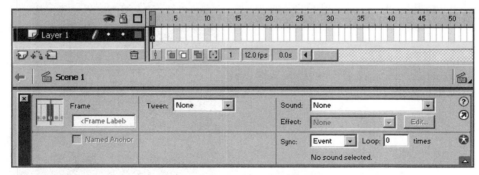

Type the word `first` in this box, over the `<Frame Label>` text:

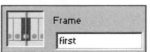

Now hold your cursor over the frame to see the new label – notice that a little red flag appears in the relevant frame to show that this frame now has a label:

As we saw briefly in **Chapter 2**, anything you can name in Flash MX can be either called to do something or go somewhere via ActionScript. Indeed, this goes for frames too – an example is in order!

In this example we'll demonstrate how you can label a keyframe and jump to that frame during a movie. Although it contains a couple of lines of ActionScript, it's nothing to be worried about, and serves as a nice introduction to scripting too. Open up spaceShip.fla and look at the timeline – it has two layers, spaceship and stars.

The spaceship layer has 24 pictures of the spaceship, and the numbers in the bottom-right corner increment to reflect the frame of the movie. The label of each frame also corresponds to the frame number:

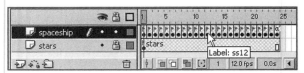

If you click on the spaceship in adjacent keyframes and look on the X-scale of the Property inspector, you will see that the ship has been moved 10 pixels to the right in each successive keyframe – this creates the appearance of motion when you run the animation.

However, on the stars layer, there is only one keyframe, labeled stars, and 23 ordinary frames that do nothing other than fill in the image between frame 1 and 24. *Note that you cannot name or access an ordinary frame.*

Now test the movie (CTRL+ENTER/⌘+ENTER). When the movie reaches the end, you'll see a button appear in the lower-left corner accompanied by the label 'Jump to 7':

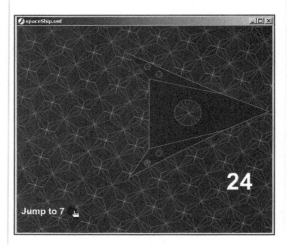

Click on this button and, lo and behold, you are 'redirected' to frame 7 of the movie:

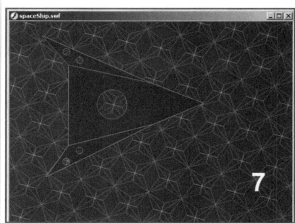

So how does this work? Well – of course – it's relying on the frame labels to be able to redirect you to a specific keyframe. Go back into the FLA and click on frame 24 of the timeline – this is where we place our button. In the Property inspector you can see that we have named this particular instance of the button myButton:

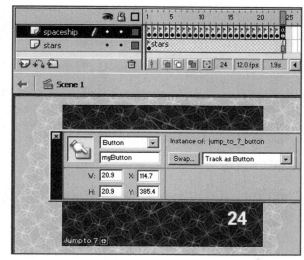

No doubt you've already noticed that frame 24 of our movie also contains some ActionScript commands, as indicated by the little 'a' symbol on the timeline:

So open up your Actions panel while frame 24 is selected (hit F9) and you should see the following information (assuming you're in the Normal mode of the Actions panel):

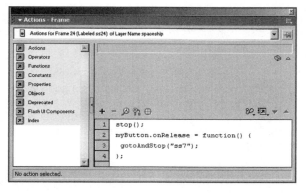

There are four lines of code attached to this frame. Don't panic! We'll explain precisely what each line of this script does in the order that it occurs. First, we have the now-familiar stop() action, which simply stops our movie from constantly looping around the 24 frames at this point:

```
stop();
```

Next, we have three potentially worrying lines:

```
myButton.onRelease = function() {
    gotoAndStop("ss7");
};
```

Let's break this down – these lines translate directly to: "When you click on and then release the button called myButton, then the Flash movie will go the frame labeled ss7 and then stop there". And this is exactly what happens when you test the movie and the button. Not so tricky, huh!?

So, at a very basic level we've learned that we can label a keyframe, reference it, and then jump to it via some simple ActionScript commands.

ActionScript	Plain English
	"OK, Flash: when someone clicks on and releases the button symbol instance called myButton, I want you to perform an action..."
myButton.onRelease = function() {	
gotoAndStop("ss7");	"...and that action is this: go to the frame that's labeled ss7 and pause the playhead there."

Comments

Frame comments are notes to yourself about what is happening – or what you intend to happen – in the frame.

You make frame comments exactly the same way you make frame labels (see previous section) except that you put a double forward slash '//' in front of the text that you enter in the Property inspector:

On entering a comment, that frame will show the double forward-slash in green to indicate that it has comments attached, and your cursor will reveal the full comment:

Adding plenty of comments – especially to more complicated movies – is a good habit to get into. Adding comments is a bit like recording a director's commentary for your movies; you can remind yourself (and other designers) what's happening in the movie at any given time.

Let's see a more realistic example – have a look at alienComment.fla. This is exactly the same animation as that which we saw earlier, but now it has been commented throughout. Hold your cursor over the keyframes to reveal the comments.

> ### Tip
> A lack of comments may not seem like a problem on the day that you're creating the content, but things might not look so clear or obvious when you come back to your FLA after days, weeks, or months.

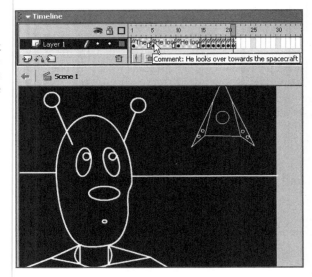

Timeline frame view options

Customizability is a pretty big deal in Flash MX, so we'll complete this chapter with a quick review of some of the options we have for changing the look and feel of our timeline.

You'll find the **Frame View** options menu by clicking the button in the top right corner of your timeline:

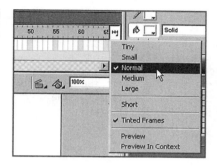

Size

The frame size options of the timeline are:

- Tiny

- Small

- Normal

- Medium

- Large

The best way to get a feel for these options is to try them out! In fact, you'll soon realize that there is a view for every occasion. For example, open up `spaceShip_sound.fla`, which is very similar to an earlier example, but with added sound effects, and have a play with the size options. Clearly, a Tiny frame size is impractical in this case: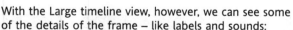

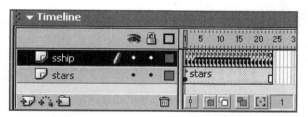

Indeed, even the Normal view is less than ideal for displaying all the information in the timeline of this FLA:

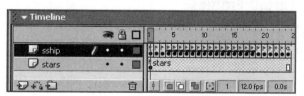

With the Large timeline view, however, we can see some of the details of the frame – like labels and sounds:

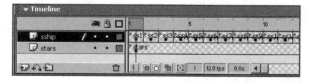

Short

The Short timeline view simply shortens the height of the frames – this option can be combined with any of the sizes to give you a bigger view of the stage when working without losing the timeline altogether. Or maybe you'll want a thinner detached bar when working at the bottom or top of your artwork:

Layer Height

It's also possible to change the height of individual layers' frames so that you can get an even clearer view:

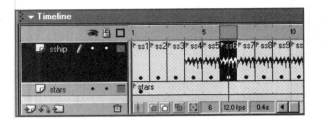

To do this, right-click (CTRL-click) on the layer name at the far left of the timeline. When the dialog box appears, select the Properties option – the Layer Properties dialog box will be revealed:

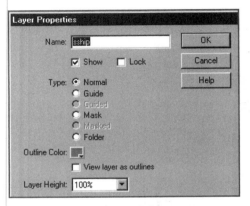

Here, select your chosen option in the Layer Height box.

You'll now have lots more space to view the content of this layer's frames.

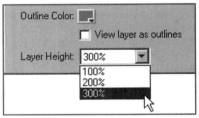

Tinted Frames

The use of Tinted/Untinted frames is essentially one of personal preference. The Tinted option is initially checked by default in Flash MX as tinting can give you a very quick view of which frames have content and which don't, especially when working with multiple layers. It's your call!

Preview

The Preview option shows you a large thumbnail picture of every object in each frame, but not to scale:

Preview In Context

The Preview In Context option is very similar to Preview, but shows small pictures of the content drawn to scale so that each frame is in proportion to its neighboring frames:

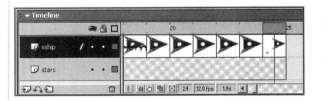

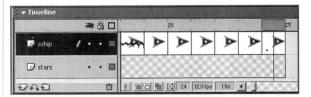

Summary

We've covered a lot of ground in this chapter:

- The **timeline, frames,** and **frame rate**, and how these affect animation

- Types of frames:
  - **Keyframes**
  - **Blank keyframes**

- Frame references and documentation:

  - **Labels** and **comments**

- **Timeline options** – different ways of viewing and using the timeline

Next

More detail on **animation** in Macromedia Flash MX!

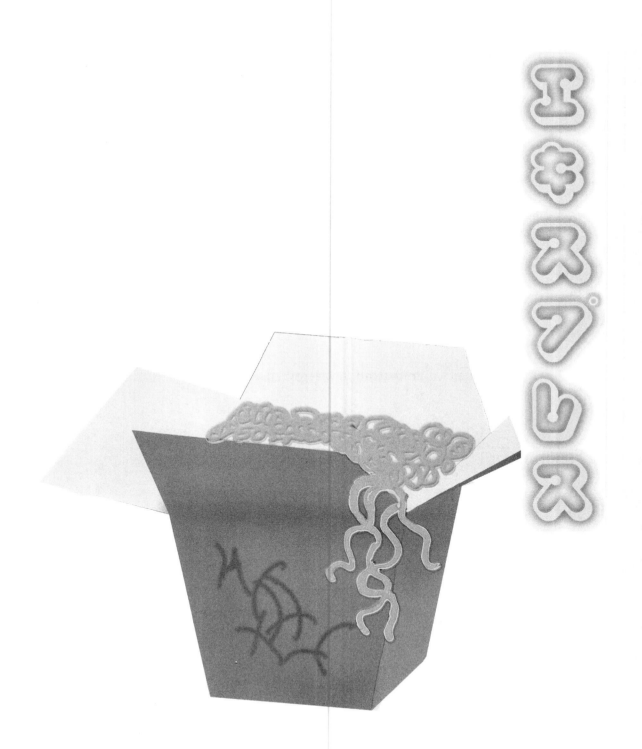

Chapter 6
Animation in
Flash MX

What's in this chapter:

- Basic motion

- Frame-by-frame animation

- Motion tweening:
  - Symbol properties
  - Skewing a tween
  - Center points
  - The frame panel
  - Auto rotation
  - Easing motion tweens

- Shape tweening:
  - Shape tweening strokes vs. fills
  - Shape hints
  - Easing shape tweens

Basic motion

Basic motion in Macromedia Flash MX is implemented by changing the position, size, or shape of symbol instances, grouped objects, or graphics placed on keyframes. Frequent changes in keyframes result in **animation**. Basic movement is *usually* linear, and in one direction only: a bouncing ball; a car traveling along a road; a plane flying across the sky.

Basic, linear motion

Frame-by-frame animation

Frame-by-frame animation is where each and every frame is a keyframe: here, every frame holds a slightly different image, just like traditional cell animation, where animators drew on different sheets of transparent celluloid and could build up a sequence of drawings over time. They would overlay these drawings – much like a transparent flick book – so that they could see the previous drawing in a sequence. This would help them judge how much to change the next drawing in the sequence; and so the cartoon would grow by the accumulation of small increments. These multilayer sets of transparent sheets gave rise to the term 'onion-skinning'.

Onion skins

Flash has a very handy tool to help you create your own frame-by-frame drawings: **Onion Skins**. There are two buttons just below the timeline that enable us to use the onion skin effect, each giving a slightly different view. These buttons are the **Onion Skin** button and the **Onion Skin Outlines** button.

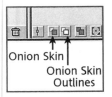

Onion Skin
Onion Skin
Outlines

We can learn the effect of these buttons easiest by seeing them in use.

Open the source file `key_lock.fla` and click on the Onion Skin button. Look at the stage and you'll see that the content of the frames surrounding the frame the playhead is currently on is visible, albeit with transparency. This is the onion skin effect:

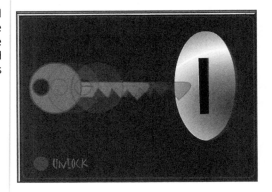

> **Tip**
> *Onion skins cannot be seen if the layer you're working on is locked.*

If you look at the top of the timeline you'll see that a number of frames are selected. These are the frames that are currently included in the onion skin.

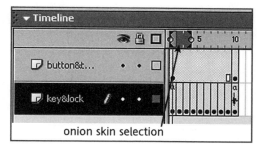

onion skin selection

You can change the span of frames included in the onion-skinning by dragging the skin selection markers (the start and end points represented by the little disks):

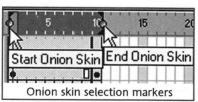

Onion skin selection markers

Drag the end marker so that the onion skins are applied to the whole timeline. Click the playhead and pull it back and forth across the frames and, as you do so, notice that the onion skins disappear as you progress forwards and *re-appear* as you pull back to frame 1. If you're working on a frame in the middle of the movie you can just as easily drag the **Start Onion Skin** marker to your required frames. With frame-by-frame animation it's often only necessary to see the current frame and previous frame when creating new content.

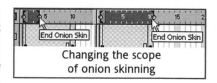

Changing the scope
of onion skinning

Instead of dragging the onion skin markers you can choose preset limits in the **Modify Onion Markers** menu:

The **Always Show Markers** option means that the onion skin markers will always be visible on the timeline – even if you haven't got onion skinning turned on. The **Anchor Onion** option just means that the onion skins won't move along with the playhead. The bottom three options allow you to skin two or five frames on either side of the playhead frame (**Onion 2**, **Onion 5**), or to skin all the frames (**Onion All**).

111

Outlines

Now click on the **Onion Skin Outlines** button and observe that the content of each frame, apart from the playhead frame, is now represented by the content's *outline* rather than by a transparent image:

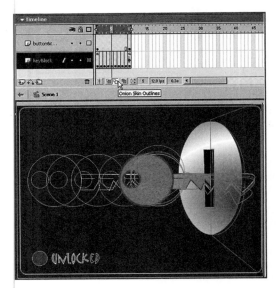

Outlines can be of greater use than the standard onion skins when you're working mainly with strokes. Take a look at `tightrope_walker.fla` for an example of this:

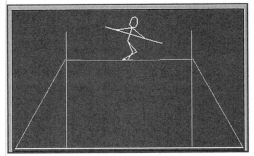

Turn the Onion Skin Outlines mode on, and select the Onion All option from the Modify Onion Markers menu:

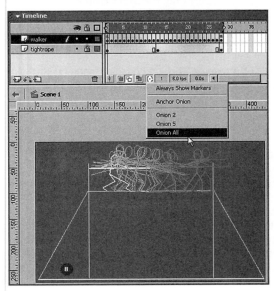

Creating frame-by-frame animation

Armed with the knowledge of how to use onion skins, creating frame-by-frame animations is simple. Let's look at a quick example. In a new movie (CTRL+N/⌘+N) draw a quick stick man on frame 1. Use the Line tool (keyboard shortcut N) to draw a body, legs, and arms, and the Oval tool (shortcut O), with no fill, to draw the head.

Create a keyframe at frame 2 (F6) and turn the Onion Skin Outlines on. You can't see the effect of the onion skin yet as the stick man hasn't been changed.

In the Modify Onion Markers menu choose Onion All so that you can see all the onion skins as the movie becomes longer.

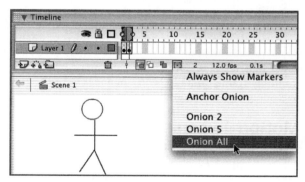

If the stick man is selected, deselect him. On frame 2, use the Arrow tool (keyboard shortcut A) to move the man's arm slightly upwards. You'll see that the onion skin outline for frame 1 is now faintly visible, showing the arm in its original position in the previous frame:

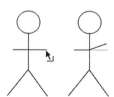

Add a keyframe at frame 3 (F6) and deselect the stick man by clicking on a blank area of the stage with the Arrow tool. Now use the Arrow tool to move the arm slightly higher, and move the opposite leg up a little too.

Continue this process of making new keyframes with the F6 key, deselecting the figure, and modifying him slightly with the Arrow tool. Make the movie ten frames long with a keyframe on each frame:

Press ENTER to watch the animation run through. You can see this finished effect in `stickman.fla`.

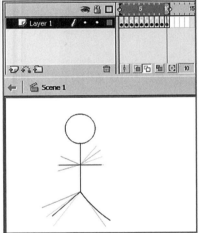

 As you can see, frame-by-frame animation is pretty labor intensive. The major benefit of frame-by-frame animation is the amount of detail that you can include. If you're doing a quick project then this traditional style of animation is not really an efficient use of time if the movie is more than a few frames long. There's a much easier and faster way to make animations where the frame-by-frame details and nuances aren't the overriding consideration: **tweening**.

Motion Tweening

 Motion tweening is a smart way of making smooth movement between keyframes in an animation. Flash automatically fills the frames inbe**tween** two keyframes to make the motion appear seamless. If you need to change a symbol's size, rotation, skew, color, or position over time, then use a motion tween. All the properties of a symbol instance outlined in the Properties inspector can be changed during a motion tween.

Tip
Motion tweening will not change an object's shape other than skewing or resizing it. Use a shape tween if you want to change a shape.

Take a look at `seal.fla` for a quick example of a motion tween. Test the movie (CTRL+ENTER/⌘+ENTER) and you'll see that the ball rotates on the seal's nose. This has been achieved with only two keyframes, and no code.

Let's emulate this rotation effect. In a new movie draw a circle that has both a stroke and a fill with the Oval tool (shortcut key O). Hold down the SHIFT key to ensure you get a perfect circle as you click down and drag the shape:

Now use the Eraser tool (E) to make a small hole in the fill – like a little highlight – so that you can see the circle rotate once you've made the tween:

Select the circle using the Select All command (CTRL+A/⌘+A), and convert it into a graphic symbol named **ball**, with a center registration point:

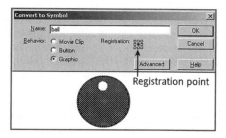

Click on frame 40 of the timeline and use F6 to insert a keyframe here.

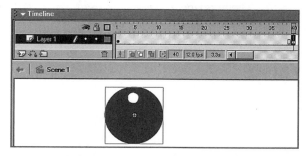

Now click on a frame in the middle of the timeline and open the Property inspector if it's not already open (CTRL+F3/⌘+F3). Choose **Motion** from the Property inspector's **Tween** drop-down menu.

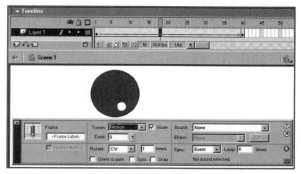

Note how the time line has changed to a blue color, and that it now has an arrow pointing to the end keyframe; this signifies that there's a successful motion tween. Select **CW** (for clockwise) in the **Rotate** drop-down menu. Leave the number of rotations as 1 (the default value):

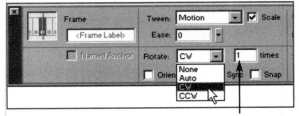

Number of rotations

Test the movie (CTRL+ENTER/⌘+ENTER) and you'll see the ball rotate once in a clockwise direction. To finish off the effect, let's make the ball look like it's rolling across the stage.

Click on frame 1 and move the ball symbol to the left hand side of the stage with the Arrow tool. On frame 40, move the ball to the right hand side of the stage, holding the SHIFT key down as you move it to ensure that the ball stays on a flat path. Test the effect once you've done this. The finished file can be found in the download code files as `ball.fla`.

Symbol properties

As we mentioned earlier, all the properties of a symbol instance can be changed during a motion tween. Look at the Property inspector when you select the ball symbol in `ball.fla` at frame 40. There are a number of attributes we can edit here:

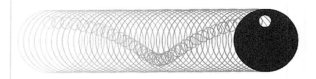

Width   Height   Y location   X location   Color Styles

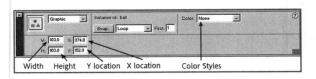

Change both the width and height values of the ball to 200 by typing this value in the appropriate boxes and pressing ENTER. Test the movie (CTRL+ENTER/⌘+ENTER) and you'll see the ball get bigger as the movie runs through.

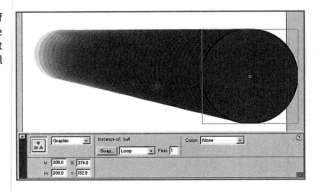

Now move the ball to the top right corner of the stage by entering 350 and 0 as the X and Y values in the Property inspector. Once again, test the movie to see the effect. To finish off, play around with the symbol's *color*. Select the **Tint** option in the **Color Styles** drop-down menu:

There are two places to select the color you're going to tint with. The first option is to enter the individual RGB (red, green, blue) values for a color – this is only really useful if you know the exact values of the color you're after. We recommend that you use the second option, the color picker. Choose a red color with the Eyedropper tool that appears when you click on the color picker:

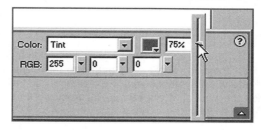

Finish the effect by clicking on the value slider to select the **Tint Amount** – set this to 75%.

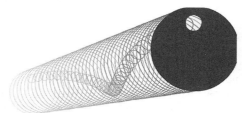

Press ENTER and watch the ball grow, change color, rotate, and move up and across the screen. This effect can be seen in `ball2.fla`.

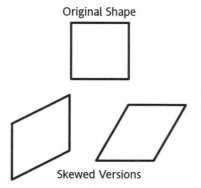

Skewing a tween

Skewing means changing the shape of the invisible bounding box that constrains a drawn shape:

Original Shape

Skewed Versions

It may not be in the Property inspector like the other symbol properties you've looked at, but the Free Transform tool can be used on symbols. This tool can rotate, skew, and scale a symbol, so it's useful in the motion tween context, too too.

Open up the `ball2.fla` file, or just continue in the file that has been built throughout this chapter. Click on frame 40 of the movie and then select the Free Transform tool (keyboard shortcut Q). This should select the ball symbol automatically, but if it doesn't, click on the symbol to select it:

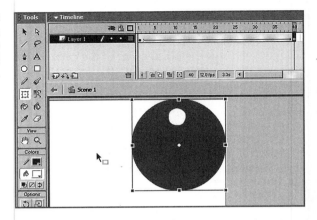

Use the Free Transform tool's skew option to move the left hand side of the symbol down. The skew tool can be used when the symbol ⌶ appears. Just click down and drag:

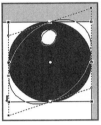 

Test the movie now (CTRL+ENTER/⌘+ENTER) and you'll see how this simple change has given the movie a 3D look with the ability to flip and spin. These results can be seen in `ball3.fla`.

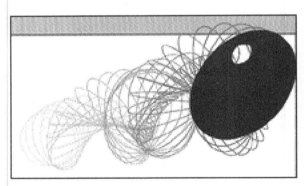

Changing a registration point

 When you first draw a picture on stage, highlight it, and convert it to a symbol (F8), you're presented with a choice of nine registration points for your newly created symbol. The black square represents the currently selected registration point:

You can change this registration point later, too, which can be useful in making your animations more convincing.

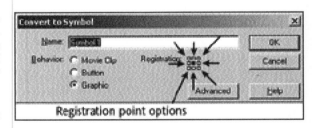

Registration point options

Open the file `transform_tw.fla`. In this file you'll see the tightrope walking man inside a movie clip. The registration point for this movie clip is the top left corner.

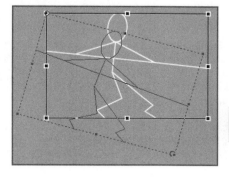
Movie clip registration point

Select the Free Transform tool (shortcut key Q) and the movie clip on the stage will be selected. Move the cursor near a corner of the movie clip until the rotation cursor appears. Click down and rotate the clip. You'll see that it rotates around the registration point in the top left corner.

This isn't really nuanced enough for creating realistic effects. Undo the rotation by pressing CTRL+Z/⌘+Z. Select the Free Transform tool again and move your mouse over the registration point of the clip in the top left corner. A little circle appears to the bottom right of the cursor arrow.

You can move this point by clicking down and dragging; move it now to the middle of the man's body. This moves the center point around which the clip rotates:

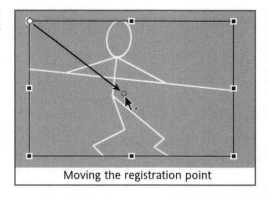
Moving the registration point

Rotate the man using the Free Transform tool again. This time he rotates around his waist, which makes for a much more realistic effect of a tightrope walker going across the rope and wobbling a bit. Take a look at `transform_tw2.fla` to see the effect.

Frame panel

Earlier, we saw how to create a motion tween and rotate a symbol as a tween; both of these techniques used the Property inspector. The Property inspector is content sensitive, and we get tweening options as part of the frame options. Open `fall.fla` and click on frame 1 of the **falling_person** layer. Take a look at the Property inspector; there are three options we're going to look at now – **scaling**, **easing**, and **auto rotation**.

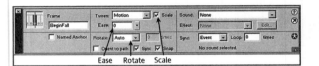

Scaling

The **Scale** option ensures that a tween scales up or down in proportion. It's an important feature, and it's switched 'on' by default. If you only wanted an object to change color, and *not* scale up or down, you'd uncheck this.

Test the movie `fall.fla` using CTRL+ENTER/⌘+ENTER and you'll see the stickman fall down into the swimming pool:

No autoscaling = no shrinkage during tween

Now click on frame 1 in layer 1, uncheck the **Scale** option, and test the movie again. This time the man *doesn't* fall – this demonstrates the value of auto scaling: there's a big version of the stickman in frame 1, and a tiny version in frame 24; without the autoscaling applied to the tween, Flash doesn't know to reduce the stickman's size and simulate his descent to the water.

Turn the option back on.

Easing

Easing is a process that makes animations look more realistic. In the real world, objects don't usually travel at a constant rate all the time when they move; for example, when you hit a golf ball, it suddenly acquires a great deal of *acceleration*, then it climbs up and through the air for a while, until friction slows it down and gravity pulls it down to earth. If you're lucky, the ball will trickle to a halt next to the pin. In Flash, unless we tell them otherwise, animations will occur at a constant rate throughout – this is a recipe for unconvincing looking motion, and the Easing feature can help us combat it.

The **Ease** option works as a value slider. Click on the downward arrow to the right of the easing value box to bring up the slider. The values range from -100 to 100, with 0 meaning 'no easing':

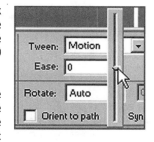

Push the slider to -100 and run the movie (CTRL+ENTER/⌘+ENTER). Notice that the man hovers in the air for a split second before accelerating to his fate. The Ease option makes the tween appear more naturalistic by speeding up or slowing down the actions at either end of the movement.

Auto rotation

Auto rotation means that you rely on the computer to rotate an object automatically during a tween. The computer figures out the shortest way to rotate the symbol between two keyframes and works out all the implementation details for you. Auto rotate can give 'unexpected' results – what you intend, and what the computer actually *does*, are sometimes two different things. Open up `seal.fla` again to see this in action...

 Click on frame 1 of the **seal** layer and make sure you have the Property inspector open (CTRL+F3/⌘+F3). This file uses a clockwise rotation, as we saw earlier, so change the rotation back to the default **Auto** setting:

The rotation frequency changes to 0 and is grayed out – the computer will now make the choice for you. Hit the ENTER key – nothing happens. This is because Flash is comparing the content of the two keyframes and sees no difference. The auto rotation feature detects the smallest discrepancy between corresponding points in the start and end frames of the animation and tweens that difference; here, there *is* no distance. To see how this works, click on the end keyframe. Select the ball with the Free Transform tool (Q) and move near a corner of the symbol until the rotation cursor appears. Rotate the ball until the hole is at the three o'clock position:

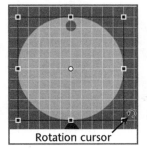
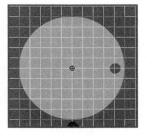

Rotation cursor

Test the movie (CTRL+ENTER/⌘+ENTER) and see how the symbol automatically rotates through the shortest distance.

> **Tip**
> *Easing in (-100 through 0) makes the tween start slowly and accelerate, and easing out (0 through 100) makes the tween decelerate towards the end. If you want to add easing in and easing out to a single animation, consider splitting the animation into sections with extra keyframes; that way, you can add separate easing settings to discrete segments.*

> **Tip**
> *Always check the auto rotate results to make sure that they're doing what you want them to.*

Shape tweening

The shape tweening process *morphs* one shape into another over the course of a series of frames:

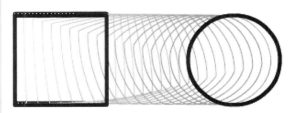

Square shape tweened into circle

The transition frames cannot be edited unless you turn them into a keyframe. Morphing via shape tweening is really a special effect – and, like motion tweening, it *can* be overused. Unlike motion tweens, shape tweens cannot be symbol instances. If you want symbol instances to morph you must break them apart first (Select with the Arrow tool and then CTRL+B/⌘+B).

> **Tip**
> *A shape tween is indicated in the timeline by coloring the tweened frames green (compared to blue for a motion tween) – there's also an arrow through from the start and end keyframes:*

Take a look at `morph.fla`. The shape tweening here occurs in the bottom layer, **Morphing**, starting at frame 76. Click on the keyframes on this layer and see the various shapes. Drag the playhead through these frames and watch the shapes morph into each other through the shape tweens:

 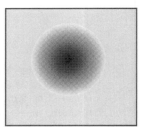

 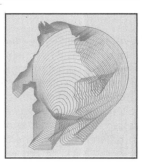

Let's start with a simple tween: a shape morphing from a square to a circle across the stage. In a new FLA (CTRL+N/⌘+N) select the Rectangle tool (R) – set the fill color to black, and the stroke to none:

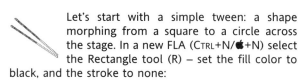  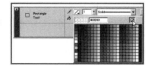

On the left hand side of the stage click down and drag out a square, holding the SHIFT key down as you do this to ensure a perfect square. Release the mouse to fill the square with black tint.

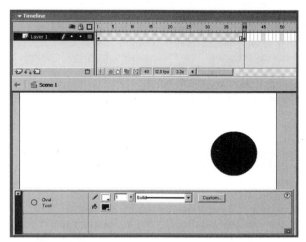

Click on frame 40 of the timeline and insert a keyframe (F6). The content of frame 1 will be replicated here. Delete the square on frame 40 by selecting it with the Arrow tool (this *should* have been done automatically when you made the keyframe) and pressing DELETE. Select the Oval tool and draw a circle on the right hand side of the stage, using the same black fill/no stroke combination. Remember to hold down the SHIFT key as you click-drag to create a perfect circle:

Click on a frame in the timeline between the two keyframes. In the Property inspector, select **Shape** from the **Tween** drop-down menu; the timeline will have turned green to signify a shape tween. Drag the playhead back to frame 1 with the Arrow tool and press ENTER to watch the movie run through. The square now morphs into the circle as it passes across the stage. This effect can be seen in morph2.fla.

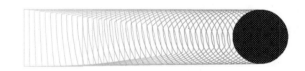

Shape tweens can create some pretty interesting (and unplanned!) effects. Take the morph2.fla and, on frame 1, use the Oval tool to draw some eyes, a nose, and a mouth on the existing square. Set both the stroke and the fill to white for these:

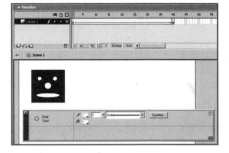

Test the movie now (ENTER) and you'll see some kaleidoscopic pictures occur as the white spaces are morphed:

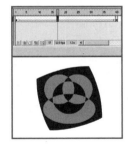

Special effects like shape tweening have their place in the Flash MX armory, and it's worth knowing about them so you can exploit them when their time comes. For years I wanted to showcase the 'Browser Shake' effect so overused by people who know a little JavaScript – if you've never seen this effect, it makes the whole browser window shiver, as if your computer were sitting on top of an earthquake – very disconcerting. For a few months, you saw this effect everywhere on the web, and then it was laid to rest. I thought it was a wonderful piece of scripting, but I hung back from ever using it publicly. Then the day came when I had to write a web site all about Apollo 10 for the Franklin Museum. The movie counted down from ten and then there was some embedded film of the launch and the sound of engines roaring – you can guess what I put in at the end just as take off was happening...

It's often worth observing effects in nature; clouds passing across a sky, wind playing over trees, or – maybe the hardest effect of all – rain. Then look again and think about how these might be stylized in Flash to suspend people's disbelief just long enough to get your message across. Never use shape tweening just for the sake of it; have a specific reason, or make it work for you in a way that no other effect can.

Shape tweening lines vs. fills

Lines are far more difficult to tween than fills, because there are more vertices to render and Flash has to take shortcuts with strokes. Unless you are extremely organized, there will just be an unsightly mess of scribble in the transitions – that's fine if it's the effect you are looking for, but it's always best to 'fillet' out the elements you wish to change; it's best to separate lines and fills altogether, and it's even better to separate lines into their own groupings as well.

Mixed strokes and fills do not look good when tweened; there's too much visual clutter that gets in the way – and the result is visually unappealing. Try drawing a stroked and filled square and circle and shape tweening them:

If you must use lines, there are several tricks that enable you to achieve a much cleaner end product.

Shape tweening mixed fills and lines

First frame   Middle frame   Last frame

For precise tweening of strokes, it's advisable to put different elements on different layers of the movie (we'll look at layers in depth in the next chapter). For now, just remember that multiple layers allow us to implement different tweens on different elements, *without* them getting all mixed up. Take a look at `jinn_morph.fla` for an example of this layer separation principle; each element is contained on a dedicated layer so that separate tweens can be applied to each stroke:

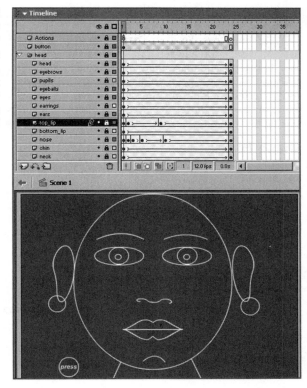

Tip
New layers are inserted by clicking on the Insert Layer icon at the bottom of the layer names list.

There's one other way you can cheat if you use strokes on different layers in this way. Because each line is on a separate layer, you can turn all the lines into fills using the **Convert Lines to Fills** option – select the lines and then choose the **Modify > Shape > Convert Lines to Fills** menu option:

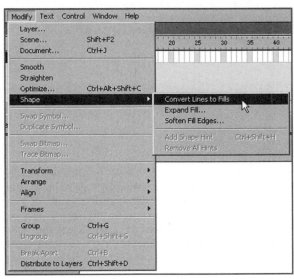

Compare the `jinn_morph.swf` with the `jinn_morph_fill.swf`. Notice that the first SWF is much sharper, but that the transitions can sometimes be a little jerky. The second SWF is a lot softer visually, and the transitions are filled morphs. And as for the raw line transition movie `jinn_morph_one.swf` without the lines separated out – don't even go there!

As you can see, a little strategic planning gives you a cleaner movie and a sharper message. So if you can, keep lines and fills separate and separate out the elements you want to morph, and make them morph cleanly and with precision. Nobody is going to thank you for giving them visual clutter to look at. The simpler you can make things appear, the better the effect, even if the effort of making things easier to 'read' takes a little more time.

Shape Hints

Shape hints are little red circle markers (automatically labeled in alphabetical sequence) – you can drag and drop onto the key morphing points of your line drawings. Markers are placed on these key points in the *starting* keyframe of a tween, and *corresponding* markers are arranged on the final keyframe. When a shape tween occurs, each labeled point in frame 1 migrates to the position of its correspondingly marked point in the *final* keyframe; the corresponding labels act as 'homing beacons' for each other. Shape hints are best used for simple enclosed polygons that you want to morph into one another.

This is best seen by trying it out...

On frame 1 of a new movie (CTRL+N/⌘+N) use the Rectangle tool to draw an unfilled rectangle fill in the center of the stage:

Insert a new keyframe at frame 40 by clicking on this frame in the timeline and pressing F6. On frame 40, the rectangle will now be selected, so click on a blank area of the stage with the Arrow tool to *deselect* it. Still on frame 40, use the Arrow tool to drag out the top right corner of the rectangle, and then the bottom right corner:

Click on frame 1 and choose **Shape** from the **Tween** drop-down menu in the Property inspector – the timeline will change to green to reflect the shape tween. Test the movie (ENTER) and watch the standard shape tween.

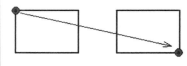

First frame   Final frame

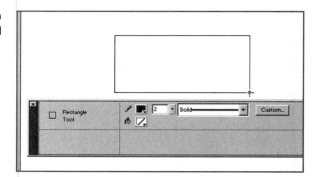

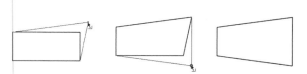

If the rectangle in frame 1 is not still selected, select it now (CTRL+A/⌘+A). Add a shape hint by pressing CTRL+SHIFT+H/SHIFT+⌘+H (or use **Modify > Shape > Add Shape Hint**). This will add a red marker named **a** in the middle of the rectangle. Drag this marker to the bottom right corner of the rectangle.

Press CTRL+SHIFT+H/ SHIFT+⌘+H three times to add three more markers, **b**, **c** and **d**. Starting from the 'a' position, arrange these counterclockwise around the corners of the rectangle:

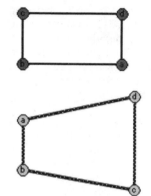

Click on frame 40 of the timeline with the Arrow tool; you'll find that all the shape hint markers are stacked in the middle of the stage. Arrange them in the corners of the modified rectangle, but this time start with **a** in the top left, **b** bottom left, **c** bottom right and **d** top right:

Watch the markers turn green as you place them, indicating that they're 'locked on' to the corresponding markers in the first frame. Click back on frame 1 and see that the markers have turned yellow. Locked and loaded!

Test the movie (CTRL+ENTER/⌘+ENTER) and observe that instead of opening like a door, the shape now appears to flip as the markers match up with each other.

 Use **Shape Hints** to manipulate drawings with lots of straight lines and polygons that need tweening. shapes_hint.fla gives an example of how you can build up a simple cube using hints. Experiment with the hints and see what is and isn't manageable.

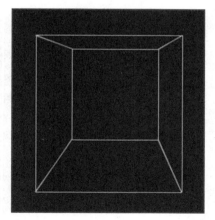

Easing shape tweens

Easing shape tweens, like easing motion tweens, allows for more realistic animation by speeding up or slowing down the actions at either end of the shape morph. Acceleration and deceleration are pretty intuitive in the real world: when a car starts its journey, it *accelerates* away from the curb, achieves a relatively constant cruising speed, and then *decelerates* as you approach your garage. The most convincing motion effects would be better achieved using ActionScript and a bit of applied physics theory, but as this is an *Express* book, easing should be enough to satisfy us here.

Open `easing.fla` to have a look at the easing of a shape tween in action. The crate has shape tween easing on it, while the weight has motion tween easing on it (we covered this earlier). Easing works on a scale of -100 to 100. Negative values represent easing in, 0 represents no easing, and positive value show easing out. The easing in this shape tween occurs at frame 7, where the easing value has been set to -100. This means that the shape will resist the crushing slightly by morphing *slower* at frame 7, but by frame 13 it will have speeded up the morph process considerably; this adds to the effect of the weight seeming to stop momentarily and then pressing down hard on the crate.

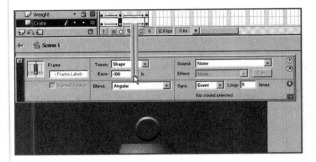

The **Angular** setting for the **Blend** option is used because Flash is dealing with lines and corners when it morphs the crate. The **Distributive** option is for use with fills.

Use the **Easing** option when you want to simulate more 'naturalistic' effects of speed and motion to a shape change. Virtually any recreation of an event that involves gravity can potentially benefit from having easing applied to the effect.

Summary

In this chapter we've covered the basics of animation in Flash MX:

- Basic motion

- **Frame-by-frame animation** (like traditional cel-based animation)

- **Motion tweening:**
  - Symbol properties – how they affect tweens
  - Skewing a tween
  - Changing center points, and why this is important
  - The frame panel
  - Auto rotation
  - Easing motion tweens to create realistic effects

- **Shape tweening:**
  - Shape tweening strokes vs. fills
  - Manipulating a tween with shape hints
  - Easing shape tweens for realistic effects

Next

Layers.

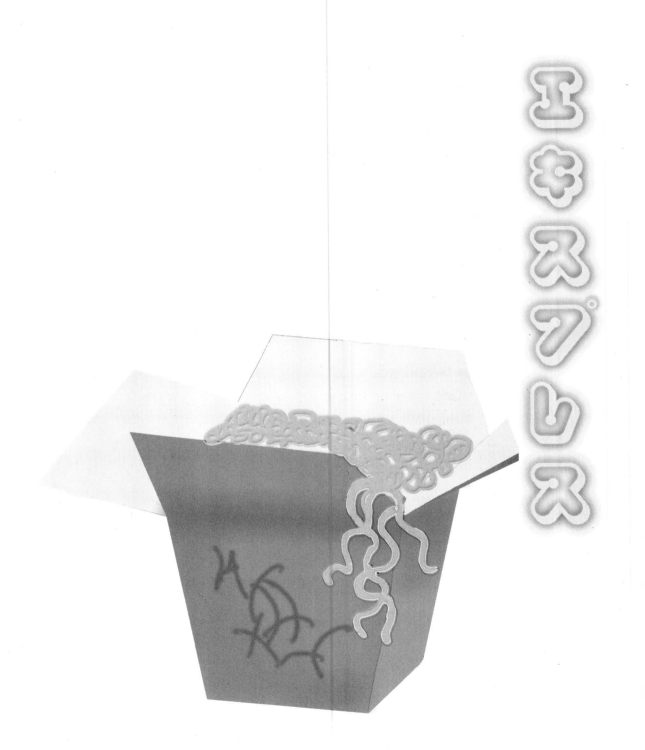

エクスプレス

Chapter 7
Layers, Guides, and Masks

What's in this chapter:

- Creating and naming **layers**

- Working with **multiple layers**:
  - **Manipulating** layers
  - **Layer options**
  - **Multiple tweens**

- **Guide layers**

- **Mask layers**:

  - **Dynamic** vs. **static** masks

Creating and naming layers

The layers in the Flash timeline act just like sheets of transparent paper resting on top of each other – you can draw on each layer, you can hide all or some layers, and you can pull layers on top of or underneath each other in any order. Even though the layers themselves are invisible, the elements you put on them are not.

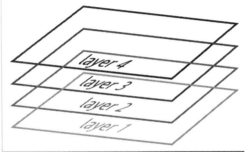

When you open up a new file in Flash MX you are initially presented with only one default layer:

If you want more layers then you have to add them by clicking on the **Insert Layer** icon:

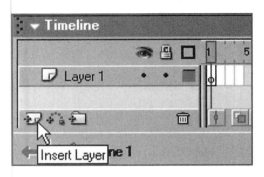

We've already seen layers used in other chapters – and indeed they can be very useful! They make the drawing of simple graphics much, much easier. Different elements in your movie, not just drawings, can be put on different layers and shown, hidden, locked, selected, or moved at will. This gives you far greater control over what happens on the Stage, and lets you achieve more sophisticated and professional effects.

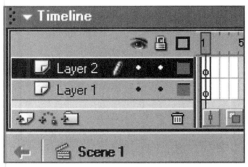

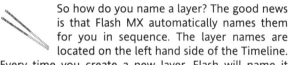

So how do you name a layer? The good news is that Flash MX automatically names them for you in sequence. The layer names are located on the left hand side of the Timeline. Every time you create a new layer, Flash will name it sequentially Layer 2, Layer 3, and so on and insert it into the timeline *above* the last layer created or highlighted:

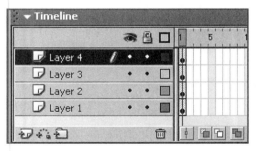

Of course, we also have the option to *rename* layers. Just double-click on the name of the layer and you can rename it as you wish:

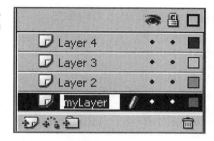

Additionally, you can insert a new layer *anywhere* within a group of layers:

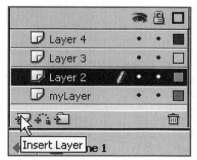

When you select the Insert Layer option, Flash will automatically make a new layer **above** the currently selected layer, continuing its sequential, numerical naming of layers:

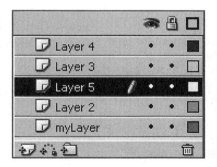

> **Tip**
> *Naming layers like this is good basic design practice – you should consider applying this principle to all your movies.*

 If you have more than one layer it's best to rename them to reflect the content that they hold. Open up layers.fla and you'll see a picture of four layers. Let's think of them as four bits of colored paper all stacked on top of each other:

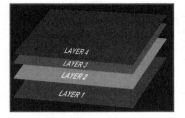

Double-click on the layer name Layer 1 and name it Green, change Layer 2 to Orange, and likewise for the other layers:

Now each layer's name reflects the content that it holds.

Working with multiple layers

When you need to put more than one drawing (or part of a drawing) or multiple elements on stage, it's wise to use multiple layers. The different layers help to separate information into bite-sized chunks. What you're doing, in effect, is putting information in different named 'containers' and, when you get more proficient at Flash MX, you can access these containers/layers using ActionScript – just like you can control symbol instances on stage.

As we saw in the previous section, to make multiple layers simply click on the Insert Layer option on the timeline (or go to **Insert > Layer** from the menu options). It's often a good idea to plan your layers in advance rather than just let them sprawl uncontrolled as the movie grows. Whatever style of design you follow, make sure you give your layers appropriate names to keep track of the objects on them.

Multiple layers should be employed when you need to separate out a lot of different symbols, groups, objects, strokes, or fills. Remember the `jinn_morph.fla` in the last chapter? This has twelve different layers just for the head of the Jinn.

Indeed, even more layers could be added – perhaps a background layer of a bazaar, and then maybe some landscape features in the distance.

The whole idea of layers is to compartmentalize all the elements on the stage so that they can be accessed and manipulated easily. One of the hardest things for beginners to grasp is that Flash allows you not only to do this on different levels but also over time on each individual level.

Tip

Many designers new to the concept of layers need to physically manipulate objects before they become comfortable with their equivalent on screen. If you find the idea of layers difficult to visualize satisfactorily, try buying a set of overhead transparencies and some water-based transparency pen; you can then draw out objects on different physical layers – this can help you get a more concrete grip on the concept. There's no shame in this – some of the best designers still work from pencil and paper as starting points.

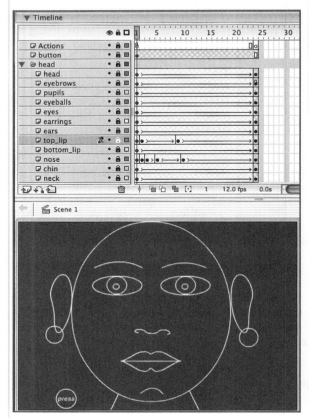

Layer arrangement

Layer arrangement is crucial to movies. Open up `layers2.fla` and you'll see there are four layers: Green Layer 1, Orange Layer 2, Red Layer 3, and Blue Layer 4.

However, no matter which layer is selected, all we can see is Blue Layer 4.

Why is this? The clue is that Layer 4 is at the *top* of the stack. In fact, this layer consists of a blue rectangle that covers the whole stage – it therefore obscures the other layers underneath.

Now click once on Green Layer 1 and drag the layer up to the top of the stack and let go – the green layer is now visible because you have taken it from the bottom and put it at the top:

> **Tip**
> You can move the layers around however much you like. Remember, the layers themselves are invisible but objects on them aren't (unless they're hidden).

Manipulating layers

Open up the file `checkerBoard.fla` and straight away you'll see that there are four layers:

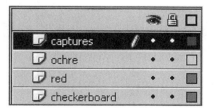

The content of the stage represents the start of a checkers game – all the checkers are different instances of the same two checker symbols.

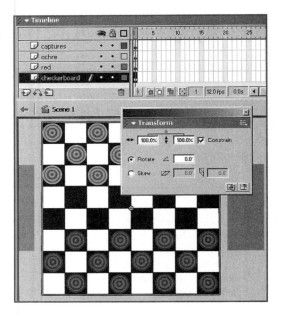

As a side note, all the symbol instances, both red and ochre, were colored using the Advanced Color option of the Property inspector (color effects in symbols were discussed in **Chapter 4**). Twelve instances have been put on the red layer, and twelve instances have been placed on the ochre layer – layers are very useful for separating elements like these for selection and coloring purposes.

But wait a minute – there's something wrong with our game already! The eagle-eyed amongst you may have spotted that the board is the wrong way round – there should always be a black square in the top-right of the board, so we need to rotate the board by 90°.

Select frame 1 of the checkerboard layer (notice that only the checkerboard on the stage will be selected) and call up the Transform tool (CTRL+T/⌘+T):

Now type 90 in the Rotate option and press ENTER – the board rotates to its correct position, but all the pieces are in the wrong places now:

Click on the 'red' layer to select all the pieces on this layer only, and use the arrow keys on your keyboard to move them en masse to their correct positions on the black squares. One will be left out on its own, so click on that one individually and pull it over to its rightful position – the vacant black square at the far right of the board:

Next, click on the ochre layer and do exactly the same thing to the ochre pieces – having similar pieces grouped on layers has saved us a lot of time.

So far so good! Now test the movie (CTRL+ENTER/⌘+ ENTER) – everything looks good and, because of a small piece of scripting within the symbols (which we'll not worry about for the moment), you can drag and drop each individual checker.

But what happens if you try and put captured pieces in the capture boxes? Well, there's another small problem – if you drop a piece on one of the capture boxes on either side of the board, the piece goes *behind* the box, and we lose sight of it:

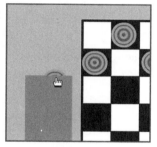

Of course, this is just not good enough! But because we've been utilizing layers, it's very easy to fix. Stop the movie and go back into the FLA. Notice that the 'captures' layer is at the top of the stack – no wonder the pieces were hidden behind it. Click on the captures layer, pull it down to the bottom of the layer list, and let go. Now run the movie again and you'll notice that the pieces sit happily on top of the capture boxes when you place them there:

Symbol layers

After playing around with this SWF file for a little while, some of you may well be thinking, "Well this is all very nice, but what about the pieces? They can cover each other as well!" In fact, it seems somewhat random that some pieces can cover certain checkers, while other checkers are hidden by some pieces. For instance, the ochre pieces can cover all the Red pieces and some of the ochre pieces cover other ochre pieces – what's going on here?

Well, the simple fact is that when you create a new layer and then drag symbol instances onto that layer, all the symbol instances are on individual 'sub-layers' – levels – too. Open up `checker_complex.fla` to see a simulated 3D representation of this – run the movie and note you can't put a red checker on the ochre level; you can *try* – but it's just not possible. Now return to the FLA and pull the red layer above the ochre level, and run the movie again – this time it's the other way around – you can't put an ochre piece above the red level.

Although it's useful to be aware of symbol levels, this book is concerned with getting up to speed with Flash MX from a beginner's perspective. Accordingly, we don't really need to go into any more details for the moment. For the record, you just need to use the magic of ActionScript to reference each piece and tell it to go to the top of the stack when clicking on it.

Layer options

There are many options that will make your life easier when working with layers:

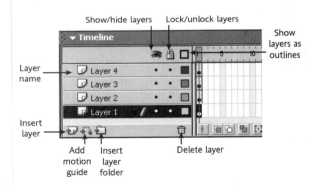

Hiding layers

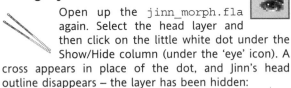

Open up the `jinn_morph.fla` again. Select the head layer and then click on the little white dot under the Show/Hide column (under the 'eye' icon). A cross appears in place of the dot, and Jinn's head outline disappears – the layer has been hidden:

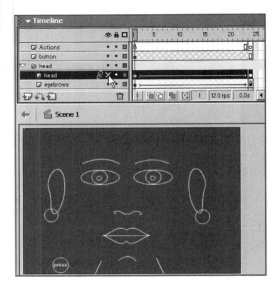

Try it with some of the other layers. Additionally, you can hold down the SHIFT key, click on several adjacent layers at once, then click on Hide for each layer to hide multiple layers. You can also hold down the CTRL/⌘ key and multi-click to select layers that aren't side by side, and then hide those as a unit too:

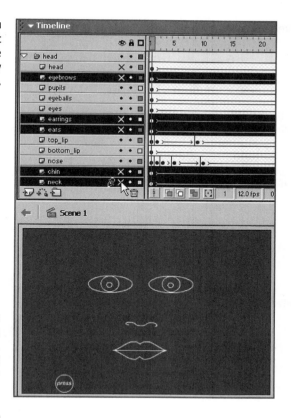

Tip
To 'unhide', or show, all the layers that you've hidden, simply hit the eye icon twice: the first hit will hide all layers, and the second hit will reveal them all again.

Hiding specific layers helps when you're trying to draw or work on one layer without being distracted by objects in other layers. The key point to remember is that hiding layers is just an *authoring-time* tool – hidden layers do not export as 'invisible' when you publish a movie.

Locking layers

You can lock layers in just the same way that you hide them. Simply click on the small dot in the Lock column (underneath the little padlock icon) to the right of the Hide/Show column:

Obviously, you use the padlock tool to lock specific layers so that you cannot overwrite or select something you shouldn't on the stage. If you *are* on a locked or hidden layer, the pencil symbol will display a red 'cancel' line through it to show that you can't edit that layer, otherwise a normal pencil appears and you are free to make alterations.

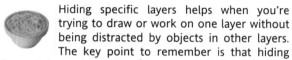

Tip
When working on a design, it's very good working practice to lock down everything except the layer you are working on.

Layers as outlines

To demonstrate this option, return to checkerBoard.fla and click on the square symbol at the top of the column to show *all* layers as outines:

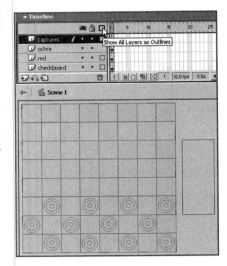

All the levels are selected and all of them become outlines. This is a quick way of selecting all your layers and applying the hide, padlock or outline to all of them at once. Notice that the outline square of each layer is color-coded to match the color of the corresponding outlined objects from that layer.

Delete

You can delete whole layers by clicking on the layer you want to delete and then clicking on the trash can icon.

Folders for layers

Layer folders enable you to put groups of layers logically together in a folder so that you can move whole collections of objects around easily. Remember that in the jinn_morph.fla all the drawings and tweens of the Jinn's head are contained in a folder named 'head'. If you click on the little triangle to the left of the folder you can collapse and retract the folder. This is useful for saving space or simply packaging your work in yet more useful little boxes.

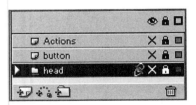

Open up symbols.fla and take a look at the timeline and stage – you'll find a four different sized boxes (symbols), each lying on an individual layer:

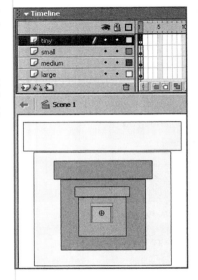

Next, click on the Insert Layer Folder icon:

Name this new folder boxes. Select all four of the layers (SHIFT and click), and drag them all into the folder.

You'll notice that if you click on the hide, lock, and outline symbols next to the boxes folder, all the objects inside the folder are hidden, locked, or outlined at the same time. Notice too the way that the layers are arranged within the folder – run the FLA to check that you cannot drag a larger box in front of a smaller one because of their layer ordering.

 Use layer folders to store whole batches of similar content: different characters in a cartoon, parts of a machine in an animated technical drawing, landscape and background features, intricate detail on artifacts – the list is endless.

Open up the apollo.fla to see an unfinished technical drawing of the Apollo spacecraft based on drawings, photos, and plans. Although this was just the first stage of the design, using a trace of a reproduction of one of NASA's drawings to get the basic information down as cleanly as possible, it could ultimately form an interactive pop-up page that labels all the parts of the craft when the mouse moves over them:

The layers of the timeline look nice and neat with the four closed folders containing all the content. Open up these folders to see just how much information the folders are hiding away:

> **Tip**
> *If you want to have fun using layers to trace scans and other objects try this; scan a picture of your face or one of the members of your family into a computer. Import the image into Flash using* **File > Import...**, *put it on the bottom layer, and lock it. Now use light blue (it shows up well and is unobtrusive on most backgrounds) to trace over the main features of the person's face. When you have got a life-like image that you are satisfied with, delete the bottom layer with the photo in. You could even take it a step further and animate the line drawing over several keyframes.*

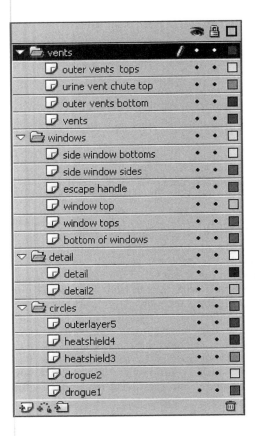

Other options

For even more options, right-click/CTRL-click (Mac) on a layer and, depending on what you have clicked on, you're presented with a context sensitive menu:

Although we've seen a few of these options already, it's quite handy to have access to them all in one place. For instance, the Show All option will reveal any hidden layers (if you have any). We'll deal with Guide layers and Masks in the latter half of this chapter.

The final option in this menu, Properties, brings up the Layer Properties dialog.

With this you can also rename, show, lock, or outline the current layer. You can change the type of layer to a guide or mask and you can make the layer into a folder. You can also edit the Outline Color box to suit your taste, and extend the height of the layer.

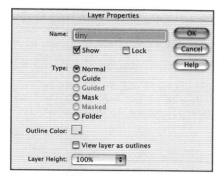

Distribute to layers

The Distribute to Layers modifier option provides a way to send objects to their own layers *automatically*. As we'll see, this works particularly well with text.

In the following example we'll study an animated birthday card and then make our own text effect. Open up the file happyBirthday.fla and run the movie.

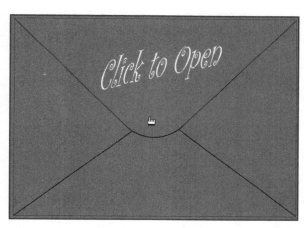

Look at the first frame – the whole envelope is one big button. When you click on the envelope, the movie plays. The ActionScript on the main timeline is basically just the onRelease action that we've used to control buttons a few times so far in this book:

```
myButton1.onRelease = function() {
    play();
};
```

Remember, this simply means, "when you release the mouse button, play the movie from this point".

Now look at frame 2 – this is where you will see the first tween. A piece of pre-prepared artwork has been imported, changed into a symbol, and put on the Post-Tween layer. This symbol has then been skewed, rotated, and motion tweened. Pull the playhead across the timeline to see the effect:

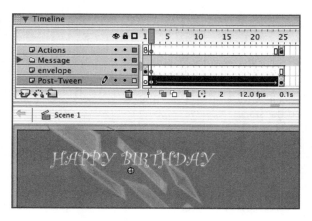

There are also more tweens going on – look in the message folder. It holds thirteen layers, one for each letter of the message HAPPY BIRTHDAY. In fact, each letter has its own layer and its own motion tween.

Click and pull the playhead across the movie very slowly, one frame at a time, and see how each letter does something slightly different.

> **Tip**
> *If you have more than one file open in Flash MX on the PC, hold down the CTRL key and press the TAB key to toggle between files.*

You might be thinking that there was a lot of tedious work involved in placing all of these letters onto individual layers, and then tweening them all. Well, not really! Let's look at how the effect was managed – open up a new FLA (CTRL+N /⌘+N).

Select the Text tool (or press T) and click on the stage, then look on the Property inspector (CTRL+F3/⌘+F3). Choose a generic font like Arial, Helvetica, or Times, and make sure the text is **static** text. Make it between 40 and 60 pt and type some text into the text box:

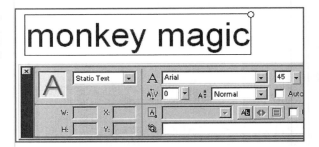

Click away from the text on stage and use the arrow tool to click *back* on the text so that a blue bounding box surrounds it, indicating that it's the current selection (or just hit CTRL+A/⌘+A to select everything on the stage). Now we're going to break the text apart. What you'll be doing here is changing the text from a text object into a *graphic*. Go to **Modify > Break Apart** (or simply hit CTRL+B/⌘+B) and you'll see a bounding box appear for every letter of your text:

The next thing you need to do is distribute these broken apart letters to different layers – one for each letter. So go to **Modify > Distribute to Layers** (or press Ctrl+Shift+D/Shift+⌘+D). Flash will automatically create a layer for *every* letter in your text, and line them up in order:

Now's an ideal time to create a folder and drop all these letters into it for ease of working; click on the Insert Layer Folder icon to create a new folder, and name it appropriately. Now, using the Shift key, highlight all the letter layers and drag and drop them into the folder. You will now be able to open or close the folder for ease of working by clicking on the little triangle.

Next, click on the first letter of your text and click on frame 1. Make a motion tween by going to **Insert > Create Motion Tween**. Now click on frame 24 and select **Insert > Keyframe**. Resize the new first letter of your text on frame 24 and then pull the playhead back and forth to see the motion tween. Follow the same process for each letter of your text:

1. Make a motion tween

2. Click on frame 24 and insert a keyframe

3. Resize the letter on frame 24

Tip
The same advice for tweens applies to the 'multiple tweens' that we're dealing with here – use them for specific projects where they can add to the effect. Don't just use them for the sake of it. Look at some adverts on the Internet and you'll most likely see tweening used quite often, but in very subtle ways. Overuse of tweening makes the viewer over familiar with the technique and they switch off mentally – the whole effect appears jaded and lifeless. Try and think of mini-narratives where a tween might surprise or shock – storyboard a movie first and fit multiple tweens in only where appropriate.

Take a look at `monkeyMagic.fla` and `name_morph.fla` to see some finished pieces of work.

Such typographical effects have been used in advertising since the dawn of animation. They are achieved in Flash MX by either turning text into a symbol instance and motion tweening, or breaking the type apart and morphing the letters.

Look at `squeeze.fla` and notice that the effect here has been achieved by breaking apart the text of the word SQUEEZE, resizing and distorting it in two ways, and then applying a motion tween. If you look on the timeline you can also see how a lot of tweaking has gone on to make the transition that much smoother:

Using guide layers

Guide layers allow you to key up and align your artwork; they aren't exported with your movie and aren't visible in the final SWF file. Although you can use guide layers to make simple motion, using a **motion guide** usually results in much smoother overall motion.

Any layer can be made into a guide layer by right-clicking on it (CTRL-click for Mac) and then choosing either Guide or Add Motion Guide – the difference between these two options will become clear soon.

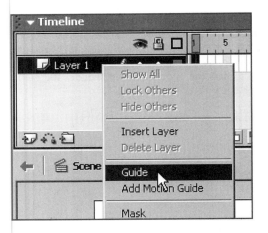

A guide *layer* is distinct from simple guides – the latter are just horizontal and vertical lines that you can pull down to help you with measurement on the stage (**View > Guides**).

Guide layers can be thought of as an extra piece of acetate that you can lay over or under your drawing to help you make small but precise refinements. The same effect could be achieved with a layer that was unlocked while all the others are locked, but with a guide layer there's no need to do this as none of its content is exported when the movie is made; this means that you can use it as a testbed for ideas and not worry about having to clean up the mess afterwards!

Creating a guide layer

Open up the file `guide_layer.fla` and you'll see three layers:

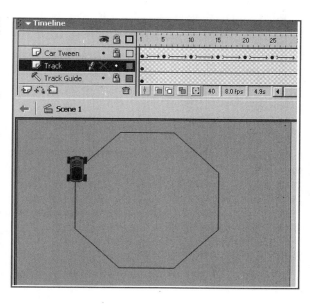

- **Car Tween** layer has an instance of the symbol `car` on it

- **Track Guide** layer has been changed to a guide layer (note the little hammer icon to the left of the layer name) and the actual guide is a simple line drawing of an octagon

- **Track** layer is hidden

The `car` symbol has been converted to a motion tween, and every five frames the car is moved above one of the vertices of the octagon so that it appears to be moving around the shape. A keyframe has been created at each point where the car is put over the corner of the octagon.

To make the motion appear more realistic the car symbol has also been skewed and enlarged when the car appears to come nearer the viewer and when it brakes around corners. A more realistic track has been drawn on the Track layer so that it isn't apparent that the car is moving around a regular octagon. These are all subtle visual tricks to help the viewer 'willingly suspend disbelief'.

Creating a motion guide

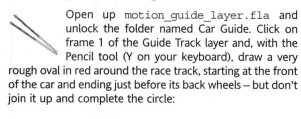

Open up `motion_guide_layer.fla` and unlock the folder named Car Guide. Click on frame 1 of the Guide Track layer and, with the Pencil tool (Y on your keyboard), draw a very rough oval in red around the race track, starting at the front of the car and ending just before its back wheels – but don't join it up and complete the circle:

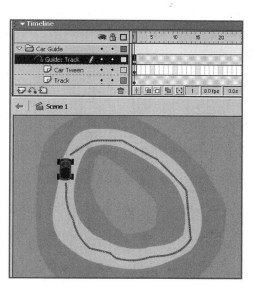

> **Tip**
> When drawing a motion guide do not cross over lines on the same layer – this breaks the stroke and will confuse Flash.

Now lock the guide track and click on frame 1 of the Car Tween layer. Click on the car and drag its registration point over the start of your red motion guide and let go – it should snap in place:

Then right-click/CTRL+click on frame 1 and choose Motion Tween.

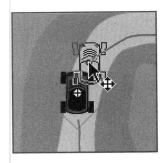

Next, click on frame 40 of the Car Tween layer and go to **Insert > Keyframe**. Still making sure you are on frame 40, drag the car on frame 40 onto the end of the track and let go – again, it will snap into place:

Don't worry, we've almost finished! Click on the playhead now and drag it back to frame 1 – notice that the car isn't headed in the right direction along the path, so bring up the Property inspector (if it isn't already visible) and check the Orient to Path option:

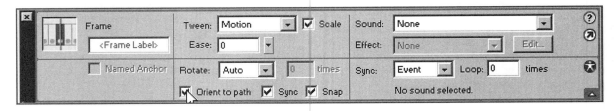

We'll learn more about this powerful option in the next section. For the moment, however, let's continue with the present example. Still on frame 1, click on the car and rotate it so that it is facing the path of the motion guide:

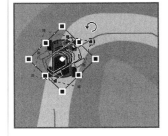

Test the movie and you'll see the car move around the track, over your now-invisible motion guide. Pretty cool stuff!

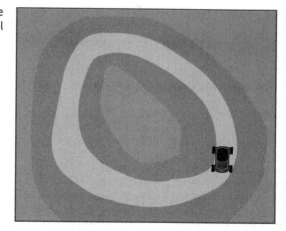

Finally, if you find the car's movement is too jerky, you can even use an unfilled oval instead of the hand-drawn guide path you drew with the Pencil tool, erasing a segment of the oval at the start and finish line so that the circle is incomplete:

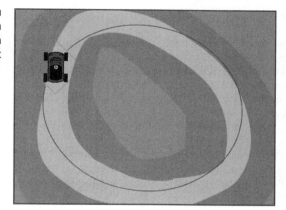

Motion guide options

Let's look at some of the options available to us when we're using motion guides in Flash MX. Open up `jump1.fla` and you'll see our old friend the jumping man who appeared in earlier chapters:

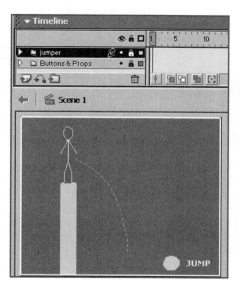

He's grown more ambitious since his earlier incarnations, and he's going to jump from a far greater height. For the moment, forget about how the animation is interacting with the buttons – we'll take a look at some scripting techniques in **Chapter 10**. Right now we want to examine some of the other options that are available with motion guides.

If you run the movie you'll see that the man jumps off the pillar onto the ground after you press the yellow button, and that the jump is perfectly synchronized. This is because the main movie's timeline is 12 frames long and the timeline of the man's jump movie clip is also 12 frames long – so they both begin and finish at the same time. Obviously, if his timeline were longer he wouldn't have finished his jump by the time he reached the ground, and if his timeline were shorter he'd have finished before he got there.

Look at the layers in the movie's timeline – there are two folders, one called Jumper and another called Buttons & Props. Jumper holds the motion tween of the jumper, the motion guide for his jump path, and there's a sound file on the last frame. Buttons & Props holds the two buttons, the white surround, and the green pillar.

Now click on frame 1 of the Jumper layer and bring up the Property inspector. We're going to change some of the options in this box to see what they do to the stick man's jump; this should give you a good idea about their functionality.

First off, you'll notice that the Scale option hasn't been checked (because the man does not change size on landing):

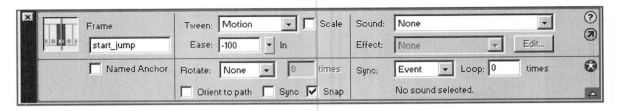

It's worth taking a quick diversion and looking at jump2.fla to see a version of this movie in which he *does* change size – try checking and unchecking the Scale box to see just why you need it. Did you spot the difference? The Scale option has the effect of changing the size of the man over the whole tween, rather than just in the final frame.

Returning to `jump1.fla`, you'll also notice that the **Ease** option is at `-100` because we want his jump to start off slow and speed up the nearer he gets to the ground. If you change it to `100` then he'll start off quick and then slow down before hitting the ground – clearly that's not what we want at all. Slide the Ease setting back to `-100` and then go to the **Rotate** option. Choose CW (clockwise) from the drop-down menu and run the movie:

The man now does a forward roll with his jump – impressive stuff! Then try CCW (counter-clockwise) and he'll flip the other way. Return the choice to None before you continue.

There are still another three boxes that concern us here called **Orient to Path**, **Sync**, and **Snap**:

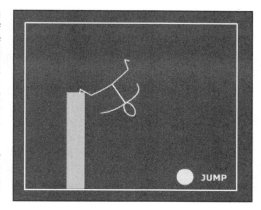

Only Snap is checked – why's that? Well, this option snaps the jumper's registration point to the blue motion guide line and guides him down to the floor while he's performing his tween. Sync is not checked because the jumper's timeline and the main timeline are both 12 frames long, so we're in sync anyway. However, even if the jumper's timeline was longer by 1 frame (thirteen frames) he would be out of sync with the main movie's timeline, so checking the Sync option would sync him back in if necessary. Any symbol whose motion timeline (the timeline inside the symbol) has an odd number of frames that won't divide evenly into the main timeline needs this feature – even then, if the result looks unnatural, don't use it.

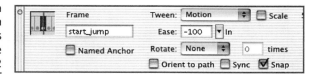

This leaves us with the **Named Anchor** (an advanced feature we won't discuss here) and **Orient to Path options**. Orient to Path has not been checked, so check it now and run the movie. The baseline of the man is following the path of the guideline – this is not what we want in this instance, but it is indeed a useful option to have.

Orient to path

As we saw in the `motion_guide_layer.fla` example, the Orient to Path option enables you to make symbol instances on the stage snap to – and follow – a certain path that you have drawn out for them. If you want an object to follow a specific line you'd use this option. The relevant check box is found in the Property inspector.

So how do you use Orient to Path? Here's another example for you to try. Open up `colony1.fla` and you'll see that there is a representation of an ant colony on the stage. There are two folders that are locked: red ant and colony:

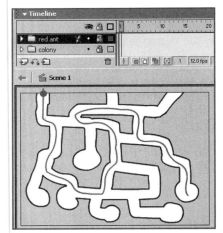

Unlock the red ant folder and open it – you'll see two layers: a guide layer called Guide: ant and an ordinary layer called red ant. Click on frame 1 of the red ant layer and the Property inspector will look like this:

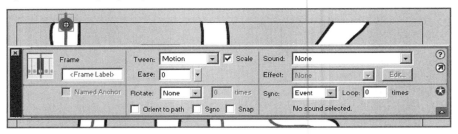

The Orient to Path box hasn't been checked, so do that now and run the movie. The ant (the red circle with the single antenna) moves along the motion path, but instead of going antennae first, it goes rear-end first around the motion track. Not exactly what we want. Click on the first frame of the red ant layer again and click on the red ant symbol (always make sure the Guide Layer is padlocked before you do this otherwise you'll end up with the guide sticking to your cursor at some point) and rotate the red ant through 180° using the Free Transform tool:

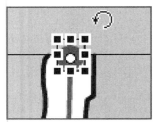

Now click on the red ant symbol instance and make sure that the Orient to Path box is checked. Run the movie again and the antenna should now point in the right direction:

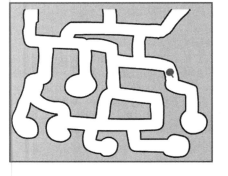

You should use the Orient to Path option when you need to point an animation the right way round to follow a path. Experiment with putting it on and taking it off for different animations to see the effects – after a while you'll intuitively get the hang of it.

Working with multiple guided layers

Multiple guided layers are simply many different guide layers on top of each other in a movie, a bit like a multistorey car park. Open up `colony2.fla` and run the movie, or just pull the playhead back and forth across the timeline. Our protoype ant colony now has ten ants running all around the nest:

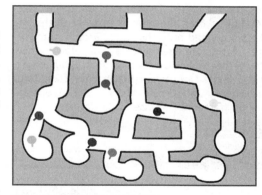

The important thing to note here is that this movie will have ten ants on ten layers with ten guide layers! Pull the timeline down to see how all the information has been neatly structured using folders.

There are ten Ant folders, which hold each ant's 'ant' and 'guide' layers. All the guide layers have been hidden, except for that of the red ant (ant 10) for this demonstration.

Let's finish off this design – click on Ant 1's folder (color-coded purple) and unlock it. Click on the 'Guide: ant 1' layer and select the pencil tool, making sure that you have the Smooth tool option selected:

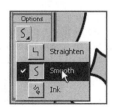

Choose a purple color and draw the ant's trail through the colony:

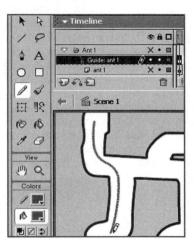

Now click on the ant 1 layer, bring up the Library (CTRL+L/⌘+L), and drag and drop an instance of the ant out of the Library and onto the stage. Drop it onto the beginning of the ant trail you've just drawn, then choose the arrow tool (A on your keyboard). Make sure you're still in frame 1 of the ant 1 layer, right-click/CTRL-click, and choose the Create Motion Tween option. Next, click on frame 48 and insert a keyframe:

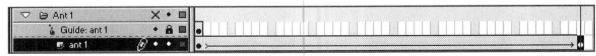

Click on frame 48 of the layer above – Guide: ant 1 and insert another keyframe. The ant trail will reappear! Now click back on frame 48 of ant 1 and, making quite sure you are in frame 48, drag the ant to the end of the trail. At this point you can rotate both ants (in frame 1 and 48) 180°, like we did earlier, and check the Orient to Path boxes in both frames. If you are feeling particularly adventurous you can tint your ant as well - if you lose your way just open up colony2_final.fla to see the completed movie:

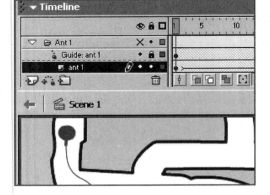

You may notice that some ants are on screen longer than others – this is because the frames in their tweens have been copied and pasted and reversed so they go back and forth. Our new ant is the slowest of the lot because he takes 48 frames to go one way, whereas most of the other ants have finished or have been round twice.

The best way to make guided multiple layers is to use the technique we've adopted in colony2.fla – put all your motion guided layers in different folders and lock and hide them when you're not working on them. Only unlock the specific guided layer you're working on at any one time. Have a good look at the FLA and make sure you understand how it works.

Use multiple guided layers when you want a lot of complex animation to be happening on the stage at the same time. Don't forget – not all of the animations have to have the same length as the main timeline.

Using mask layers

A mask screens out parts of the background or layer it's immediately above and linked to. It's the equivalent of putting a plain piece of paper with holes cut out over a photo or drawing underneath so that only part of the image is revealed. In Flash you have to imagine flipping the opaque mask shape in your head into a negative image – whatever is opaque will be transparent and vice versa.

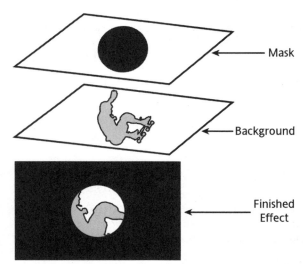

Mask

Background

A mask is used to screen out unwanted parts of a background or picture. It can achieve a clipped sharp outline. As we shall see, it's even possible to animate both the mask *and* the background below it. You cannot nest a mask *within* a mask in Flash MX, but you *can* put separate masks in separate folders, and put them on different levels. Also, you can change masks into movie symbol instances, but you cannot put a mask inside a button.

Finished
Effect

We've already seen a movie using mask layers earlier in this book – flickBook.fla in **Chapter 5**, which uses a static mask – a large circular mask – to clip off parts of flickBook.fla's star field.

It would have been hard to achieve such a clean resolution with a circle and fill. In this section, we'll explain exactly how to create these masks and talk about why they're useful.

Making a mask layer is very similar to making a motion guide. Open up a new FLA and rename the first layer 'background'. Choose the brush tool and paint or scribble lots of different colors onto the stage. Don't worry about artistic merit – just do it quickly until most of the stage is covered:

Now create another layer called 'circle mask' above the background layer. Draw a nice big black circle on this layer:

Now right-click on the circle mask layer and choose Mask – both layers will change color to a crosshatched dark green and will be locked automatically.

Note that it's possible to see the effect of any mask by choosing the Show Masking option when right-clicking/CTRL-clicking on a mask layer. Run the movie now (mask1.fla) and you'll see that everything that was opaque in the mask layer is now transparent, and everything else that surrounded the mask on the mask layer (everything but the circle) is opaque. Create a new folder, call it 'mask', and then drop the two layers into it.

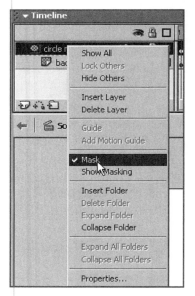

Use a mask layer to mask out parts of the picture on the layer immediately under it. You can add other layers to a mask layer by dragging and dropping them onto the mask layer. It's advisable to either: keep your mask layer with the layers it's masking in a separate locked folder; or, keep the mask layer and layers under it at the bottom of the layer stack to prevent other layers dropping onto it accidentally.

Dynamic vs. static masks

Static masks are shapes that remain in one position and obscure the same part of a background (unless the background is moving). Effects such as framing a piece of cartoon action in a certain style of silhouette can be achieved quickly and easily – the mask remains static for the duration of the scene or movie.

Let's now take a glance at the other type of mask that Flash MX makes possible – a **dynamic**, or animated, mask. To make an animated mask, turn the opaque shape on any mask layer into a symbol and then create a motion tween:

Tweened mask layer

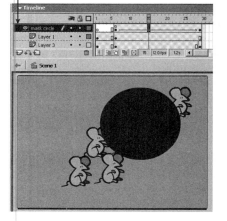

For instance, open up `cartoon_mask.fla` – in this movie we've shape-tweened the circular black mask to achieve that shrinking spotlight effect that has been used in cartoons for decades:

Multiple masked layers

 Multiple masked layers, like multiple tweens and motion guides, are best set out in different folders. Remember, you cannot have a mask *within* a mask. In fact, a mask is fairly limited in what it can do: it can move, it can change shape, and it can be opaque and transparent in different places – but that's all. The *background*, however, can change shape, color, orientation, motion, hue – so when using multiple masks you should ask yourself what effect you want to achieve and try to achieve that by optimizing the background first.

 Have a look at `multiple_masks.fla`. This movie consists of two backgrounds with the masks of two planets (little and big) above their respective backgrounds. Each planet, their masks, and backgrounds are in two separate folders:

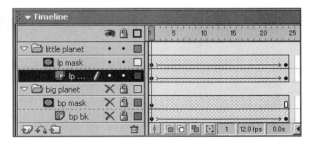

Note that the big planet's mask is *not* moving but the mask's background is. The small planet's mask *is* moving and so is its background – both are motion tweens. Skewing the little planet's background during the tween makes it look like it is revolving about an imaginary axis.

 Use multiple masks for transition effects between different movie clips, or when you want people to focus on one particular area of your FLA.

Summary

In this chapter, we looked at:

- Creating and naming **layers**

- Working with **multiple layers**
  - **Manipulating** layers
  - **Layer options**
  - **Multiple tweens**

- **Guide layers**

- **Mask layers**: **dynamic** vs. **static** masks

Next

Animated movie clip symbols.

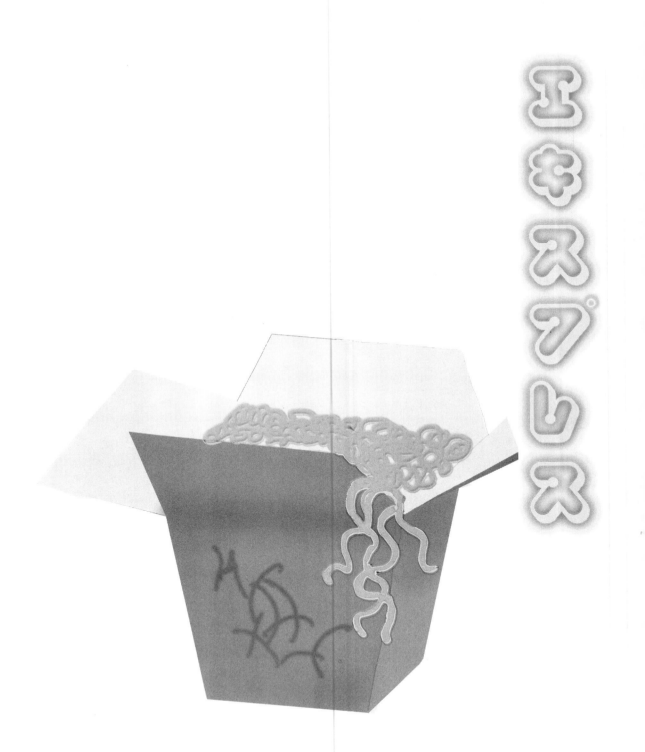

エクスプレス

Chapter 8
Animated Symbols

What's in this chapter:

- The difference between **animated graphic** symbols and **animated movie clip** symbols

- Linked vs. independent timelines

- **Creating** animated graphic and movie clip symbols

Animated symbols: graphics vs. movie clips

As a starting point, let's define these terms:

- **Animated graphic symbol** – An animation that has been converted to a graphic symbol (rather than a movie clip or button); a Graphic cannot be given an instance name and its timeline is tied to the main, or *root*, timeline of the movie. Accordingly, it has rather limited properties. The only real control you can have over an animated Graphic is being able to change the color, or specify the frame for the animation to start at.

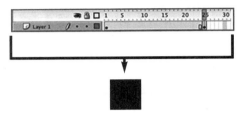

Tied to main timeline, limited functionality

- **Animated movie clip symbol** – An animation or movie that has been turned into a movie clip and therefore has its own timeline, completely independent from the root timeline of your FLA. Essentially, an animated movie clip operates in its own 'time zone' and it therefore has much more scope; you can name them, change a number of their properties, and you can control their movement using ActionScript.

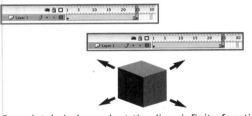

Completely independent timeline, infinite functionality!

We'll dive straight into an example now to demonstrate this difference – open up the file anim_symbols.fla:

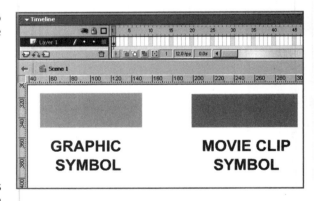

Here we have two symbol instances on the stage: one is a graphic symbol, and the other is a movie clip – have a look in the Library (F11) to see the original symbols. Click on the graphic symbol instance and check out your Property inspector:

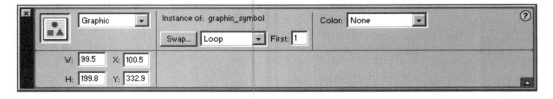

This confirms that the symbol is indeed a graphic symbol and, as you may have noticed in the Library, it is called `graphic_symbol`. Now double-click on the graphic to see what it consists of:

By double-clicking on it, we are 'drilling down' into its core elements – this opens up another timeline *nested* within the root timeline. Notice that the timeline of `graphic_symbol` has a shape tween six frames in length. Next, let's take a look at the movie clip instance – use the little Back arrow on the navigation bar to return to the root timeline:

Select the movie clip on the stage, and look to the Property inspector again:

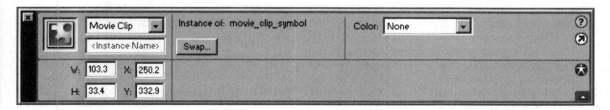

This time we see that the symbol is a movie clip called `movie_clip_symbol`. Note also that we can now give the symbol instance its own instance name; as we'll see later in this chapter, being able to name each instance of a movie clip symbol can be very useful. Double-click on the instance of the movie clip symbol on the stage to see its timeline.

Our movie clip symbol also has a shape tween in its timeline, this time sixty frames long.

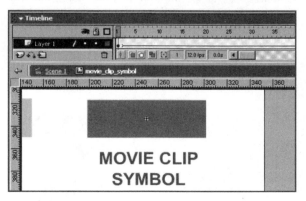

Let's see our two animations in action! Hit CTRL+ENTER/⌘+ENTER to test the FLA:

The movie clip symbol is nicely animated – it grows in length as defined by the shape tween in its timeline. But wait – what about the graphic symbol? Surely that was also animated by a little shape tween in *its* timeline? At present it looks pretty much dead! Well, so much for the animated *graphic* symbol...

GRAPHIC SYMBOL   **MOVIE CLIP SYMBOL**

Don't give up on it yet, though – let's find out what's going on here. Return to the FLA file and look at the timeline. Remember that when we looked at the timeline of the graphic we noted that the animation took place over six frames. So, let's add some frames to the main timeline and see what happens. Select frame 1, and go to **Insert > Frame** (or hit the F5 key) five times to add some new frames. You should now have a total of six frames in the main timeline of anim_symbols.fla:

Test the movie again now. You'll immediately see that both of our symbols are now animated! As before, the movie clip is quite happy to play all 60 of its frames, and now the graphic also plays its six frames (note that it runs through ten times during each play of the 60-frame movie clip, as you'd expect). When we only had one frame on the main timeline, the graphic symbol was effectively locked into only playing only its first frame. After adding the new frames to the root timeline of our FLA, the graphic animation can now play.

GRAPHIC SYMBOL   **MOVIE CLIP SYMBOL**

So what have we just learned? **Animated movie clip symbols have timelines that do not depend on the main timeline** – they can be any length, and will still play right through on a single-framed root timeline. Animated graphic symbols, on the other hand, will only display their full cartoon if the root timeline has at least the same number of frames as the graphic symbol. Indeed, this is the fundamental difference between these two types of animated symbol.

Using animated graphic symbols

As we learned in **Chapter 4**, we can create a new animated graphic symbol by going to **Insert > New Symbol**, or pressing CTRL+F8/⌘+F8, and choosing Graphic from the three choices available:

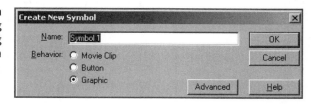

Press OK, and you'll then be taken to a fresh 'canvas' that, as you can see from the navigation bar, is one level down from the root timeline:

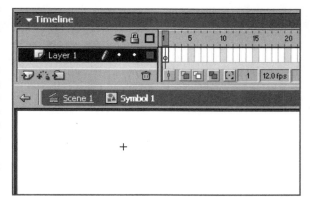

Here you can add as many layers and frames as you want on the symbol's timeline. You can create shape tweens and frame-by-frame animation, and all will be locked into the timeline of the main FLA – there is no way that an animated graphic symbol can be independent to the root timeline. Once you have created an animation inside the symbol, you can return to the main stage using the navigation bar. Your symbol will be happily residing in the Library, from which you can drag it onto the stage as and when you need it.

Remember, you can just click on the symbol and use the Property inspector to change its basic properties, like color, size, and the frame from which it can start its animation:

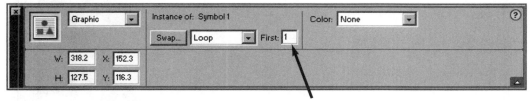

Start frame number

Creating effects with animated Graphic symbols

Let's look at an example – open up the file `lava_lamps.fla`:

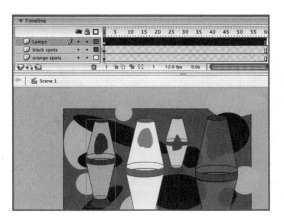

Double-click on any of the lava lamps and you'll see that the `lava_lamp` graphic symbol instance is made up of 60 frames and three layers:

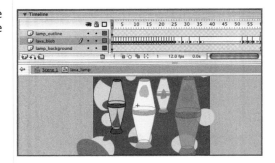

Back on the main stage, use the Property inspector to compare the properties of two different instances of the same `lava_lamp` graphic symbol. For instance, the lava lamp on the far left of the stage has a start frame value of 20...

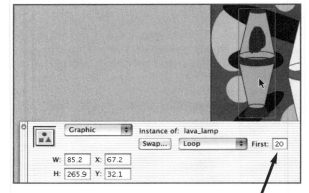

Start frame

...while the yellow lamp in the centre has a start value of 45:

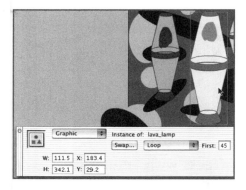

Additionally, the color properties of each lamp instance have also been changed. This exploits the limited features of the animated graphic, making each instance appear unique. Test the FLA now using CTRL+ENTER/⌘+ENTER:

The important point to notice here is that the lava in each lamp appears to have a slightly different state of flow. This is because each individual lamp instance has its animation start point set to a different frame, so no lamp starts at the same time as any other. The lava is a

staggered and tweaked shape tween (the animation is fairly jerky as a result) to give a passing similarity to the hot wax effect. In fact, this animation could probably even be scaled down and used as a background for other 'whacky' events happening on stage. Another noteworthy issue is how big the FLA file size is compared to the final SWF output – in this case, the SWF is nearly 70 times smaller than the original FLA! This is because of the file-size saving aspect of utilizing symbols – although we clearly have four versions of the animated Graphic symbol in our movie, it's only the `lava_lamp` symbol in the Library that takes up some file space!

The best time to use animated Graphic symbols is as we have seen above – when you need file-size reducing background features. To get the best out of them in your movies, subtle alterations to some of the basic properties of each instance – changing their appearance, and staggering their animations, for example – can go a long way towards producing simple, yet captivating designs.

Using animated movie clip symbols

Animated movie clip symbols are capable of far more than just following the main timeline of a movie and having their colors changed. We can combine movie clip symbols with buttons, input text boxes, other movie clips, and link them via ActionScript, to make independent and complex interactions happen at *any* time in the main movie. Animated movie clips are far more powerful than their more limited cousin the animated graphic symbol because they have independent timelines that you can call upon them to perform a wider variety of tasks. And, because you can give them instance names, you can also control the movement, appearance, and behavior of each individual instance on the stage with ActionScript.

As with the graphic symbol, you can make a new animated movie clip symbol by pressing CTRL+F8/⌘+F8, choosing the movie clip option, and then creating your clip:

But before we get involved in how to create useful and interesting effects with an animated movie clip, it's worth taking a moment to reinforce our understanding of the independent nature of a movie clip's timeline, and how we can name – and call upon – each individual instance.

Tip
Animated movie clip symbols – often used with ActionScript – are the real power-house of great Flash design; many of the best Flash designers use animated movie clips to add life, variety, complexity, randomness and interactivity to their movies.

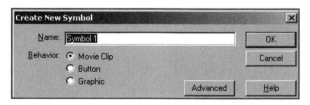

Creating effects with animated movie clip symbols

You can create a multitude of effects using animated movie clip symbols. We should utilize their independent timelines when we want different events happening at different times – or simultaneously – on stage. To achieve this, it's always important to name each movie clip instance, button, and variable so that you can have the optimum level of control.

The movie clip's independent timeline

Every symbol we create has its own timeline and, as we've established, the movie clip's is particularly special because it acts independently to the root timeline.

Open up the file `jump_timeline.fla` - it's our friend the incredible jumping stick man, who we've seen throughout this book.

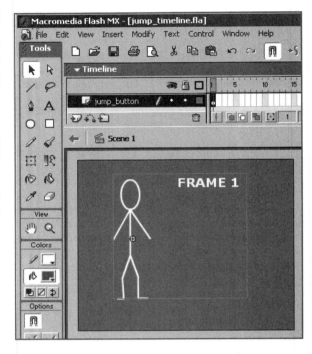

Notice that the root timeline of `jump_timeline.fla` has only one frame. If you now select the symbol instance on the stage and look in the Property inspector you'll see that this instance has been named `jumping_man` – it'll soon become clear why this is useful:

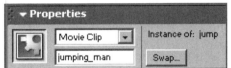

Open up the `jump` movie clip symbol by double-clicking on the instance on the stage:

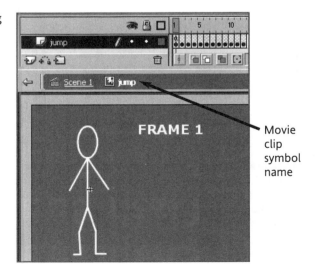

Movie clip symbol name

Now you're on the `jump` movie clip's timeline, which is nested within the root timeline of the movie (referred to as Scene 1 on the navigation bar). Looking at this timeline, you can see that it has twelve frames – pull the playhead across all twelve frames and back again – the stickman goes through his familiar jump. Return to the main timeline using the Back button on the navigation bar, and test this movie (CTRL+ENTER/⌘+ENTER).

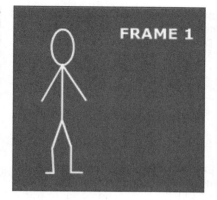

Hmm, not much action there! Our movie doesn't do anything, even though we've used an animated movie clip symbol which, because its independent timeline, should still play properly from a *root* timeline that only has one frame in it.

Go back into the FLA, and then dig down into the timeline nest by again double-clicking on the instance of the movie clip symbol that is on the stage. This time, pay close attention to the timeline:

You probably actually noticed it the first time – there's a little 'a' symbol on frame 1 indicating that there is some ActionScript present on this frame. Open up your Actions panel by selecting **Window > Actions** (F9) to view the code.

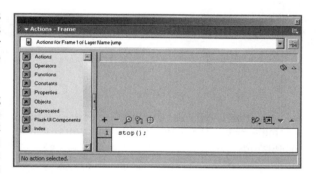

As you can see, there is only one line of code containing the `stop()` command – this is telling our movie clip to stop on frame 1, so `jumping_man` is stopped before it even has a chance to begin! OK, so we could just delete this line, and test the movie to see that everything works as expected this time. But instead, let's go one step further; this *is* a powerful movie clip, after all.

We can control the `jumping_man` symbol instance in a different way; let's take a button from the Library and add some ActionScript to control the movie clip symbol's internal timeline.

Controlling a movie clip's timeline

Take a look at `jump_butt_timeline.fla`. In this version we've created a simple button symbol by hitting CTRL+F8/⌘+F8 and selecting Button (we've called it `jumpButton`):

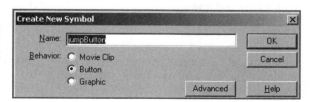

In the Button authoring environment, we've then drawn a simple circle and turned each frame of the button's states (Up, Over, Down, and Hit) into a keyframe (F6):

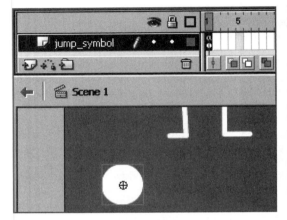

Next, back on the root timeline of the movie, we dragged an instance of `jumpButton` from the Library onto the stage, and added a little ActionScript to frame 1 (look for the telltale little 'a'!). We'll describe the script shortly:

Note also that we've given this instance of `jumpButton` a name – `myButton` – to allow us to control it with ActionScript code:

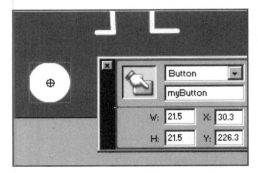

Let's now look at the ActionScript in frame 1, and see what it does and how it works. Select frame 1, and then hit F9 to bring up the Actions panel:

We've got some fairly complicated looking code in the Actions panel, but don't worry – as is normal with ActionScript, it's actually fairly straightforward to translate:

```
myButton.onPress = function() {
_root.jumping_man.gotoAndStop(7);
};
```

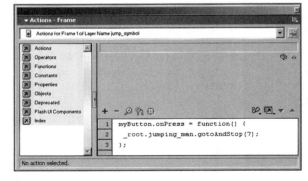

What this means is: "When you click the button named `myButton`, go to frame 7 of the `jumping_man` symbol instance and stop there." The second line here is critical:

```
_root.jumping_man.gotoAndStop(7);
```

This is essentially feeding detailed, tailored directions into the generic `gotoAndStop()` action. The word `_root` refers to where we start – the root timeline of our movie, and is included for completeness. So `_root.jumping_man` means "the instance of the `jump` Movie Clip symbol called `jumping_man`, which lies on the root timeline". The entire line thus means "Apply the method `gotoAndStop(7)` to `jumping_man`, which lies on the root timeline". Actually pretty simple, right? Such script is referred to as a 'dot notation' hierarchy.

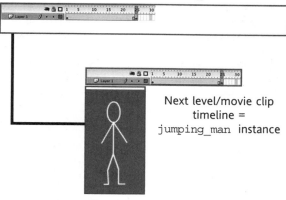

Top level/main timeline = `_root`

Next level/movie clip timeline = `jumping_man` instance

We can refer to the instance as `_root.jumping_man`

Tip
'Dot notation' refers to the little dots (periods) that separate parts of ActionScript statements. This notation style lets us specify paths to particular objects, regardless of where they are in the nested movie hierarchy.

Finally, we've added a static text box with a brief description of what the button does – this is always a good standard practice:

Jump to Frame 7 in jumping_man's timeline

Run the movie (CTRL+ENTER/⌘+ENTER) – hit the button and you should see the `jumping_man` animation jump straight to frame 7:

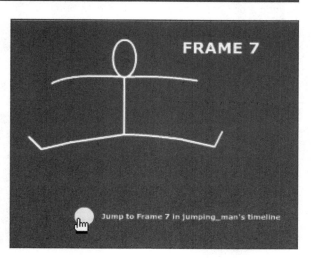

FRAME 7

Jump to Frame 7 in jumping_man's timeline

The ActionScript that we've used here is very basic and only two lines long, but it demonstrates that the animated movie clip symbol has the potential to be very powerful – because we can name an instance of a movie clip, we can also call on it to do things. No matter where the movie clip is inside the main movie, we can target it (and any movie clips nested inside it) and tell it what we want it to do.

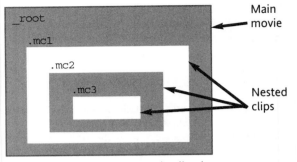

We can get to the `.mc3` movie clip via the path `_root.mc1.mc2.mc3`, and tell it what we want it to do

Now that we're a bit more familiar with the nested timelines of animated movie clip symbols, and the use of the navigation bar, let's increase the pace a little. We'll look at one more version of our jumping man FLA. The ability to jump to only one frame, as seen in the previous version, is clearly somewhat limiting. How about being able to jump to *any* frame in the movie clip? How would we do that with ActionScript? Well, in short, we'd use a **variable** – instead of telling the button to make the movie go to frame 7, we can tell it to go to frame "`frameNo`", for instance, which we define as being any frame number that we can specify at runtime. With just a small change in the script, it makes life a lot easier and we get a much larger range of options.

Let's see how it works – open up `jump_butt_timeline2.fla` and you'll see a new object on stage – a white input text box. This is where we want users to enter in their frame number and have it processed by the ActionScript. Click on this text box so that a blue bounding box appears around it and then bring up the Property inspector (CTRL+F3/⌘+F3):

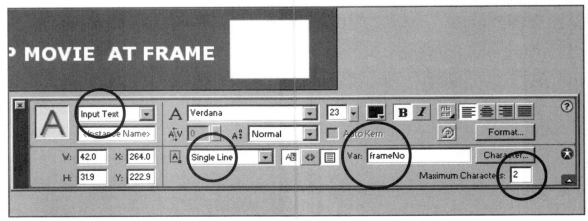

Look at the circled options: Input Text has been chosen because we want people to input text at runtime; Single Line because we want the inputted text on one line only; Maximum Characters is 2 because our text will actually refer to the frame number (1-12). Lastly, look at the Var box – this is where we declare our variable as `frameNo` (in fact, you could use any name, but it's easier to understand if the name refers to what it is for). If you click the Character button you will see that we have specified that only numerals 0 to 9 can be used.

These settings mean that whenever a user puts in a single or double digit number it will be recognized by the ActionScript.

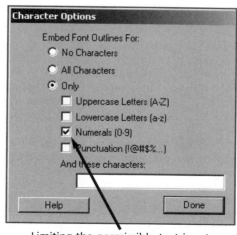

Limiting the permissible text input

Now look at the code attached to frame 1 of the root timeline. As usual, select it and open up the Actions panel (F9):

Although this code is very similar to the previous version, we're using our new variable `frameNo` as the parameter in the `gotoAndStop()` method, instead of just stating – hard coding – a fixed frame number. We also have the additional line:

```
FrameNo = "";
```

This is telling the input box to take an input of 'no characters'. This effectively wipes away the number that a user enters in the box (after it has been processed) and replaces it with nothing, and ensures that we have a blank box ready and waiting for the next input each time we enter a new number.

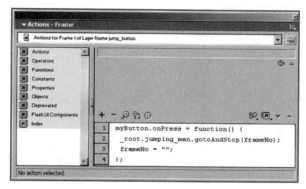

OK, run the movie now to see how the ActionScript, variables, instance names, and timeline nesting all fit together to produce the desired effect:

As with our simple stick man example, it's clear that if we name everything carefully we can reference and control any movie clip animation. Although our example was rather basic in that our 'nest' of timelines was actually only one timeline deep, it serves to demonstrate how you can navigate around the hierarchy to control what's happening on stage. The simpler the level of control and understanding you have of that map, the faster you can get around and design your own more complex routes.

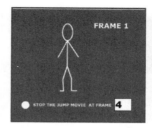

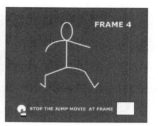

Automatic looping

As we have seen, if you create a movie with more than one frame in its timeline (and no scripting), it will automatically play to the end and loop back to the beginning – it will do this forever unless you put a piece of ActionScript in the timeline to stop it and control the endless looping.

Open up `surfer.fla` and you will see a lot of the elements that we have explored in the book so far put together to make a fairly simple 24-frame movie that will play endlessly unless we tell it to stop. Play the movie now (CTRL+ENTER/⌘+ENTER) and watch the surfer do his stuff on the huge waves (apologies to Hokusai!). The surf action is achieved using a simple motion guide with the surfer locked onto it – we covered motion guides in the previous chapter:

There are two buttons in this movie – one to stop (**S**) the action and one to play it again (**P**). Try them out! When the **S** button is pressed, the surfer stops but is still balancing atop the wave crest. Go into the FLA to see why the surfer's arms are still wobbling away, even though we've stopped the movie:

After double-clicking on the surfer movie clip instance we can see that he has a 2-frame timeline that will automatically continue to loop even when the root timeline is stopped. This gives the impression that the surfer is balancing, waiting to start surfing again. While you're here, call up the Actions panel to show the script attached to frame 1 of the root timeline. Nothing too controversial here:

```
1  stopButton.onPress = function() {
2    stop();
3  };
4  playButton.onRelease = function() {
5    play();
6  };
```

But wait! Because the surfer is a movie clip, we can actually give it an instance name (surfer, in this case) and control exactly when to start his balancing, just like the Stop and Start buttons. This isn't really rocket science, is it? All we need to do is add another named button (let's call it balanceButton), along with the relevant actions and the correctly named path (to target this movie clip through the movie hierarchy using dot notation). Here're the changes to the existing ActionScript that we need to make to frame 1 of the actions layer:

```
stopButton.onPress = function() {
   stop();
   _root.surfer.stop();
};
playButton.onRelease = function() {
   play();
   _root.surfer.play();
};
balanceButton.onRelease = function() {
   _root.surfer.play ();
};
```

Open up surfer2.fla – the changes have already been made in this version. For both the Stop and Play buttons, not only are we stopping and starting the root timeline, but now we're digging down to stop/start the surfer movie clip as well. For example, the code _root.surfer.stop() jumps down the hierarchy from the main timeline to the surfer and tells him to stop moving. In surfer2.fla we have a new button, called **B** for balanceButton, which now controls the boarder's timeline according to the last couple of lines of code. Run the FLA and try it out – if you want to see the boarder do his balancing act while his board has stopped, just hit that **B** button.

Multiple Movie Clip instances

This is another example of using multiple copies of a single symbol. This is useful for keeping file sizes down.

As usual, we'll demonstrate by example – open up canoodle.fla and run the movie:

First of all, if you look carefully at the little animated noodles on the title page, you'll see that although they're all very similar, they appear to be going through different animations. In fact, by looking in the FLA you'll soon realize that they are actually all different instances of the one animated `noodle` movie clip symbol in the Library, and that they've been skewed, rotated, resized, and generally pulled about to achieve the impression of individuality and complexity. Double-click on the `noodle_box` symbol and try selecting a few different `noodle` instances – in the Property inspector you'll see how the properties of each instance have been altered slightly to make them appear independent:

To see a good example of nested timelines, we can even double-click on the `noodle` instances to edit this symbol. Try it out and, again, watch how the navigation bar lets you know where you are within the nesting hierarchy at all times:

OK, use the Back arrow of the navigation bar to get back to the root timeline, then test the movie again. This time, notice that if you roll over the box of noodles with your mouse cursor, you get a message:

So go ahead and click the yellow button:

You'll then be taken to a new page, with a game on it. As you roll over each noodle box you trigger a button that controls the rotation property of another noodle box movie clip. This means that it becomes quite hard to click on all the boxes and put them back the right way up – the boxes act as both buttons *and* movie clip instances, and one box will control the rotation properties of another one in a different row. So the object of the game is to make all the boxes upright. Actually, it's a rather frustrating game and, admittedly, somewhat pointless! But it is good for demonstrating some more of the uses of movie clips.

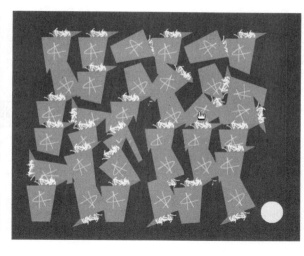

The animation in this game comes about by using ActionScript again. So, as an aside, let's take a quick look at how it's done. If you're not such a big fan of ActionScript, you can just skip this section anyway!

Actually, there is some code on every object in this movie – rather than the single piece of code that we're used to being attached to frame 1 of the root timeline, in this example we're demonstrating that you can also attach code directly to each instance (this is what's know as using 'attached scripts'). After you've played the game, have a look at the code in each noodle box and see what effect it has on other clips in the game. For example, making sure that you're in frame 2 of the root timeline, select the noodle box in the lower-right corner of the stage:

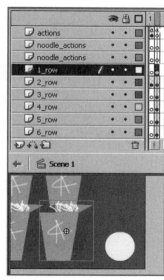

Bring up the Property inspector now (CTRL+F3/⌘+F3), and notice that all the noodle boxes are different instances, and that each one has an individual instance name. Now, with the lower-right noodle box still selected, take a look in the Actions panel and you'll see the attached script that is controlling some other boxes:

```
1  on (rollOver) {
2    _root.noodle_box23._rotation = -90;
3  }
4  on (press) {
5    _root.noodle_box1._rotation = 0;
6  }
```

So, what this is saying is that when you rollOver this noodle box with your cursor, the noodle box instance called noodle_box23 will rotate by minus 90°. Similarly, when you press (click) on our selected box (noodle_box1) it rights itself by putting its rotation property back to 0°. Pretty simple, huh!?

While we're here, it's also worth noting that the instance of the noodle box we've selected is inside a button called `noodleShifter` and inside the `noodle_box` are multiple instances of the `noodle` animated movie clip symbol. In fact, nearly every single noodle box on stage is an instance of this setup:

This whole movie could have been made a lot faster with much less scripting by randomizing some functions and using arrays in our ActionScript, but it's useful for getting us to look at the paths in the script – try and work out which `noodle_box` is controlling which other noodle box, and see if you can get them all the right way up.

Summary

In this chapter, we've looked at the basics of animating movie clip symbols in Flash MX. Key points:

- The difference between animated graphic symbols and animated movie clip symbols

- Linked vs. independent timelines

- The ins and outs of creating animated graphic and movie clip symbols

Next

Flash button basics.

Chapter 9
Flash Button Basics

What's in this chapter:

- **Button states**: **Up**, **Down**, **Over** and **Hit**

- Creating a button

- Testing buttons

- Editing buttons

- **Invisible** buttons

- **Animated** buttons

- Buttons – the next steps

Introducing buttons

There are three types of symbol in Flash: movie clips, graphic symbols and **buttons**. Buttons allow users to interact with movies via mouse events and keystrokes. Just like movie clips and graphic symbols, buttons have their own timeline. But *unlike* other types of symbol, a button's timeline is unique in its own way. You can think of buttons as interactive movie clips with four distinct frames. These four frames, **Up**, **Over**, **Down** and **Hit**, enable you to create the kind of JavaScript-type rollover effects that litter standard HTML pages, and to do this without any scripting.

Button state:	Up	Over	Down	Hit
Internal timeline frame number:	1	2	3	4

Buttons will help you to create *non-linear* movies – movies that the user can interact with, and where they can control things such as the play order. Interactive movies can also accept text and other input that affect the way that they behave and play back. Non-linear movies are thus unlike purely sequential movies, which can only be watched passively. The non-linear Flash movie is the ideal basis for a Flash web site or Flash web application.

Buttons do a multitude of things inside of Flash and aren't limited to a stereotypical hyperlink. In combination with ActionScripting they can set properties for other objects, accept information, or calculate equations. They are the means by which users can communicate with your movie and its functionality through **mouse events** – rollovers, clicks, and so on.

Dissecting buttons

Buttons work through simple mouse events. When the user interacts with the Button, its playhead moves to a corresponding frame on its internal timeline and pauses, awaiting further instructions. Let's take a look at these four frames, which can be referred to as **states**.

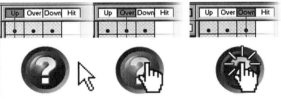

Up, Over, and Down states

Up

The Up state (first frame) represents the dormant state of every button. This is what each individual button will look like when it's sitting on your main timeline, waiting for the mouse to interact with it.

Over

The Over state (second frame) is what the user will see when their cursor rolls over the button. When the cursor enters the button's Hit area, the playhead on the button's timeline jumps from its current state to the Over state. After the cursor leaves the button's Hit area, it jumps back to the Up state.

Down

The Down state (third frame) is shown when the mouse button is pressed down. When a user clicks down on the button, its playhead jumps from the Over state to the Down state. After the user releases the mouse button, its playhead jumps back to the Over state.

Hit

The Hit state (fourth frame) is the only frame *never* seen by the user – it's invisible in the published SWF. The Hit frame allows you to define the area that the mouse can interact with. When the Hit frame is not explicitly defined, Flash uses content from one of the button's previous frames to specify the area that responds to the mouse. If no artwork is defined on any of the previous three frames, the button is unable to respond to the mouse.

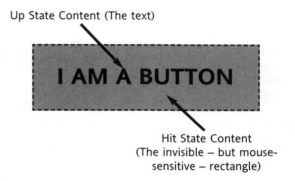

Up State Content (The text)

I AM A BUTTON

Hit State Content
(The invisible – but mouse-
sensitive – rectangle)

Creating a button

You create buttons in the same manner as you would a movie clip or graphic symbol. Let's make a simple button.

Open up Flash and use **Insert > New Symbol** or CTRL+F8/⌘+F8 to start making the button. The Create New Symbol dialog box will appear; enter 'My First Button' as the symbol name in the Name box and choose the Button radio button in the Behavior options:

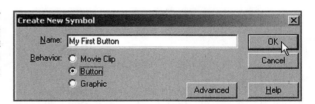

When you click on OK, a button symbol is created and you'll find yourself on that button's dedicated internal stage. There are several indicators telling you that you're on the button's internal stage and timeline; the most obvious clue is that you now have a blank stage with a crosshair in the center of it. As with all types of symbols, the crosshair represents the center point (0,0 coordinate) of that symbol's stage:

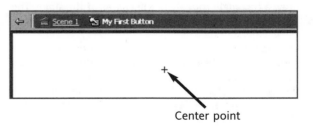

Center point

The next clue is in the timeline. Instead of the standard numbered timeline, you can now see the four button states instead. The information bar at the top of the stage also tells you you're in the button's edit mode. On the information bar you can see the name of the current timeline on the right (My First Button). There's also a 'quick link' button to Scene 1 (the main movie stage) and a back button to the last stage that you were on, which in this case is also Scene 1.

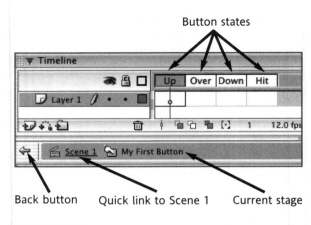

Back button   Quick link to Scene 1   Current stage

If you look in the Library (F11) you'll see that the button has been added. Note the icon that's used to represent a button:

The button symbol icon in the Library

Now that you have a button symbol created in the Library you can start adding artwork to each state. Just like all other symbol timelines, a button starts off with a blank keyframe at the first frame. Here, inside a button, it's in the Up state rather than in frame 1 (as it is in a regular movie or movie clip symbol).

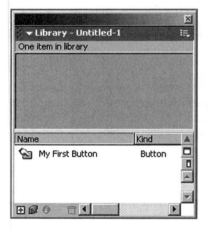

The Up state

Select the Rectangle tool (keyboard shortcut R), and draw a rectangle roughly in the center of the stage. The Up state of the button now has some content.

The Up state is the only state that absolutely *must* have some content added to it to make the button work – all the other states (especially the Hit state) can derive their content from this frame. Granted, the button will not visually reflect rollovers or clicks with content in the Up state alone, but drawing the rectangle there has enabled two essential button features already:

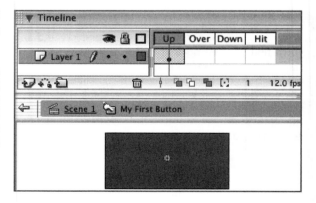

- You have a visual element for your users to interact with.

- You've defined a default area for the mouse cursor to interact with.

Although you *can* define an area in the Hit frame for interaction, by leaving it empty you force Flash to use previous keyframe content for this purpose. Neither the Over or Down frames have had content placed on them, so Flash will use the artwork in the Up state for the Hit area. Let's test this out. Move back to the main stage of the movie by clicking on the Scene 1 button in the information bar:

If you didn't do it earlier, open the Library (F11). Click-drag a copy of `My First Button` out of the Library and onto the stage:

Testing a button

There are two ways to test a button. The first is to use the standard Test Movie procedure (CTRL+ENTER/⌘+ENTER), which will open the file as a SWF. Try this, and notice that when you move the cursor over the button it changes to the 'pointing finger and hand' mode:

The second testing method allows you to test buttons in the authoring environment itself. Choose **Control > Enable Simple Buttons** or press CTRL+ALT+B/OPTION+⌘+B, and then try rolling over the button on the stage – the hand cursor appears over the button, even inside the FLA. While Simple Buttons are enabled you won't be able to edit your symbol as you could before. It's best to turn this off after you've tested your button using the same menu path or keyboard shortcut.

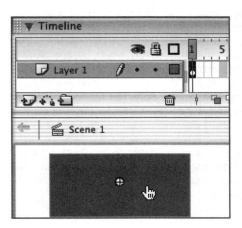

Editing a button

Now that you have a functioning button you can add some effects to it. Let's explore the other states on the timeline and create a simple color change for the other states. There are two ways that you can edit a symbol: editing it in the main timeline, or editing on the symbol's own timeline.

Editing on the main timeline

This is known as **editing in place**. The main advantage of editing a symbol on the main timeline is that you can see how the changes you make will affect the look of the whole movie (and not just the symbol itself). In this mode, the symbol's timeline is displayed, but the stage has all the other elements visible too – albeit with a transparent effect on them:

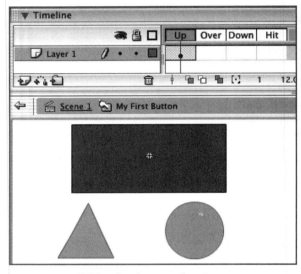

Editing in place on the stage:
the triangle and circle are on the main stage

There are two ways to enter the edit in place mode. You can double-click on the symbol, or you can select the symbol with the Arrow tool (V) and choose the menu option **Edit > Edit in Place**.

Editing on the button's timeline

This is the mode where you first created the button content inside its dedicated stage and timeline. Only elements actually in the symbol are visible; what's on the main stage can't be seen. This is advantageous when you need to focus on the symbol exclusively and don't want the distraction of what else is going on in the movie:

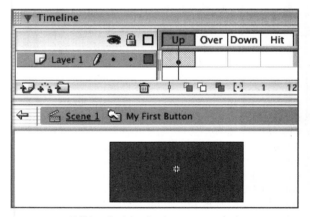

Editing inside the button symbol

You enter this editing mode by one of two methods: (1) You can select the object on the stage with the Arrow tool and choose the **Edit > Edit Selected** menu option; (2) You can open the Library (F11) and double click on the icon of the button you want to edit.

For the moment, do the editing in the button's own timeline. Select the `My First Button` instance on the stage and use the **Edit > Edit Selected** option to move into its timeline.

The Over and Down states

Once you're in the button's timeline you can add additional content to its four predefined state frames. To do this effectively, you'll need to add keyframes for each different state that you want to create content for.

You can either insert a blank keyframe (F7) and create totally new content, or insert a keyframe using F6 to copy the previous frame's content. This second option is more useful with buttons as you often need the button states to line up to ensure correct button behavior. Click on the Over frame in the button's timeline and press F6 to create a keyframe. Now click on a blank area of the stage to deselect the rectangle.

The Over state frame is where the rollover effect lives – whatever content we put here will be displayed when the button's rolled over in the finished SWF. Choose the Paint Bucket tool (K) from the Tools panel. Now use the Property inspector to select a fill color that contrasts with the rectangle's fill color in the Up state, then click on the rectangle to change the fill's color.

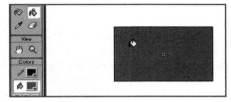

Changing the Over state's fill color

Now repeat this process for the Down state:

- Select the Down state frame.

- Press F6 to insert a keyframe.

- Click on a blank area of the stage to deselect the rectangle.

- Select the Paint Bucket tool.

- Change the fill color to (another) different color in the Property inspector.

- Click in the rectangle in the Down state frame to change its color.

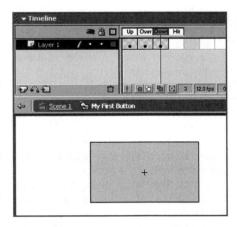

Test the movie now (CTRL+ENTER/⌘+ENTER). Move the mouse over the button and click. Note how the three different colors indicate that you've moved through the three different states:

At this point you're probably wondering why a fourth frame is needed for the Hit state. Let's look at that now.

Up   Over   Down

The Hit state

The Hit frame's content, up until this point, has been defined by the previous frame's artwork. Note that this is *not* the same as inserting a blank keyframe in the Hit state: a blank keyframe in the Hit state's frame results in the button not working at all, because that blank keyframe has no content on it to act as a hit area. Try this and see: click on the Hit state in the timeline and press F7 to insert a blank keyframe (this will override the 'inherited' content from the previous frame which had been defining the hit area). Now test the movie (CTRL+ENTER/⌘+ENTER). Nothing happens when you roll over or click on the button, because its Hit state is completely blank:

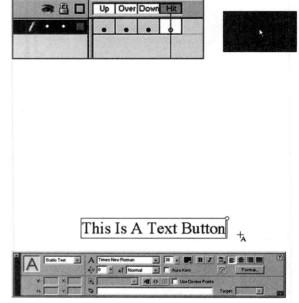

Let's try an example that takes advantage of the Hit frame.

Start a new movie (CTRL+N/⌘+N). This time, we'll use an alternative method to create a button. In the last example you made the symbol and then put the content into it. This time, we'll create some content first and *then* convert it into a symbol.

Select the Text tool (shortcut T) and click in the approximate center of the stage. Type 'This Is A Text Button' into the text box that appears. Use the Times New Roman font here (this is set in the drop-down menu in the Property inspector):

Now select the Arrow tool in the Tools panel to terminate the text entry mode – a blue box will appear around the text to show that it is selected. If this blue box doesn't appear, click on the text once with the Arrow tool. Convert the text into a button by using F8 or **Insert > Convert to Symbol**. A dialog identical to that you made your last button in (except for its title) will appear. Select the Button behavior, make sure it has a top-left registration point in the Registration grid, and name the symbol My Text Button:

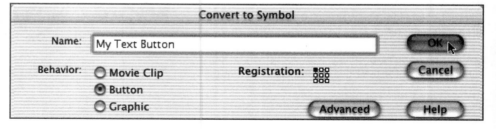

Click OK to finish creating the symbol. This method of creating a symbol has the added benefit – in this case – that the button's already on the stage and doesn't need to be dragged from the Library. Select the button on the main stage and use the **Edit > Edit Selected** option to go into the button's timeline.

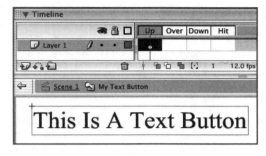

Before you go any further, test the movie (CTRL+ENTER/⌘+ENTER). Move the cursor over the button and you'll see the problem of having no Hit state; the cursor only changes to the hand cursor when you're over a stroke of the text – if the mouse pointer is over a gap between the letters' strokes it doesn't register that this is part of the button.

The white gaps in the text don't register as 'hittable'

Only the lines in the letters themselves are acting as 'hittable' areas. Consequently, this is a very tricky (and annoying) button to use.

You can imagine how frustrating this could be on a navigation consisting of text buttons. Luckily, it's possible to define the Hit state to make the whole text area – not just the stroke – act as the button. Click on the Hit frame of the button's timeline and press F6 to convert this into a keyframe. Note that this will fill the Over and Down states with the same content as the Up state as well, which is fine for the purposes of this exercise:

You could always convert these to individual keyframes too, as you did earlier, and change their style or color if you wanted to make each state distinctive. The Hit state will now contain the replicated content from the Up state. This is the content that was acting as the (implicit) hit area until we created this (explicit) Hit state by making it a keyframe.

Select the Rectangle tool (R) and draw a rectangle that covers all the text in the Hit frame:

You won't be able to see the text once you've done this, but don't worry – the Hit state content is invisible in the SWF, and just defines a mouse-sensitive *area*, not visible content.

The finished hit state area

Test the movie again. You'll now find that the button functions properly: the white space between and around the letters is now a mouse-sensitive part of the button, and there's none of that irritating 'cursor flicker' when you move the mouse over the text:

This demonstrates why explicitly defining the Hit area can be important.

This Is A Text Button

Invisible buttons

Not every movie you create will require a custom button with every state defined. Creating individually customized buttons is not only time consuming, but it *can* be unnecessary and may also add extra weight to your movie's final size. In many cases, defining a simple clickable area is all that's needed to give the user something to interact with. You can create clickable – or 'hot' – areas using invisible or 'clear' buttons. You create these by inserting artwork *only* on the button's Hit state frame. This will allow you to create a single button in your Library that you can use over and over again, without worrying about rollover state effects or size issues.

Create a new movie in Flash (Ctrl+N/⌘+N). Create a new button using the technique you learnt earlier:

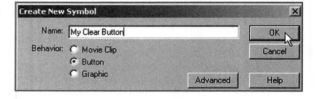

● Choose **Insert > New Symbol** (Ctrl+F8).

● Set the behavior to Button.

● Name the button My Clear Button.

● Press OK to create the button and move into its timeline.

Ignore the first three states of the button and click on the Hit state. Insert a blank keyframe here (F7).

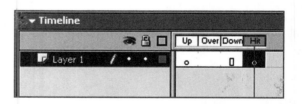

Select the Rectangle tool (R) and draw a square on the stage. You can ensure the perfect square by holding down the Shift key as you click and drag the shape out. Select the square's stroke and fill by double-clicking on it with the Arrow tool (V). Now use Ctrl+K/⌘+K to open the Align panel. Check on the To Stage box in this panel and align the drawn shape to the center of the stage using the align vertical center and align horizontal center buttons:

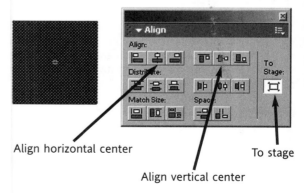

Align horizontal center

To stage

Align vertical center

What you have just done is define only the Hit state frame of the button. As the other three frames are empty, Flash won't have anything to display on the stage when your mouse interacts with the button. But, since you have defined the Hit frame, there's still an interactive area for the button, allowing you to rollover and click on it. Let's go back to the main timeline and use this invisible button.

Click on the Scene 1 button in the information bar to return to the main stage:

Open the Library (F11) and drag a copy of the invisible button onto the stage. Once you release the button you'll see the square you drew turn a transparent aqua color. Flash renders the Hit area of the button in this fashion so that you, as a developer, can locate it and see what area the Hit frame will encompass on the stage:

Select the Text tool (T) and click somewhere over the invisible button on the stage. Ensure that the text color in the Property inspector is black, and type 'This is some text' into the text field:

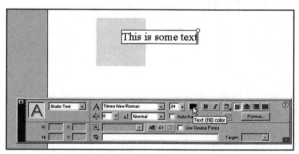

When you've finished typing the text, select the Arrow tool from the Tools panel. This will place a blue border around the text to show that it is selected. From the **Modify** menu, choose **Arrange > Send to Back**. This will move the text behind the invisible button:

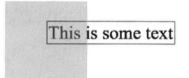

You should now clearly be able to see that your invisible button is transparent, and that the area in the Hit frame partly covers your text. Test the movie now (CTRL+ENTER/⌘+ENTER):

This is some text

The first thing you'll notice is that the aqua shape is gone, but the text remains. Try rolling over the area where the button was placed. When your mouse cursor is over the button it will change to a hand icon, notifying you that the area is clickable. Where the invisible button *doesn't* overlap the text, the text isn't clickable.

You can use invisible buttons in your movies to great advantage. You can create one generic button and then drop instances of it throughout your movie, saving both file size and production time. Since it's invisible, you can use Flash's scaling tools to change each instance without affecting the other instances. In addition, you will save on file size by reusing one symbol many times – only the original Library version gets downloaded with the finished SWF.

Creating animated buttons

At this point you should feel comfortable making a simple button with several different static states. This is accomplished by Flash moving the button's playhead to a frame that corresponds to the current state of the cursor and waiting for another event. But with only three frames available in each button (excluding the invisible Hit state) how can we accomplish an animated effect? The answer is to use *movie clips* embedded in the button states. Movie clips run independently of other timelines and, as a result, they can be placed in any frame of a button to create an animated state. Let's try making a simple animated rollover state with a movie clip.

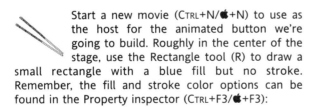

Start a new movie (CTRL+N/⌘+N) to use as the host for the animated button we're going to build. Roughly in the center of the stage, use the Rectangle tool (R) to draw a small rectangle with a blue fill but no stroke. Remember, the fill and stroke color options can be found in the Property inspector (CTRL+F3/⌘+F3):

Select the rectangle with the Arrow tool (V) and covert it into a symbol (F8). This time, make it a graphic symbol called 'rectangle'. Make sure you choose the Graphic radio button for the behavior and – very importantly – that you select the top-left registration option in the Registration box before you click OK:

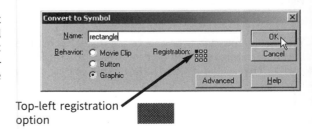

Top-left registration option

With the graphic symbol still selected on the main stage, select the Convert to Symbol option again (F8). This time choose the Movie Clip radio button, select a top-left registration point again, and name the symbol 'animation':

With the new movie clip still selected on the main timeline, press F8 one final time. This time, make the behavior the Button type, choose the usual top-left registration point again, and name the symbol animated button:

Once you press OK you'll be left with a button with a symbol nested inside it, and another symbol nested inside *that*. It's a bit like those Russian dolls where one is placed inside of the other...

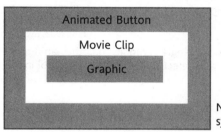

Nested symbols

If you test the button now you'll see that the button works, but nothing really happens. It's now time to make the animation come alive. Open the Library (F11) and double click on the movie clip icon next to the animation symbol to go into the movie clip's edit mode.

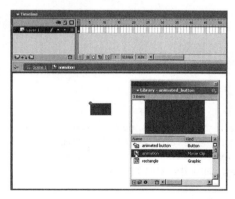

On the stage you'll see the rectangle graphic symbol. Click on frame 10 of the timeline and press F6 to insert a keyframe. Now click back on frame 1 and open the Property inspector (CTRL+F3/⌘+F3). In the Property inspector, select Motion from the Tween drop-down menu. The frames with content on them will turn blue in the timeline to signify a motion tween:

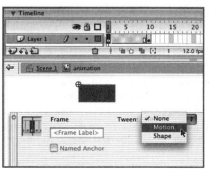

A Rotate option will now be available in the lower half of the Property inspector. By default it is set to Auto, but choose CW (clockwise) from the drop-down menu. The default number of times for a clockwise rotation is 1. Leave this value as it is:

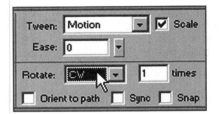

If you press ENTER to play the clip (or test the movie) you'll see that the rectangle now rotates once clockwise inside the button, using the top left corner as the center of rotation. This could be a bit tricky for the user, as they have to try and catch the rotating rectangle with the mouse to click on the button. It would be much better if the rotation was around the *center* of the rectangle, giving the user a better button target to aim at. This can be achieved with the Free Transform tool, which lets you move the center point around which the rotation occurs. Select the tool (keyboard shortcut Q) and the rectangle should become selected. If it doesn't, click on it.

> **Tip**
> *Be careful when clicking on nested clips: it's easy to click too any times and end up working on the wrong symbol. Keep your eye on that navigation bar and check where you are!*

Click on the rectangle graphic on the animation symbol's stage and select the Free Transform tool in the Tools panel:

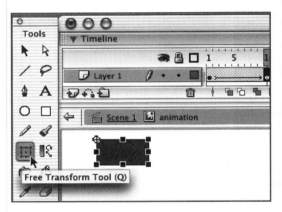

Note that the rectangle now shows the Free Transform tool's selection handles at its edges. The center point of rotation is revealed when you move the mouse over the top-left corner, and the cursor display shows a small white circle:

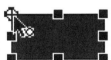

Move the cursor over that corner until the cursor changes to its 'white circle' form, then drag this rotation point to the *center* of the rectangle:

Click on the keyframe at frame 10 and move the center point into the middle once again, using the same Free Transform tool technique. If you now press ENTER the rectangle should rotate around its new center point, making a much easier target for the user's mouse to point at.

Still on frame 10, click on the `rectangle` symbol and look at the Property inspector. To the right of the panel you'll see a Color drop-down menu. Choose Tint from this menu.

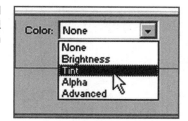

Some more options will now appear in this area of the Property inspector. Leave the Tint Amount slider as 100%, but choose a totally different color in the Color box:

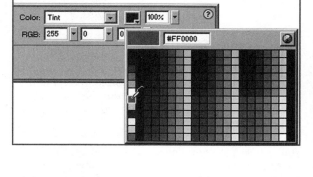

The color of the rectangle on the stage will change, but it's only at this frame – the actual color of the symbol is still what you set it as earlier.

If you press ENTER now, you'll see the rectangle change color as it rotates. This will be the animation for the button rollover. To make the animation stop when it reaches frame 10, rather than looping, open the Actions panel (F9). We'll cover Actions in more detail in the next chapter; for now you just need to add a stop action.

On the left hand side of this panel there are a group of folders. Go into the Actions folder, and then the **Movie Control** folder. In here, you'll find the stop action. Double-click on stop and this action will be added to the script window on the right hand side:

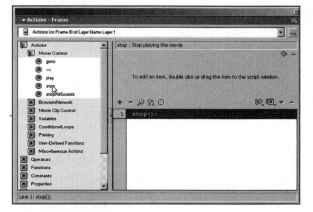

That's all the coding for now.

If you now test the movie (CTRL+ENTER/⌘+ENTER), you'll see the rectangle change color as it rotates, and then stop. There's one problem here: the animation is supposed to be a rollover, but currently it's running in the Up state rather than the Over state. To correct this you need to go into the button's edit mode. In the Library (F11), double-click on the button icon next to the `animated button` to go into its edit mode:

If you look at the timeline you'll see that the movie clip is on the Up state and the other states are empty.

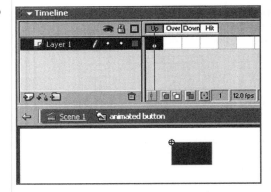

With the Up state still selected on the timeline (highlighted in black), click on the black frame and drag it across to the Over state. This transfers the content from the Up state to the Over state, leaving the Up state as a blank keyframe:

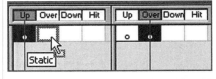

You've now got the rollover, but no content on the Up state, meaning that the button isn't visible in the SWF (unless you roll over it by accident). To fix this, you need to place a copy of the `rectangle` symbol in the Up state. Select the Up frame in the timeline and drag an instance of the graphic symbol from the Library to the stage.

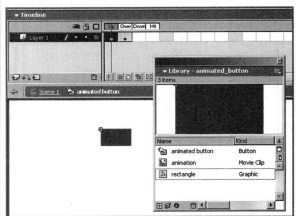

The final task is to align the graphic so that it sits in the same position as the animation. To do this, open the Info panel (CTRL+I/⌘+I). Because you set up all the nested symbols with their registration points in the top left hand corner, all you have to do is match up the top left corner of the symbol with the (0,0) coordinate. With the `rectangle` graphic symbol selected on the stage, type 0 into both the X and Y boxes of the Info panel:

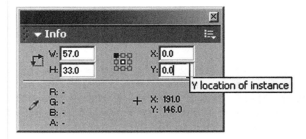

Test the movie again now (CTRL+ENTER/⌘+ENTER). The rectangle symbol will be visible on the stage in its static form, and it will rotate as you roll over it. This effect can be seen in `animated_button.fla`. It's just as easy to make an animation on the Up or Down states; you just have to place your animation movie clip on the appropriate frame.

You'll find that several things will affect the length of time for development of your buttons and other symbols. The biggest factor here is the type of animated effect you make, and its complexity. As with all things, practice makes perfect; try experimenting by making some additional animation clips and putting them in the different button states.

More advanced button uses

We've introduced the basic topics associated with buttons in this chapter. With time and experimentation, you'll find new ways to use them and new effects that you can apply to them. There are many other things that buttons can do, but these are a little beyond the scope of this *Express* book. However, we'll just whet your appetite for some of these uses here, so that you'll have a starting point for pursuing these subjects as your Flash knowledge and confidence grows.

Track as Menu Item

Once a button is placed on the stage, that instance of the button has two possible settings in the Property inspector. It can be set to either Track as Button or Track as Menu Item:

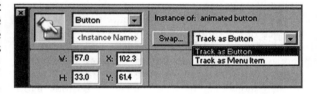

By default, the instance is set to Track as Button. This means that the button's events are independent of other buttons, and that the button will only accept mouse events for one button at a time. For example, you could have two buttons on the stage with separate event actions assigned to each for something like a press event on one and a release event on the other. In this case, it wouldn't be possible to trigger both events by pressing one and dragging to the other and releasing over the second.

On the other hand, the Track as Menu Item setting will allow two separate button events to occur. A good example of this is a drop-down menu. The user could press down on a main menu item to open a sub-menu and then drag the mouse down to another button and release it to open a URL. This would require two events, with only one 'press and release' cycle. Open Track_As_Menu.fla so you can take a closer look at this feature.

Clicking on the first menu item, navigating through the drop-down list, and releasing on the third item

Mouse events

When you begin to explore ActionScripting in the next chapter you'll be introduced to **event handlers**. Buttons have their own event handlers that allow you to assign code to them and define which mouse event will trigger that action. These handlers surpass simple Press and Release events. You can apply things like Keypress events and Release Outside. After you've become familiar with the basics, explore these handlers and see what types of interactions are possible. Open file `Assigning_Actions.fla` for a closer look of this effect.

Instance names

Much like Instance names for movie clips, which allow you to target them and retrieve properties, the 'name' property for buttons allows you to take advantage of the 'event model' – how the movie reacts to mouse events – in Flash MX. In previous versions of Flash, designers were forced to attach mouse event actions *directly* to the instance of the button symbol on the stage. This led to scattered code placement, added difficulty in the debugging process, and got in the way of effective collaborative development. The new Flash MX ability to give individual instance names to buttons allow us to consolidate code in one location, and to apply actions to buttons *elsewhere in the movie* by targeting them with ActionScript. This makes it easy to debug, and helps other developers come in after you and edit your code. This event-based button functionality can be seen in `Assigning_Actions2.fla` in the download package:

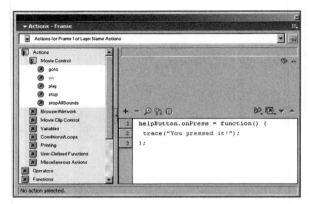

Button instance names can thus be referenced in code, and allow us to use buttons much more directly and flexibly than was possible before MX came along.

Layers and symbols

After you get more acquainted with Flash's interface and become more familiar with symbols and nesting, you'll start learning methods that will help you organize your content and reduce overall file size. Organization is key in any development process for many reasons. For example, if you work on a project and come back to it six months later you may have forgotten where things are or what does what. One of the easiest ways to organize content is by using layers on your timeline. Take the animated button that you just made. You could organize this by placing the animation instance on a layer named Animation and have the text on another layer named Text. It may seem like extra work, but what about buttons that contain ten symbols and a few pieces of text? By naming and organizing as you go you can come back to that button and edit it with little effort. Open `Track_As_Menu.fla` again so you can take a closer look at how this can be done in several buttons:

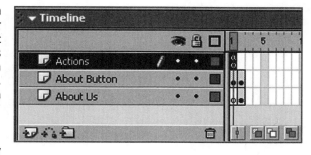

In addition to organization, optimization is another very important factor to consider in your development process. Symbols have been mentioned over and over again in this book. They are a key element in every movie because they can be reused adding very little to your file size. In the case of a button you could reuse the graphic elements that they're built from, saving file size in a large navigation. For example, you could create a background graphic and a glossy highlight graphic and reuse those in every button, and add new text for each one, making them appear different. Simple tricks like this can save you a lot of time in the long run. Take the time to experiment with different set-ups and find out what works best for you in each project.

Adding sound

 You can add sounds to your buttons that will enrich a user's experience by giving audible clues about which events are happening. Adding sounds is a simple process; inserting a separate layer in your button will allow you to organize your sounds and separate them from your artwork. This is covered in more detail in **Chapter 12**.

Summary

In this chapter we've seen:

- **Button states**: what they are and how to use them:
  - **Up**, **Down**, **Over** and **Hit**

- Creating a basic button:
  - Testing
  - Editing

- Making **invisible buttons**, and why they're useful

- Creating **animated buttons** using nested symbols

Next

Basic ActionScript.

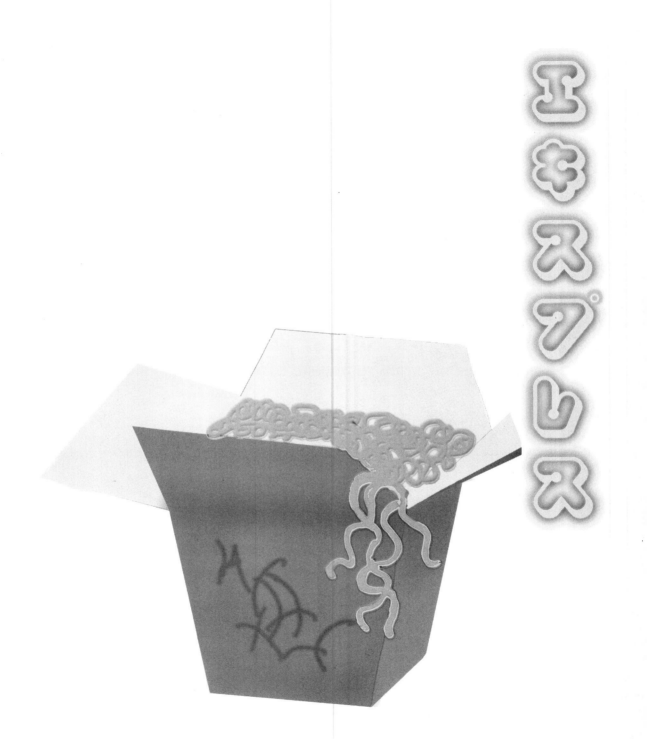

Chapter 10
Essential ActionScript

What's in this chapter:

- Using **the Actions panel**

- Basic **timeline-based actions**

- Scripted button behaviors

- Navigating the timeline with buttons

- Web and e-mail links

- How ActionScript can power a simple web site

The Power of ActionScript

 When it comes to making Macromedia Flash MX sites truly shine, nothing is more powerful than ActionScript. If you've heard many scary things in the past about ActionScript, don't worry; it's really quite a simple concept.

Imagine that you've paid the latest auto designer to create the most state-of-the-art, futuristic looking automobile for you. They spend weeks developing, testing aerodynamics, drawing, molding, and then finally creating the most beautiful and space-aged machine you've ever seen.

Testing day arrives, and they bring the car to the racetrack. The driver climbs in, and you wait with anticipation to see your creation come to life and do amazing things. The driver turns the key, and... nothing happens. One of the lead designers opens the hood of the car, scans the engine compartment, and says, "There's no engine in this vehicle. You've got perfect exterior, but the car has no heart." You realize that you've only done half the job – no engineer was assigned to create the cutting-edge, ultra powerful engine system.

The engine is somewhat like ActionScript. You are only harnessing half the power of Flash MX if you create static, pre-animated keyframed graphics. Sure, you can make a Flash site look great with just frame-by-frame animation, but that is akin to merely pushing the car along the track, giving the illusion of internal motor power. The other half of the process comes in what lies beneath the hood.

With ActionScript, we're able to make our movies and web sites act as if they're truly alive, operating under their own power, or perhaps at the guidance of the driver – the *user*.

Working with ActionScript

 So now you'd like to put something under the hood. We've already touched upon ActionScript in some of the earlier chapters in this book; here, we're going to look at ActionScript a little more systematically. In this chapter, we'll see how to use some simple ActionScript to control elemental yet vital aspects of our Flash creations. We're going to look at controlling movie timeline flow with ActionScript, responding to user interaction via the mouse, and using ActionScript to open up web pages and send simple e-mail with the `mailto:` tag.

By the time we're done this chapter, you should be able to create a simple Flash web site with forward and backward navigation, links, and an e-mail feedback facility.

The Actions panel

The Actions panel is our window into the scripting brain of Flash. It's through the Actions panel that we input our commands, and tell Flash to do what we want it to do.

Open up a new blank movie in Flash MX. Press F9 (or use the **Window > Actions** menu option), and you'll see the Actions panel appear:

The Actions panel

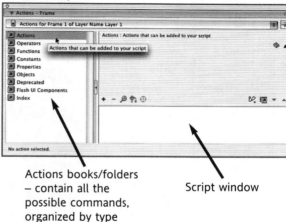

Actions books/folders – contain all the possible commands, organized by type

Script window

The white box bottom right of the Actions panel is the **script window** – any ActionScript code you create will appear here. At the left hand side of the panel, you can see little 'books' (or folders) that contain the full lists of the available actions. From here, the entire ActionScript language is accessible. Things go pretty deep here, but for now we're mainly going to be interested in the **Movie Control** and **Browser/Network** folders:

These two folders group together the ActionScript commands that let us (a) control the basic flow of a movie, and (b) let our movies talk to other web sites. Each of these little folders can be opened and closed by clicking on them once.

The Movie Control and Browser/Network folders

Adding ActionScript

ActionScript can be entered into the script window in a few different ways. The three main ones are:

1. Click-drag the action from the left hand pane into the script window; you can place it above or below other lines of ActionScript code in the script window. Alternatively, double-click on an action in the left hand pane – it will insert itself into the script window:

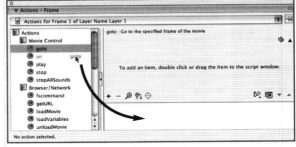

Dragging an action

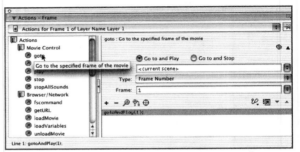

Double-clicking an action

2. Click on the "+" button above the script window to bring up a list of all ActionScript commands. You can navigate through the different ActionScript categories and get to the command you want to add:

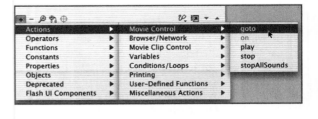

3. ActionScript can also be entered in **Expert Mode** – this allows you to enter the ActionScript code *manually*. This is how the majority of experienced ActionScripters enter their scripts. To switch to Expert mode, press CTRL+SHIFT+E/SHIFT+⌘+E. Alternatively, click on the View Options button (located above the script window) and choose the Expert Mode option:

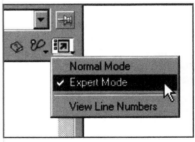

If you select this option, you can type in your ActionScript code at will.

View Options and Expert Mode option

As you're a beginner here, let's stick with the Normal mode. If you've switched Flash into the Expert mode, you can change back by pressing CTRL+SHIFT+N/SHIFT+⌘+N.

Now that you know how to put ActionScript into the script window, let's look at some of the simple commands and how we can use them in an interactive movie.

Frame actions

Frame actions are actions that you attach to the frames of a movie's timeline. Typically, these actions get triggered as soon as the movie's playhead hits the frame that the action is sitting on – they run automatically, with no intervention from the user. We'll start with the most basic actions: those that control the timeline.

Open up Flash (or, if you've already got Flash open, create a new movie CTRL+N/⌘+N. Use this movie to work through the following exercises on the goto, play and stop commands.

> **Tip**
> There's a working version of this FLA in the download files for this chapter – Ten_Frames.fla

On frame 1 of the movie, use the Text tool (keyboard shortcut T) to write frame 1 in the top left corner of the stage:

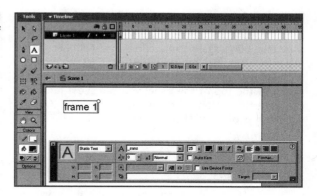

Insert a new keyframe at frame 2 (F6). The content of the first frame will be replicated on this frame. Edit the text on frame 2 by double-clicking on the text field, and replacing the '1' with '2' so that the text now reads 'frame 2':

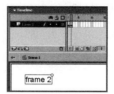

Now select the Arrow tool (V) – the border of the text field will turn blue. Use the Arrow tool to click-drag the frame 2 text field off to the right and down a little – this will help you to distinguish between the content of different frames:

Press ENTER to watch the two frames play. If you *didn't* move the text on frame 2, the only differentiator between the two frames would be the number in the text field changing from 1 to 2 and, unless you've got a really low frame rate, spotting this change won't be easy.

Insert a keyframe at frame 3 (F6), replicating the frame 2 content. Using the same process as before, change the text so that it reads 'frame 3' and then move the text field to a new position. Continue this technique to make the movie ten frames long, with the labels reading from 'frame 1' through 'frame 10'. Remember, for each frame insert a keyframe (F6), double-click on the text field and change the frame number, and use the Arrow tool (A) to move the text field. When you've finished this process, test the movie by pressing CTRL+ENTER/⌘+ENTER. The screenshot shows how this effect looks with onion skinning turned on:

Onion Skin button

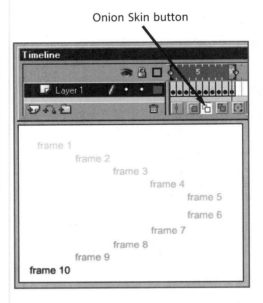

There's nothing earth shattering here; the movie just runs through the frames and then loops back to the start and plays again. Let's add some ActionScript to make things a little more interesting. Click on frame 5 of the movie's timeline and press F9 to open the Actions panel. At the top of the panel you can see a reminder of where the ActionScript code will be added: 'Actions for Frame 5 of Layer Name Layer 1':

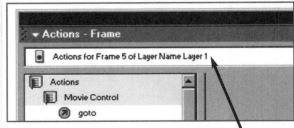

Identifies which frame the script is being added to

gotoAndPlay

Double-click on the goto option in the **Actions > Movie Control** folder in the Actions panel's left hand pane. Clicking on the goto option inserts a `gotoAndPlay` command into the script window. The line of code reads:

```
gotoAndPlay(1);
```

So, what does this code do? What are we expecting to happen? Test the movie (CTRL+ENTER/⌘+ENTER) and you'll see. You'll notice that text is flying across the screen as before, but you can also see that once it has displayed

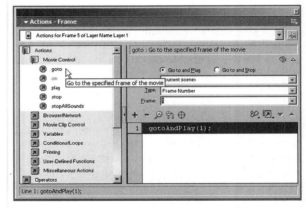

'frame 4' the movie then returns to frame 1 again and repeats, rather than running through the remaining frames. So the gotoAndPlay(1); instruction is clearly telling Flash to "go to frame 1, and then continue playing". gotoAndPlay(2); would send the movie to frame 2, and so on. You can edit the frame the movie goes to by typing the frame number in the Frame box, ensuring that the Type selected is Frame Number.

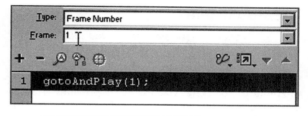

> **Tip**
> If you look at the timeline you'll see that a small 'a' has appeared at frame 5. This signifies that there is ActionScript on the frame – this identifier appears on all frames that contain ActionScript.

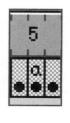

You've seen how gotoAndPlay can create a simple loop in a movie, but that's not its only use. This command can be used to jump to any point in movie, either forwards or backwards. You can even jump to another scene entirely using the Scene drop-down option:

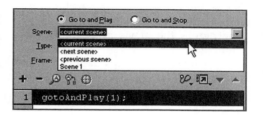

gotoAndStop

You now know how to make a movie go to a certain frame and play, and it's just as simple to make it *stop* in the target frame you specify. When you enter a goto command you'll see that there are two radio buttons at the top of the command options. Click on the Go to and Stop button to change the code to a gotoAndStop action:

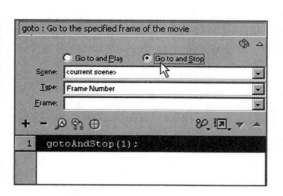

    gotoAndStop(1);

Test the movie and note that instead of looping when it reaches the frame 5 code, the movie now stops back on frame 1.

Why use gotoAndStop instead of gotoAndPlay? There are a number of circumstances where this is of more use. A major use is where you want the movie to pause and wait for some user input or an **event**, such as a button press. Typically, you'd do this when a movie loads up into a user's browser and you present them with the movie or site's main options screen.

> **Tip**
> Code lines in ActionScript are terminated with a semicolon. A semicolon indicates that this is a complete, self-contained chunk of ActionScript – a complete 'statement'.

The stop action

When creating a movie you don't always want the movie to jump somewhere else and stop, like it does with the `gotoAndStop` command. You often want the movie to stop where it is currently. Luckily, Flash provides a stop command especially for this:

```
stop();
```

In the FLA you've been playing with, select the goto action you added earlier; click on it in the Actions panel, then press DELETE to remove the action. Now add a stop action by double-clicking on stop in the **Movie Control** book of the left hand pane of the Actions panel. This will add the action to the script window:

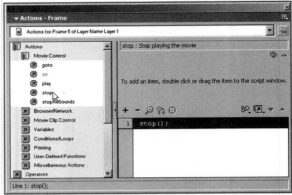

Unlike the `gotoAndStop` action, where you could set the frame to stop on in the parameters section there are no options here – none are needed, as this command simply stops the movie in its tracks, right where it is. Test the movie (CTRL+ENTER/⌘+ENTER) and you'll see that the movie now stops at frame 5 and nothing else happens.

The play action

The final action to look at to complete the basic actions is the play command (`play();`). This is entered in the same fashion as the stop command, this time double-clicking on play in the **Movie Control** book. The use of this command is a little less intuitive than the other commands we've looked at so far. Why would you want a play command sitting alone on a frame? The movie should already be playing, after all. Its use lies in restarting a timeline after an **event** such as a mouse click. This is the second time I've mentioned events. Don't worry; the next section will reveal how we use events and how they are used in conjunction with the basic commands that we've just looked at.

Object actions

We've just looked at how to apply actions and ActionScript to *frames* so that the actions are triggered when the playhead hits that frame. Flash isn't just linear however, and we can also attach actions to *objects* like as movie clips and buttons. These actions can then be triggered by the user interacting with these objects – say, by using

Tip

It's good practice to keep all your code on a separate layer set aside just for ActionScript. This practice helps you clarify exactly where your code is, and means that you don't have to go digging around on different layers to piece the whole code picture together. It also makes things easier for anyone who has to look through your FLAs at a later date and understand what's going on.

their mouse. These simple object actions allow you to create true interactivity in your web sites.

The main object we're going to focus on here is the **button** object. Since most links and clickable images on a web site are all 'buttons' – conceptually at least – then this is a good place to start.

Controlling playback with buttons

Open the `Ten_Frames.fla` download file. You'll recognize this file as the example we built earlier in this chapter, before we added the ActionScript. Rename Layer 1 of this movie to `frame text` by double-clicking on the layer name in the timeline and typing in the new layer name:

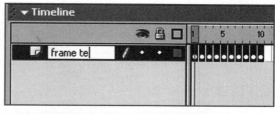

Add two new layers by clicking on the Insert Layer button at the bottom left corner of the Timeline panel. Name these layers `buttons` and `actions`.

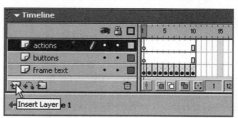

The next task is to add some buttons to the movie – you can then use these to create some interaction with. Luckily, Flash has some great built-in buttons for you to use. Choose **Window > Common Libraries > Buttons** and the buttons library will open in front of you:

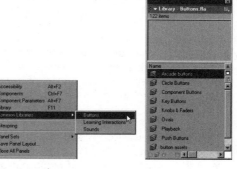

This library contains a number of folders holding different style buttons. Double-click on the Arcade buttons folder to open it – you'll reveal the predefined buttons we'll be using in this exercise.

Select the buttons layer on the timeline and drag an instance of the blue arcade button onto the stage. Place it on the left hand side of the stage, halfway down. Now drag instances of the green and orange red buttons out onto the stage and arrange them in line next to the blue button, clear of the ten bits of frame text – you might want to leave onion skinning on so you can get the placement right:

Each of these buttons lives on the keyframe in frame 1, but they're visible (and usable) throughout the timeline, as the gray coloring of the buttons layer indicates.

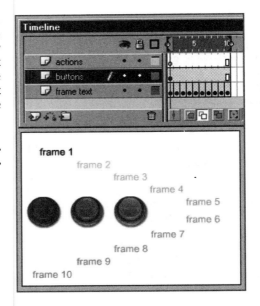

Open the Property inspector (CTRL+F3/⌘+F3) and select the left-most button on the stage (the blue one). For the subsequent code to work you need to assign the button an **instance name** to identify it uniquely. Go to the Instance Name input box on the left of the Property inspector and type the instance name blue into this box:

Assign the instance names green and orange to the other two buttons in the same way. Now that the symbols have got individual instance names we can refer to them – *target* them – with ActionScript. Select frame 1 of the actions layer and open the Actions panel (F9):

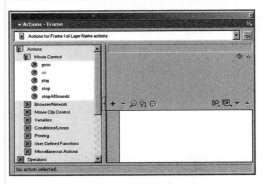

 The first thing we'll do is add is a stop(); action on frame 1. In this movie, different 'events' will occur when different buttons (objects) are pressed, and these events will trigger ActionScript that makes the movie run in a particular way.

You therefore need a stop action, right at the outset, to make sure the movie doesn't run through all its frames in a linear fashion – remember, you want the movie to sit and wait for the user to trigger an event. This doesn't mean that our movie has aborted or completely halted, it just means that the main timeline playhead has *paused*, waiting to spring into life once something – some use interaction – happens.

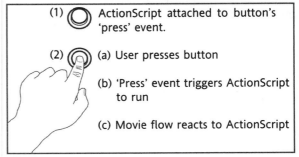

(1) ActionScript attached to button's 'press' event.

(2) (a) User presses button

(b) 'Press' event triggers ActionScript to run

(c) Movie flow reacts to ActionScript

Click on frame 1 of the actions layer, then double-click on the stop action in the **Actions > Movie Control** folder, as you did in the earlier exercise:

Now for the interactive code. The options you'll use for this are in the left hand pane, in the **Objects > Movie > Button > Events** folder:

Mouse Events

 The options available in this folder are known as **onMouseEvents**. They occur in relation to mouse movements – clicks, rollovers, and so on. The most important mouse events are:

- **Press**: Occurs when the user presses down on the mouse button while the cursor is over the top of a Flash button:

- **Release**: Occurs when the user releases the mouse button while it's above a Flash button:

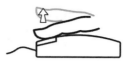

- **Roll Over**: Occurs when the mouse cursor moves anywhere *over* the event-sensitive 'hit' region of the Flash button:

- **Roll Out**: Occurs when the mouse cursor *leaves* the hit region of the button.

These event-based actions let us replicate most of the interactive functionality that people expect from a web site.

Still on frame 1 of the actions layer, double-click on the onRelease event. The function created here is run when the mouse button is released, hence onRelease. Note that the start of this line in the script window has turned red where it says <not yet set>. This is where we supply the instance name of the button that we want this code to act upon:

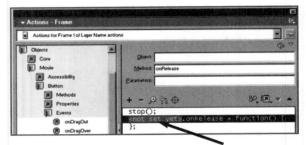

Placeholder for instance name

Note the three input boxes (just above the script window) for **Object**, **Method** and **Parameters**:

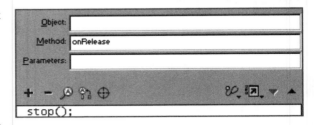

You use these boxes to enter the details of exactly how you want this code to operate. Here, we don't require any additional Parameters to modify the way the code runs. The Method was automatically defined as onRelease when you double-clicked to enter the code. The Object box is where you enter the name of the object that you want the selected method to apply to; in this movie, that's going to be the instance name of a button.

> **Tip**
> *We don't want to execute this code when the mouse button is pressed down (although onPress is valid), because in most computers buttons behave by reacting when you release the mouse button, not when you press it. Usually this is so that users who've clicked on a button, can change their minds, drag the mouse off the button, and then release the mouse button without triggering the actions that the button performs.*

Click on the input area of the Object box. This makes another feature available to you: the Insert a target path button:

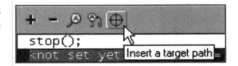

You *could* just type the instance name in the input area, but this button allows you to ensure that you refer to the right object and use the correct path to target it, wherever it happens to be in the movie. We recommend that you use this button while you're still learning ActionScript.

Click on this button to open the Insert Target Path dialog box.

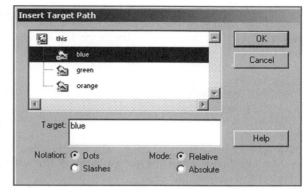

You'll see a list of all available objects in the movie that *could* act as the target for this piece of ActionScript. The entry right at the top of the list – this – refers to the timeline the code exists on.

We *could* have written the earlier gotoAndPlay action as this.gotoAndPlay();

To select the blue button as the target, click on blue in the dialog box and then press OK.

The object box will now have blue in it, and the code in the script window will look like this:

```
blue.onRelease = function() {
};
```

In plain English, this means "when the blue button instance is clicked on, and the mouse button released, the function we define next will be triggered and run".

The actual code that we want to run when this onRelease event occurs will go between the opening brace on line 2 of the script window and the closing brace on line 3. The function we specify here will thus be run when the user clicks and releases on the blue button.

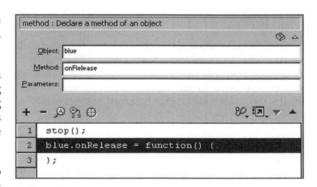

Now to define the code for the function triggered by that mouse click event. This is where the basic gotoAndStop action you saw in the earlier section comes in.

With the line containing the onRelease handler still highlighted, go to the **Actions > Movie Control** folder and double-click on the goto action. This will insert a gotoAndPlay action inside the function. Anything that you want to happen when the button is released has to live within this function – between the braces. A gotoAndStop action is required here, so click on the radio button to change the code.

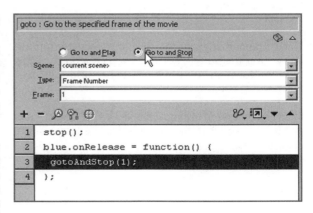

Leave the '1' that's specified in the Frame box; this is the frame number that we want to 'go to and stop' at. This may seem strange when you bear in mind that this code is being attached to frame 1, but object actions can potentially be activated from *all* the frames in the timeline (unless you write code in a later frame changing their behavior). Here, only the stop action will be run automatically in frame 1 – the other code is *event*-driven, and won't be run automatically when the playhead hits the frame. Your ActionScript should now look like this:

```
stop();
blue.onRelease = function() {
    gotoAndStop(1);
};
```

To recap once more for total clarity: when the playhead gets to this frame when the movie loads, Flash will interpret this code as follows:

● Stop on this frame (and wait for an event to occur before you do anything else)

● When someone presses and releases the blue button instance (this is the triggering event)...

● ...go to frame 1 and stop there

Test the movie (CTRL+ENTER/⌘+ENTER) – nothing will happen when you click the blue button. The movie is already on frame 1, so `gotoAndStop(1);` will have no impact. You need to put code on *another* button that moves the movie off frame 1 before the blue button will work properly.

Still in the Actions panel, click on the bottom line of the frame 1 code. You need to do this so that the new code is added *after* the current block. Go back to the folder containing the button events in the left hand pane (**Objects > Movie > Button > Events**). You could just add another `onRelease` command, but so that you see something else in use, double-click on `onRollOver` instead:

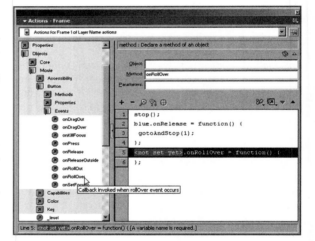

This command triggers the function when the mouse moves *over* the button, not when you click on it, so this time the function will run when the mouse rolls over the green button.

Specify the green instance name in the Object box, either by typing it straight in, or using the Insert Target Path method.

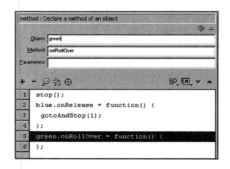

Next, insert a `gotoAndStop` command into the function by double-clicking on the goto option in the **Actions > Movie Control** folder. Remember to change the action from `gotoAndPlay` to `gotoAndStop` using the radio button. This time, change the number in the **Frame** box to 5 so that the movie skips from frame 1 to frame 5.

Test the movie again. Move the cursor over the green button – the movie will skip to frame 5 and stop. If you then click on the blue button, the movie will go back to frame 1.

Frame box   Go to and Stop radio button

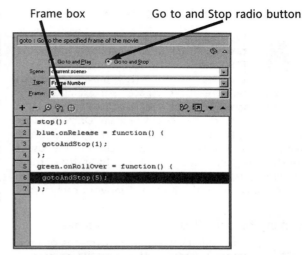

For the orange button, add another `onRelease` command. You know the technique by now:

- Click on the bottom line of the current code to ensure that the new code is added after this.

- Go to the **Objects > Movie > Button > Events** folder.

- Double-click on the `onRelease` option.

- Type the instance name orange into the Object box, or select this instance in the **Insert Target** Path dialog:

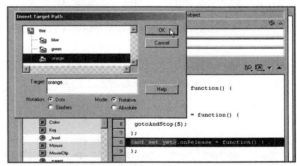

This time, instead of a `gotoAndStop` action, add a standard play action. Click on the play option in the **Actions > Movie Control** folder to do this:

Test the movie (CTRL+ENTER/⌘+ENTER). Hitting the orange button makes the movie play through and stops it at frame 1 when the `stop();` action is read. It doesn't matter whether the movie is at frame 1 or at frame 5 (due to the green button having been rolled over) – the movie will play through all the remaining frames when you click on the orange button. This shows the power of Flash scripting: you can have code that affects just one frame (the `stop();` command here), as well as code that can be triggered from *any* frame (the **onMouseEvent** functions, kicked off when we click – or rollover – one of our three buttons). Furthermore, all these actions can live in one script on a single frame. This completed file can be found in the download code as `Ten_Frames_with_Buttons.fla`.

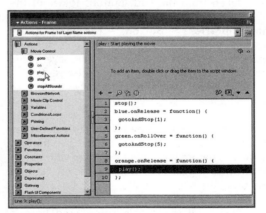

> *Tip*
> *You can move lines of code up and down using the arrow buttons at the top of the script window.*

Buttons for links and e-mail

We've looked at creating buttons that can take us to different locations within our Flash movie, but what if we wanted to send the user *out* of the Flash movie, to another location elsewhere in cyberspace? For example, many web sites have dozens of links, which can redirect the user to a completely different domain. Or perhaps we want to display a button saying "click here to e-mail me", and which automatically opens up the user's e-mail program when clicked. To satisfy these requirements, we're going to use the second book in the **Actions** folder; the **Browser/Network** category:

Linking to web sites from Flash movies

The ActionScript command that is of most interest here is the getURL command. You're going to use this to open up links to external web pages from inside a Flash MX SWF.

Open the source file Link_to_URL.fla from this chapter's download code.

This movie consists of three layers; the bottom layer houses three push buttons taken from the Push Buttons folder of the buttons common library (**Windows > Common Libraries > Buttons**). The layer above contains text labels describing each button's purpose. The top layer is currently empty, but from its layer name I'm sure you can guess what it's for: **actions**. Adding code to this layer will make this deceptively simple page become *interactive*.

As you discovered when making buttons to control the playhead in the last exercise, you need to give buttons instance names before you can target them with scripts and use them to trigger actions in the movie. Let's do that, and bring the buttons to life.

Stick with the simple color-based naming convention that you used in the last exercise. Open the Property inspector (CTRL+F3/⌘+F3) and click on the blue button at the top of the stage. Type blue into the Instance Name box:

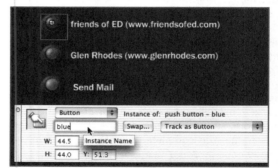

Now give the middle button an instance name of green and call the bottom one orange. Remember, now that the buttons have instance names you can target them with some ActionScript code.

Click on frame 1 of the actions layer and press F9 to open the Actions panel. Once again, start the code with a stop action to stop the movie looping. Looping is not much of an issue here because it's a one frame movie, but the stop action will reduce CPU strain – a constantly looping movie will take up processor resources. If you recall, the stop action is added by double-clicking on **stop** in the **Actions > Movie Control** folder of the left pane of the Actions panel.

The onRelease method should be used to create a standard link effect on a button. This option can be found in the **Objects > Movie > Button > Events** folder. Insert this method by double-clicking on onRelease. The next step is to add the object that the method will affect; in this case, that's the blue button. Type blue into the Object box:

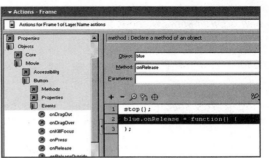

Now it's time to add the getURL command; this will enable the button to point at a URL out on the web sosmewhere. Open the **Actions > Browser/Network** folder and double click on getURL to add the code into the function:

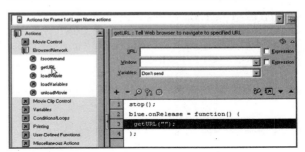

Above the script window you can see the specific parameters that we can use to tell getURL what to do; that is, where we want it to jump to on the web, and how. The first parameter, the URL box, contains the actual web site address to which we wish to navigate. Type http://www.friendsofed.com into this box:

This is just like any standard URL typed into a web browser's Address box.

> **Tip**
> You **must** start the name of the web site with 'http://', otherwise Flash won't be able to open up the site. Without the http:// prefix, Flash will look for the named location/file on the hard drive/server where the SWF's being run from.

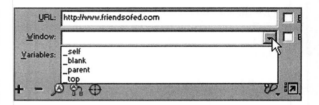

The next parameter is the Window parameter. With this parameter, we tell Flash how it should go about opening up the web page. There are four options for the window parameter:

● **_self** – When you open a window with the Window parameter set to '_self', you're telling Flash that it should open the target URL in the window currently holding the SWF. This means that the Flash movie calling the URL will no longer be loaded and visible – the browser will be taken over by the target URL.

● **_blank** – When you set the Window parameter to '_blank', you're telling Flash to open up a brand new browser window and load the URL into it.

● **_parent** – This specifies that the URL should be loaded into the parent window of the current window.

● **_top** – This specifies that the URL should be loaded into the top most window in the current frameset. This is handy if you're ever designing a web site that uses frames to separate content.

> **Tip**
> When the movie is tested (CTRL+ENTER/⌘+ENTER) in local mode all settings have the same effect as using _blank.

For this exercise, choose _blank to open the web site in a new browser window. This way, you don't lose the Flash page when a link is clicked on. Note how the code changes when you select this option:

```
1   stop();
2   blue.onRelease = function() {
3       getURL ("http://www.friendsofed.com", "_blank");
4   };
```

The final parameter is the Variables parameter. This can be set to either Don't send, Send using GET or Send using POST.

This has the effect of sending all variables within the timeline containing the button to the URL specified. We're not going to get into this with too much detail. If you've ever worked with HTML forms before, this is the same thing as GETting or POSTing hidden variables to a specific URL. For our purposes right now we're going to keep it set to Don't send.

> **Tip**
> These functions can be crucial for sending data backwards and forwards between the user's machine and the web server that's hosting your Flash site. You'll probably come across these more advanced features later in your Flash career.

Back in the FLA, press CTRL+ENTER/⌘+ENTER and watch what happens when you press the blue button next to the 'friends of ED (www.friendsofed.com)' text...

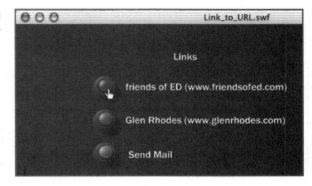

The friends of ED web site opens in a new browser window:

You've successfully made a link to an external web site. Repeat the process for the green button to see if you've mastered this technique. This time, enter the address for my web site, `http://www.glenrhodes.com`:

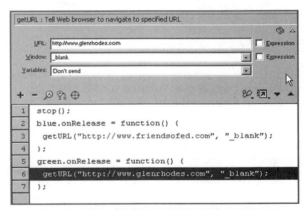

```
1  stop();
2  blue.onRelease = function() {
3    getURL("http://www.friendsofed.com", "_blank");
4  };
5  green.onRelease = function() {
6    getURL("http://www.glenrhodes.com", "_blank");
7  };
```

Opening e-mail programs from Flash

Let's now take a look at how you can make Flash open up a blank e-mail window; once again, this uses the `getURL` command, but with some different parameters. The basic process is very similar to the one you've just used to create a web link.

Here's a summary of the steps to take:

● Double-click on the `onRelease` option in the **Objects > Movie > Button > Events** folder to insert the `onRelease` handler into the script window.

● Set the instance name of the button as the object in the Object box. In this case it's orange.

● Double-click on getURL in the **Actions > Browser/Network** folder.

● Type in the address in the URL field. Since you want this link to open up the user's e-mail program, type in the address in this form:

```
mailto:name@address.com
```

The `mailto:` syntax specifies that we want to invoke a mail contact rather than jump to a URL. Once you've entered an address into the URL field in this `mailto:` format, test the movie and click on the orange button. A new mail from your default mail program will open, and the To field will be populated with the address you just entered in the `getURL/mailto` ActionScript.

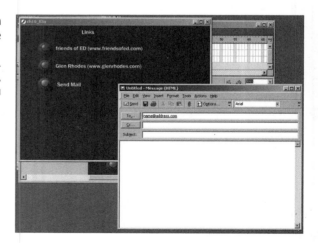

> **Tip**
> *If the button doesn't work, even after you've double-checked your code, check that your Publish Settings are outputting to HTML, then publish the movie (SHIFT+F12); some machine/ software setups require the SWF to be embedded in the HTML template for this function to work.*

Close the mail program and return to the FLA by closing the SWF. By appending some code at the end of the e-mail address in the URL field it's possible for one click of the orange button to add a subject line and message content into the mail message. Look at the following line of code:

```
mailto:name@address.com?subject=Hello
➥there!&body=I think the site's great
```

Enter this line of code into the URL field. The ? defines the end of the e-mail address and is followed by `subject=` and then the content for the mail message's subject line. You could just leave it there, but the & says, "I want to add something else as well". This something else is the message text. It takes the same format as the subject (`subject=content, body=content`):

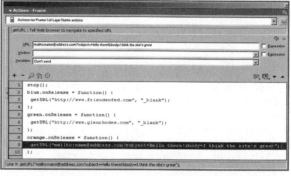

Test the movie now. When you press the orange button a mail message will appear with an e-mail address, the filled out subject line, and the message content that you appended in the URL field. The final effect of this file set up like this can been seen in `Mail_Content.fla` in the download package.

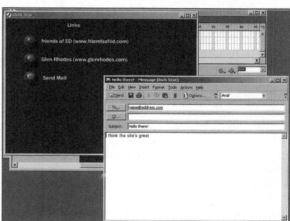

 This technique is useful for creating pre-filled, user-friendly automatic feedback, or for predefining easily identifiable requests for more information about a Flash web site, or for product requests.

A simple web site

 You've learnt a lot in this chapter about the elementary workings of ActionScript. Let's finish off by seeing the techniques you've used in practical use on a mock web site, 'the color site'. This site has been created using only the code examples you've used in this chapter, and it's the code that we'll focus on here, rather than the design aspects. The site can be found in `Color_Site.fla`.

This movie/site consists of six screens: a homepage and a page for each of the five colors displayed on the front page. Open up the movie from the download package and test it (CTRL+ENTER/⌘+ENTER) – you'll be greeted by the homepage:

This page only contains text, graphics, and one button; the Enter button, which has been given an instance name of `enter`, and whose controlling code lives in frame 1 of the actions layer. Here's that frame 1 code:

```
stop();
enter.onRelease = function() {
  gotoAndStop("blue");
};
```

As this is an entry page, there's the now-familiar stop action that prevents the movie from running through to the later pages and rendering the navigation buttons pointless. We've then got the standard `onRelease` handler that we've used throughout the chapter, linking the `enter` button instance with the function that will run when the button is released. In this case, that function is a regular `gotoAndStop` action. There's one slight variation from the way you've used this command earlier; instead of specifying a frame number to go to, there's a label instead – "`blue`".

Frame labels

Frame labels are used to give a specific frame a customized *name* in addition to the default number it derives from its position on the timeline. Using these customized, intuitive names helps you keep track of exactly what's going on in the timeline. The additional benefit we gain is that frame labels can be used to target the frame in code. This is especially useful if you use meaningful, descriptive labels, since you don't need to look at the frame's *content* to see what's happening on that frame – the name should give you a pretty good idea.

Take a look at the color site's timeline. On the Backgrounds layer, the keyframes have little red flags, followed by the name of a color. A red flag indicate that the frame has a frame label, and the text following the flag is the assigned label:

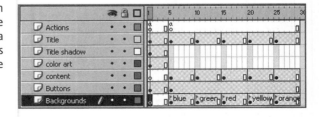

Labels are assigned to frames in the Property inspector. Click on the keyframe you want to add the label to in the timeline and open the Property inspector (CTRL+F3/⌘+F3). The Frame Label box is on the left hand side of the panel (just below the word Frame). To create a label, you type the label text into this box. Easy, eh?

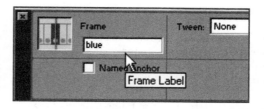

So how do you refer to a frame label in code, rather than a frame number? Let's see how to add the frame label reference to a goto action.

Click on frame 1 of the Actions layer and open the Actions panel. Select the line with the goto action and look at the properties above the script window:

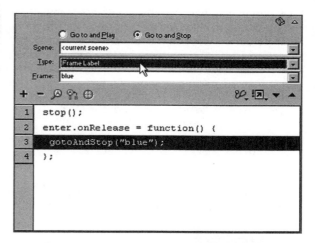

In the Type field, you've previously been using the default Frame Number setting. In this movie I've changed this setting to Frame Label using the drop-down menu. Changing this option means that all the frame labels I've added into the timeline are now listed in the Frame option drop-down menu. It's a case of choosing the frame you want to go to from this menu and adjusting the code to reflect the frame choice.

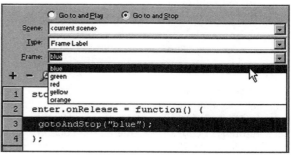

Each of the remaining five sections of the web site is for a different color, so the frames where they start have been labeled accordingly. Choosing 'blue' on the enter button sends the user to the blue section of the site.

> **Tip**
> Note that in the code, labels are enclosed within quote marks.

The color pages

The color pages all have the same structure; there's the color title at the top, text in the middle (with color definitions from www.dictionary.com), and the buttons on the left:

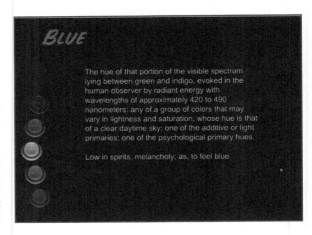

These buttons are introduced at frame 5 on the timeline and run throughout the rest of the movie – there are not separate instances on each color page. This allows us to use the same code for these buttons throughout.

Each button has been given an instance name that corresponds to its color and to its frame label. The code for these buttons lives on frame 5 of the actions layer; it's not on frame 1, since these button instances don't *exist* on frame 1. The frame 5 code is in the standard format that we've come to know and love:

```
blue.onRelease = function() {
    gotoAndStop("blue");
};
green.onRelease = function() {
    gotoAndStop("green");
};
orange.onRelease = function() {
    gotoAndStop("orange");
};
yellow.onRelease = function() {
    gotoAndStop("yellow");
};
red.onRelease = function() {
    gotoAndStop("red");
};
```

You can see here that the use of frame labels makes it very easy to link the correct frames to the correct buttons. The benefit of an actions layer is also apparent here. Although I couldn't include all the code in frame 1 as I would in the ideal world, it *is* all contained in the same layer, and is just as easy to find.

Test the movie (CRTL+ENTER/⌘+ENTER) and click on each of the buttons to see how easily this navigation works. You may now feel a little less daunted when you hear the word 'ActionScript', as you've now got the knowledge to script your own basic web sites.

Summary

In this chapter we've learned the following:

- How to use **the Actions panel**

- **Frame actions**: how to **goto**, **stop**, and **play**

- Scripting basic **actions on buttons**

- **Navigating** the timeline with **buttons**

- **How to open a URL** in a web browser

- **How to invoke e-mail** with Flash MX

- Applying basic scripting to create a simple web site

Next

Working with bitmap images.

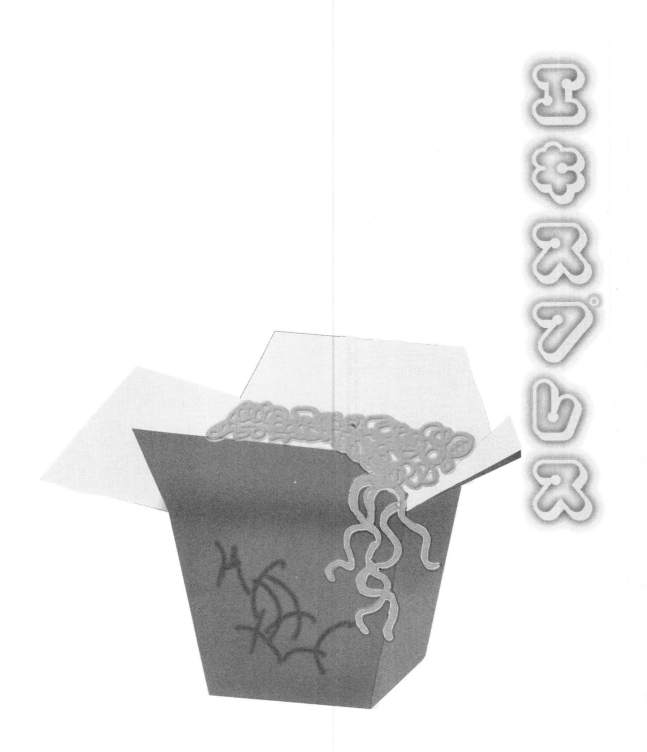

エクスプレス

Chapter 11
Working with Bitmaps

What's in this chapter:

- **Bitmap** vs. **vector** graphics

- **Importing** bitmaps and bitmap sequences

- Bitmap **properties** and **compression options**

- **Performance considerations** when using bitmaps

- Converting bitmaps to **symbols** and creating effects:
  - **Buttons**
  - **Tweening**
  - **Looping**

- Converting bitmaps to **vector** images

- **Editing images** using the Break Apart function,
  the Lasso tool, and the Transform Fill tool

Bitmap basics

Let's take a moment to recap what exactly a bitmap image is. As we mentioned in Chapter 1, bitmap images are made up of a grid with units called pixels. These pixels store color information and, when they're arranged on a grid, these make up the complete image that we see. Because they're made up of pixels, bitmaps are *resolution-dependent* – you can see this by looking at the inset of the photo below where we've zoomed in:

At normal magnification, this bitmap image looks fine. However, when you zoom in you see the grainy limitations of its pixel-based nature.

Vector graphics, on the other hand, are composed of points and color information that precisely describe lines and fills. They are therefore *resolution-independent* because they will be rendered with the same clarity at any size through some pretty clever math:

So, if vector graphics are resolution-independent, why would you want to use bitmap images at all? Well, for one thing, bitmaps are better for displaying photographic images. They can contain millions of details and represent photo realistic material much better than vector graphics. Vectors are better for icons, diagrams and stylized visuals. This is not to say that vectors can't be used to draw realistic looking images, but that bitmaps are the standard for complex color variations and photos.

Bitmaps have other advantages within Flash. While vector graphics are better for displaying content that needs to be resolution-independent, the belief that vector images are *always* smaller than bitmap images is not always true. Take the previous two images, for example. The first (JPEG) image, when exported from Flash at 50% quality, is 16KB, while the vector rendering of it weighs in at 36KB. This is because the compression technique used on the bitmap involves losing some of the finer details of the image for the sake of its file size (this is known as 'lossy' compression), whereas the vector version retains all of its complex math.

Another case where bitmaps may be preferable to vectors is when performance and detail are a top priority. When you read about publishing your Flash movies later in this book (**Chapter 13**) you'll learn about the Quality option of the HTML Publish Settings. With this option you can set your movie to play with a lower quality setting, meaning that speed takes priority over rendering, resulting in pixilated lines and fills. When bitmaps are used in the low quality setting their quality remains and only Flash's smoothing technique is dropped. This results in clean, crisp, and detailed images. Try it out for yourself:

- Open the `vector_vs_bitmap.fla` file from this chapter's source code files (all of which you can download from `www.friendsofed.com`).

- Test the movie by choosing **Control > Test Movie** (Ctrl+Enter/⌘+Enter)

- In the Preview Window, choose **View > Quality > Low**.

- Observe the subtle, yet potentially important, change in the two renderings:

Let's now list a few examples of when you'd use each type of image.

When to use bitmap images

- When photo realistic renderings are a must, such as product photos or pictures of people

- When file size is crucial – compression techniques can reduce the file size of a bitmap dramatically in comparison with a vector rendering

- When your movie will not be scaled at runtime and you need to include photos

- When crisp, non-scaling renderings are needed at low quality

When to use vector graphics

- When simple icons or illustrations are required

- When simple graphics are needed for small file sizes

- When movies will be set to allow scaling

- When lightweight graphics are needed for optimal speed in a low quality setting and rendering crisp images is not a priority

- For motion graphics

Types of bitmap file formats compatible with Flash

Flash supports a wide variety of bitmap image formats, but these types can vary depending on whether or not you have QuickTime 4 (or higher) installed on your system. Having QuickTime installed adds support for additional file formats to both Macintosh and Windows platforms – go to www.apple.com/quicktime/download/ to download the latest version.

The following lists show the possible bitmap file types Flash supports on its own, and the additional formats that you have access to via QuickTime.

Without QuickTime installed

- Bitmap
- GIF
- JPEG
- PICT (Mac only)
- PNG

With QuickTime installed

- MacPaint
- Photoshop
- PICT
- QuickTime Image
- Silicon Graphics Image
- TGA
- TIFF

Importing bitmap images

Importing bitmap images is very simple and for the most part is the same as importing sound files and other vector artwork. Let's import an image right now.

First, open up a new document in Flash MX by choosing **File > New** (or just hit CTRL+N/⌘+N), and then open the import dialog by **Choosing File > Import to Library**.... Once you're in the Import to Library window, locate the image file empire_top.jpg within your downloaded code directory, and click on Open:

If your FLA's Library isn't already open, select **Windows > Library** (F11), and check that your image has indeed been imported:

So, using Import to Library adds the image directly to the movie's Library without placing it on the stage. On the other hand, choosing **File > Import**... (CTRL+R/⌘+R) will add the bitmap to the Library *and* to the currently selected keyframe. Either method will achieve the actual importing of the file into your movie.

It's worth noting that you can even import more than one file at a time from the Import window. On a Macintosh you can click on Add, which will allow you to include a number of files for import. On a Windows-based system, just hold down the CTRL key to select multiple files.

Importing bitmap sequences

In addition to importing multiple images by selecting them all individually, you can import bitmap *sequences*. A bitmap sequence is a number of files named in a sequential order. For example, it's possible to export video as a sequence of still images, and most video editing programs that allow this will export the images with a distinctive naming convention such as fileName001, fileName002, fileName003, and so on. If you have a large number of images to import, selecting each file individually can take an excessive amount of time. Fortunately, Flash will recognize the sequence for you. Let's try importing a sequence of images. In this example you should use Import

(CTRL+R/⌘+R) rather than Import to Library to show how Flash can speed up your production time.

 Press CTRL+N/⌘+N to open a new file in Flash, and make sure that the first keyframe of this FLA is selected. Open the Import window using CTRL+R/⌘+R, locate the folder Intersection within the downloaded source code files of this chapter and then select the file intersection01.jpg:

After hitting Open, you'll see the following prompt:

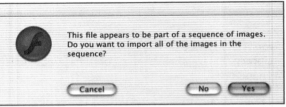

Click Yes, and Flash will import all 20 of the bitmaps and place them individually on their own keyframes in the correct order (we've saved this file as intersection_seq.fla):

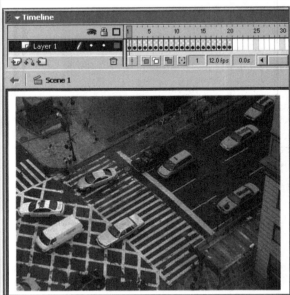

Once all the images have been imported you'll see that that each bitmap has been placed on the main timeline on its own frame, and in sequential order. You can see the sequence without exporting the whole movie by simply hitting ENTER. Note that Flash will only import the files that are after (and including) the file that you select in the sequence. For example, if you had selected intersection17.jpg in the previous Import window, Flash would only import the four subsequent images in the sequence, resulting in only four keyframes in your FLA file.

Importing sequences of images can give the illusion of video within Flash, or save time when importing a large number of bitmaps into a movie. One of the topics we'll turn to in **Chapter 13** is essentially the opposite of this – *exporting* our Flash movies as a sequence of bitmap images.

Bitmap properties

Once a bitmap has been imported you can view its properties at any time in the Library – so we'll now study these properties and the associated compression options that are available to us before publishing our movies. As we've learned so far, although Flash is mainly a vector-based graphical design package, it also includes robust support for bitmapped images.

Open up `bitmap_properties.fla` – this is a very simple movie with a bitmap on the stage. However, as we'll soon see, we have more options to select with this bitmap than initially meet the eye:

Press F11/⌘+F11 to open up the Library, and then choose the bitmap image `gameshot.jpg`:

Next, click on the Properties icon at the bottom of the Library window:

The Bitmap Properties dialog box will appear:

The first thing we see is some information about the imported image: its current name (this is automatically named at the time of import, but can be renamed at any time), the location of the directory from which it was imported, the date and time of import, and the dimensions and bit depth of the image. Additionally, notice the Test button on the right-hand side of this window – we'll be using this button shortly.

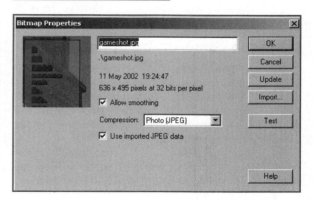

As ever, there are also a few options that control how the image is handled:

- **Allow Smoothing** – This option determines whether or not Flash will apply anti-aliasing around the edges of the bitmap so that its pixels blend in with the rest of the SWF.

- **Compression** – Here, there are two types of compression to choose from:

  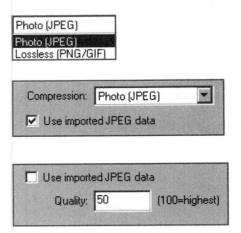

  - **Photo (JPEG)** – This is a 'lossy' compression, meaning that in our final SWF file, some image data is discarded in favor of file size. If we have Photo (JPEG) compression selected, then we see another option:

    With this selected the image will be exported at the same quality as the original JPEG image itself. If we de-select this option, we get this display:

    Here, you can enter a desired compression quality, where 100 is the best and 0 is the worst. As you'd expect, higher quality yields a larger file size, while lower quality makes the file size smaller.

  - **Lossless (PNG/GIF)** – When we choose this option, we're telling Flash to include the image in the SWF using lossless compression (that is, the GIF and PNG file formats specifically). This method preserves each individual pixel of an image, and doesn't lose *any* of the image in favor of file size.

 For images that have a great number of colors, like photographs, JPEG compression is recommended. On the other hand, files that have simple shapes and large areas of solid color are ideal for lossless compression.

Using the compression options

When setting the compression quality of JPEG images, it's recommended that we use the Test button to determine how the final image will look, and how large the file will be. Let's play around with the options using the file `bitmap_properties.fla`:

Try a JPEG quality of 5, then hit Test to preview the image:

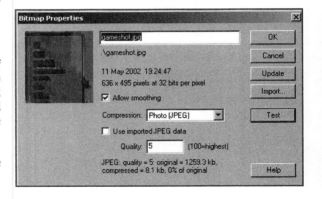

As you can see in the little preview box at top left, the image looks terrible, but it will be exported at a mere 8.1 KB in size. Considering that the original, uncompressed file at '636x495 pixels, 32 bit color' was about 1.2 MB, that's a substantial compression! Unfortunately, it results in an unacceptable image quality in this case. Note that you can zoom in and out of the preview pane by right-clicking (or CTRL+click on a Mac) on the preview image:

```
Zoom In
Zoom Out
100%
Show All

Quality      ►

Settings...

Print...

Debugger
```

Here, we've used a quality setting of 30:

The image looks nicer, although there is still some artifacting (the ring shapes around the blue pieces), which can look ugly. The exported file size has increased to 16KB for this image. That's quite small, but the image quality is still unacceptable to us perfectionists!

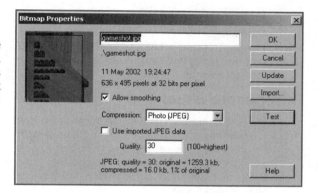

In this image, we've used a quality of 80, and the results are clearly much nicer:

The image is smooth and clear, and the file size is still only going to export at 32.5 KB. This is probably a good setting to use. For completeness, let's try one more...

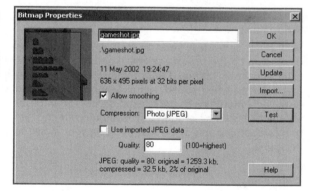

This image is, for all intents and purposes, perfect:

But we pay a price for 100% quality: the file size has climbed to 105.2 KB. It's still only 8% of the original uncompressed file, but may well be too large depending on the task at hand.

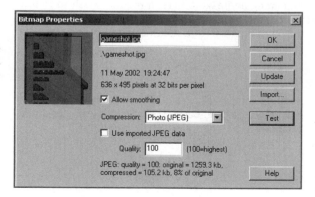

One last feature of the Bitmap Properties window that you might want to take notice of is the Update button. You can use this feature at any time in your development process – if your bitmap needs to be changed outside of Flash for any reason, you can make your changes and save it again. Then use Update to automatically locate and re-import that bitmap while retaining the current settings that you've applied to that image in Flash.

When it comes time finally to test, export, or publish the final movie, you'll be glad that you went through and took the time to manage the compression settings of your bitmap images. This simple task can save us hundreds of kilobytes of disk space and can, in turn, greatly enhance the performance of our Flash design.

Performance issues

Earlier in this chapter, we mentioned that bitmaps can render faster than vector graphics if we set the quality output to Low – let's now take a moment to consider some of the things that can affect our playback performance when using bitmap images.

Smoothing

Smoothing can affect your performance dramatically, depending on the size of the image and the amount of color variation. Flash uses smoothing to blend pixels so that bitmaps, when scaled, will appear less jagged and distorted. Smoothing requires extra processing in order for the image to be rendered. You should refrain from using smoothing unless you'll be allowing your movie to be scaled.

Animating

Animating an image onscreen requires Flash to redraw the bitmap on every frame. This places extra strain on the Player and it thus takes longer to complete the animation.

Rotating

Rotating images also requires extra processing. Flash must render a pixel-based grid at multiple angles during rotations.

Quality

Selecting Low Quality will reduce the amount of effort Flash applies to rendering the bitmap. Flash will use the image's default pixel grid, and doesn't need to enhance it in any way.

Alphas and other graphics

When Alpha effects are applied to bitmap symbols (discussed later in this chapter), Flash must render both the bitmap and the content behind it. To do this, Flash has to calculate new colors for each pixel in the image by comparing a percentage of the pixel's color with the color of the content below it. This can become quite complex when fading one bitmap on top of another. It's best to limit the activity on the screen at times when Alphas are applied, and to do it in areas that don't have complex material behind them.

Although bitmaps may create headaches when it comes to performance, in many cases they can be made to perform better. You will need to experiment with your bitmap usage on a case-by-case scenario to find the best possible playback setting at that point in your movie.

Converting a bitmap into a symbol

Importing a bitmap into Flash will allow you to reuse that image throughout your movie. But although it appears in the Library after it's been imported, it's not yet a symbol you can use to tween or apply effects to within the movie. Making a bitmap into a symbol uses the same process as all the other symbols you've made so far:

● Make a new symbol by choosing **Insert > New Symbol** (CTRL+F8/⌘+F8)

● Enter a name for the symbol:

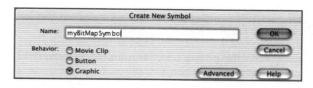

Select the Graphic behavior, and then click OK.

As usual, you'll be taken to the new symbol's stage. To complete the process, drag an instance of a bitmap that you've already imported into the Library onto the symbol's stage. This places the bitmap inside of that symbol and allows you to reuse it as an instance in your movie as much as you want, without increasing your file size dramatically.

Creating effects with bitmaps

Now that your bitmap's a symbol, you can apply effects to it and create motion tweens to each instance you create from it. An example of when you might apply effects to a bitmap could be when creating different Button states – you could use one bitmap symbol and apply numerous effects to it making it seem like a different image.

Buttons

Let's try making a button using a bitmap image and some the effects we've mentioned.

1. In a new FLA file, choose **Insert > New Symbol** (or press CTRL+F8/⌘+F8).

2. Enter a name (myBitmapButton) and select Button for the behavior:

3. Click OK – this will take you onto the new Button's stage.

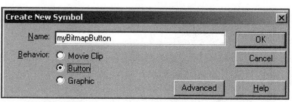

4. With the first frame (Up) selected, got to **File > Import...** (CTRL+R/⌘+R) and locate the file button_backdrop.jpg in the source code download for this chapter:

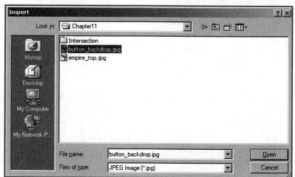

5. Hit Open, and this will import the bitmap directly onto the first frame of your FLA:

6. Select the bitmap and go to **Insert > Convert to Symbol** (F8). This is another way to create a symbol in Flash, as we saw in **Chapter 4**. It will allow you to convert the current selection into a symbol and leave it on the current timeline.

7. Enter a name for the bitmap symbol and select the Graphic behavior:

8. Click OK – this will leave you with the new symbol on the Button's first frame and it will also insert a copy of it into the Library.

9. Now highlight the Over frame and go to **Insert > Keyframe** (or hit F6). This will replicate the Up state in the Over frame:

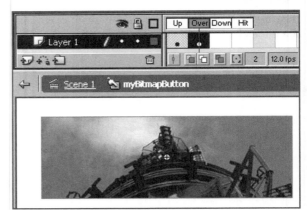

10. With the bitmap symbol still selected, take a look at your Property inspector. You will see a Color drop-down menu (we looked at this in **Chapter 4**) on the right-hand side:

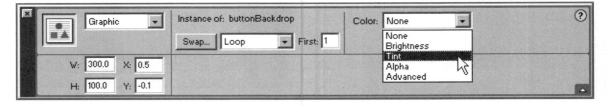

11. Choose the Tint option, select white in the swatch selector, and then enter a value of 50%:

12. You'll then see the bitmap change color to appear more faded on the stage:

13. Use the Back button on the navigation bar to get back to your root timeline, then open up the Library (F11) and drag an instance of myBitmapButton onto the main stage:

14. Finally, test the movie (CTRL+ENTER/⌘+ENTER) to preview your Button's rollover and see the effect you've created. Our version of this example can be found in your source code files as bitmap_button.fla:

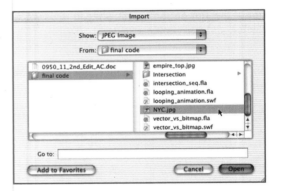

Tweening

Let's take a look at how we can apply some similar effects to a motion tween and make an image fade in.

1. In a new FLA, import a bitmap onto the stage by choosing **File > Import**... and locating the file NYC.jpg in your downloaded source code directory:

2. Click OK to place the image on the stage. Select the imported image and choose **Insert > Convert to Symbol**... (F8).

3. Name the symbol NYC and select the Graphic behavior. This will place the symbol in your Library and leave the converted bitmap on the stage in frame 1:

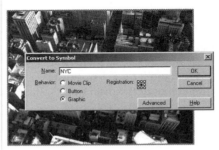

4. Highlight frame 20 further down the timeline and insert a keyframe (go to **Insert > Keyframe**, or just press F6). This will place a duplicate of frame 1 on the timeline at frame 20:

5. Now select frame 1 and create a motion tween using the Tween drop-down menu of the Property inspector (you could also go to **Insert > Create Motion Tween** instead):

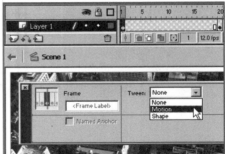

6. You'll now see a blue tint to the frames in between the two keyframes, and a solid arrow on the timeline linking these two keyframes:

7. Now for the effect – select the instance of the bitmap symbol in frame 1. In the Property inspector, choose the Color drop-down menu again, select Alpha this time, and enter 0%. You'll immediately notice that your bitmap graphic symbol seems to have become invisible:

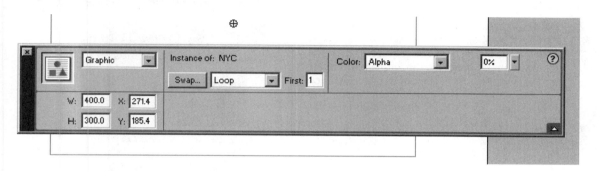

After you've done this you can play your movie by pressing ENTER to see the 'fading in' effect. The finished version of this example is available in your source code directory as `bitmap_fade_effect.fla`. Remember, you'll follow the same process with all of your motion tweens and instance effects – each one requires a start and end keyframe, a motion tween, and an applied effect.

If you choose to test your movie (CTRL+ENTER/⌘+ENTER) you may notice that your 'fade in' effect plays back rather slowly. This will vary depending on your processor speed and video card. In general, Alpha effects with bitmaps are very processor-intensive and may seem sluggish at times.

Looping

 Looping in almost any medium refers to the repetition of an element. In Flash we can create animation loops by beginning and ending our animation with similar images, resulting in a smooth transition from beginning to end. Let's take a look at how we can do this by crossfading two images. Before you begin you can take a look at file `looping_animation.fla` in the source code directory for an example of what we're going to create.

1. In a new FLA, import two images from the source code download: use the **File > Import to Library...** technique, and select `Cityscape1.jpg` and `CityScape2.jpg`. This will import both images into our Library:

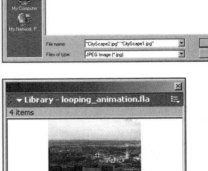

2. In order to create our crossfade tween you need to create a symbol for each image. So, use **Insert > New Symbol** (CTRL+F8/⌘+F8) to create the symbols without dragging the bitmaps onto the root stage; instead, drag copies of `CityScape1.jpg` and `CityScape2.jpg` onto their respective *symbol* stages. Your Library should then look like this:

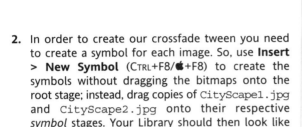

3. On the main timeline you should have a blank stage. Drag over an instance of your first symbol in frame 1 and resize it so that it fits on the stage. Now select frame 50 and insert a frame (F5). This will increase our timeline duration to 50 frames. Rename this layer so that it reflects the content:

4. Insert a new layer above this one by choosing **Insert > Layer**, or by clicking on the Insert Layer icon:

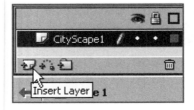

5. Highlight frame 20 on the new layer and go to **Insert > Blank Keyframe** (F7). This'll give you a keyframe to place your second image on and start the crossfade – so drag an instance of the second symbol you made for `CityScape2.jpg` onto frame 20 of the second layer:

6. Now highlight frame 30 of the CityScape2 layer and insert a keyframe (F6). This'll make a copy of frame 20 here.

7. Return to frame 20 of layer CityScape2 and select the `CityScape2` symbol. In the Property inspector, select the Alpha effect in the Color dropdown menu and set it to 0%. This will serve as a starting point to fade in the second image. Next, still using the Property inspector, create a motion tween that will cause a fade in from frame 20 to frame 30:

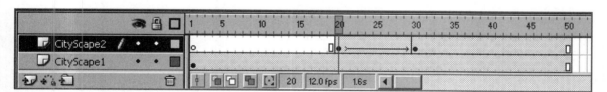

8. Insert two additional keyframes on frame 40 and 50 of the same layer. These will outline your second fade:

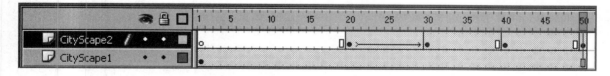

9. On frame 50, select the `CityScape2` instance and set the Alpha to zero here (in fact, Flash will probably remember the last time you used it and set it to zero automatically). Lastly, highlight frame 40 of the CityScape2 layer and create another motion tween using the Property inspector. This will create a fade out effect and return you to the image that you started with, producing a smooth animation loop.

Test your animation loop with CTRL+ENTER/⌘+ENTER. Remember that if the fading in and out is too slow for your needs, just change the frame rate by selecting the stage of your document and entering a higher value in the Property inspector:

Changing the frame rate

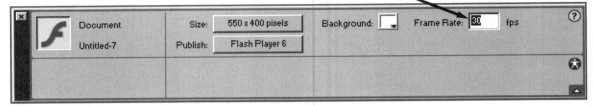

Converting bitmap images into vectors

 Bitmap images can be effectively traced in Flash – this process converts a bitmap image into a vector image by analyzing bitmapped areas of color and converting them to solid fills created with vector-defined points.

The results will vary, based on several settings in the Trace dialog box. Let's import an image and apply a trace to it.

 Open a new FLA (CTRL+N/⌘+N) and import (**File > Import**...) the bitmap empire_top.jpg (again!) from your source code files – this will place the bitmap on the root timeline of your new FLA.

With the bitmap selected, go to **Modify > Trace Bitmap**.... This will open a Trace Bitmap dialog box with several settings.

Let's take a look at how these settings will affect our final result.

Color Threshold

 Color Threshold represents the difference between two pixels that are next to each other in a grid. When the two pixels are compared, if the difference in the RGB color values is *less* than the color threshold setting, then the two pixels are considered to be the same color. If the difference in the two values is *greater* than the threshold then they are considered different. As you increase the threshold value, you decrease the number of colors in the finished trace.

Bitmap

Traced bitmap

The difference is best seen by comparing a low Color Threshold value, for example 30:

With a higher value – 200 for instance:

Minimum Area

This field indicates the number of pixels that Flash will compare when considering the Color Threshold.

Curve Fit

The Curve Fit setting influences how smooth your trace will be. You have a number of options, like tracing units as small as every pixel, or very smooth tracing:

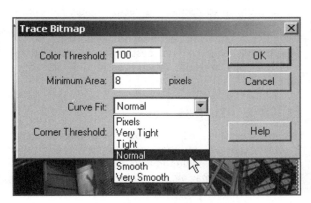

The differences are subtle, but can be important. For example, a Curve Fit set to Pixels would yield this result:

Whereas when set to Very Smooth, we'd get the following:

Corner Threshold

 This setting determines the amount of points in your trace. Choosing Many Corners will produce more points and a more ridged look, while choosing Few Corners will have less points and appear more curved:

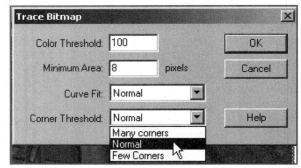

Take a moment to play with all of these settings – you'll see that a variety of results can be produced. In addition, you'll soon notice that lower thresholds, more corners, and so on, will take longer to render out. This is a direct result of the increased number of calculations that Flash has to perform to render the vector image. Note also that with the same settings your vectors are larger in SWF file size when you test them out. Depending on the desired style and the final destination you'll need to find a happy medium when considering size and appearance.

Editing images

Like many graphic editing programs available today, Flash includes a number of features specifically designed to make editing images as simple as possible. For instance, you may already be familiar with the Lasso tool and its associated options; they're useful for selecting different areas of both vector and bitmap images. Let's take a look at the different selection types each tool can perform and what they can do for you in the bitmap editing context specifically. Then we'll use an example to study another useful function for editing images – Break Apart.

Lasso tool

The Lasso tool, by default, allows you to draw freeform areas for selection:

This is good for quick selections or for making selections that aren't based on color or shape in existing artwork.

Magic Wand option

The Magic Wand option of the Lasso tool allows you to select areas in bitmaps that have been 'broken apart' – we'll describe what that means in just a moment.

With the Magic Wand you can select irregularly shaped colored regions in your bitmap and adjust several settings to vary the amount of the image that's selected. To the right of the Magic Wand tool you will see a properties button. Pressing this will open an options box and allow you to adjust some settings:

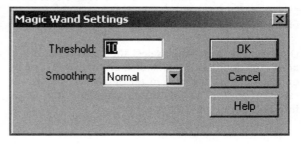

The first setting, Threshold, determines the difference in pixel color value that Flash uses to distinguish colors when making a selection. The other setting is Smoothing, with which you can choose a number of settings ranging from Pixels to Smooth, allowing you to decide how tight your selection will be in comparison to the bitmap's grid.

Polygon mode

Additionally, once the Lasso tool has been selected, you have the option of using Polygon mode:

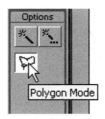

This allows you to draw straight lines with the Lasso tool in a point-to-point method until you come back to the starting point. This is useful for making straight-edged selections in your artwork that aren't based on color or shape.

The Break Apart function

Flash MX has a unique feature that allows you to break an image apart, but what exactly does it break images up *into*? Well, breaking apart a bitmap separates each pixel in the image into discrete areas that can be selected and modified separately from one another. This allows you to modify the bitmap with the Flash drawing and painting tools, such as the Paint Bucket and Fill Transform tools. As you have just seen, the Lasso tool, combined with the Magic Wand option, let you select areas of a bitmap that has been broken apart. Let's try and break an image apart and select a region with the Lasso tool.

Open up a new FLA file and import the `empire_top.jpg` bitmap into it, as we've been doing throughout the examples in this chapter. Once your image is on the stage, try this:

Select the bitmap on the stage with the familiar Arrow tool. Then go to **Modify > Break Apart** (or press CTRL+B/⌘+B). This will produce a pixelated dot pattern on the selected image:

On the main Tools panel, select the Lasso tool (or just press L on your keyboard) and choose the Magic Wand option. Click on the broken up bitmap area. This will select a portion of the image based on the color threshold settings for the tool:

Clicking in additional areas will select more of the image. While the areas you've chosen are still selected, hit the DELETE key on your keyboard. As you might expect, this will remove the selected areas from the bitmap:

Now that we've learned how to break apart a bitmap image and deleted specific regions of it, we should look at filling areas back in...

Bitmap fills

Bitmap fills are a good way to produce patterns in your artwork. They are simple to create, but should be used sparingly as they can reduce playback performance. Let's try making a bitmap fill.

1. Open a new FLA file (CTRL+N/⌘+N). We're actually going to import a pattern to use as our fill, so go to **File > Import**... (CTRL+R/⌘+R).

2. Locate the file canvas.jpg in the source code directory and click Open. This will place the bitmap on the stage for you.

3. With the bitmap seleted, choose **Modify > Break Apart** (CTRL+B/⌘+B) to break the image up into separate color areas and allow us to select it as a fill.

4. Select the Eyedropper tool on the Toolbar:

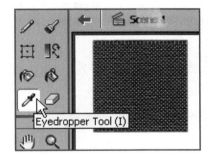

5. Hit the bitmap's pattern with the Eyedropper:

6. You'll now see the bitmap pattern in the Fill Color setting of the Color Mixer panel. If this panel isn't currently open, choose **Window > Color Mixer** (CTRL+F9/⌘+F9):

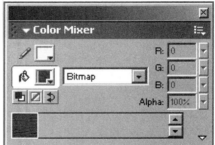

7. You now have this bitmap fill pattern selected and can use it to fill other shapes. Try it out – select the Oval tool on the main Toolbar (or just hit O on your keyboard), and draw a circle on the stage – it'll then be filled with your recently selected bitmap:

8. You can then select the Fill Transform tool (press F) to resize or rotate the 'tile' of the bitmap as well – you can use the frame that appears to adjust the scale of your fill pattern and the angle it is within the object. Try it out for yourself:

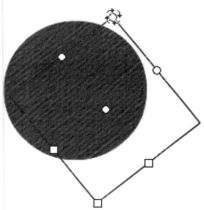

Summary

In this chapter we've covered all the major issues associated with using bitmap images in our Flash designs. To recap:

- Bitmap images differ from vector graphics because they're based on a pixel unit grid system and not a math-based point system.

- Bitmaps are good for creating movies with photographs or any other 'realistic' style; they work best in movies that are not set up to be scaled. However, with Flash MX you can actually choose to smooth the pixels in each bitmap's properties box if need be.

The major topics that we've covered include the following:

- Importing bitmaps

- Bitmap properties and compression options

- Performance issues

- Creating effects with bitmaps through buttons, tweening, and looping

- Tracing and editing bitmap images

Take a look back over the usage breakdown covered early in this chapter, and keep in mind the performance considerations when you start your next project using bitmaps. You can then compare how you intend to use them and what settings will work best for your movie. Remember, however, to use bitmaps strategically and sparingly, as they can slow down your animation and increase file size significantly.

Next

Adding another dimension to your designs – using sound with Macromedia Flash MX.

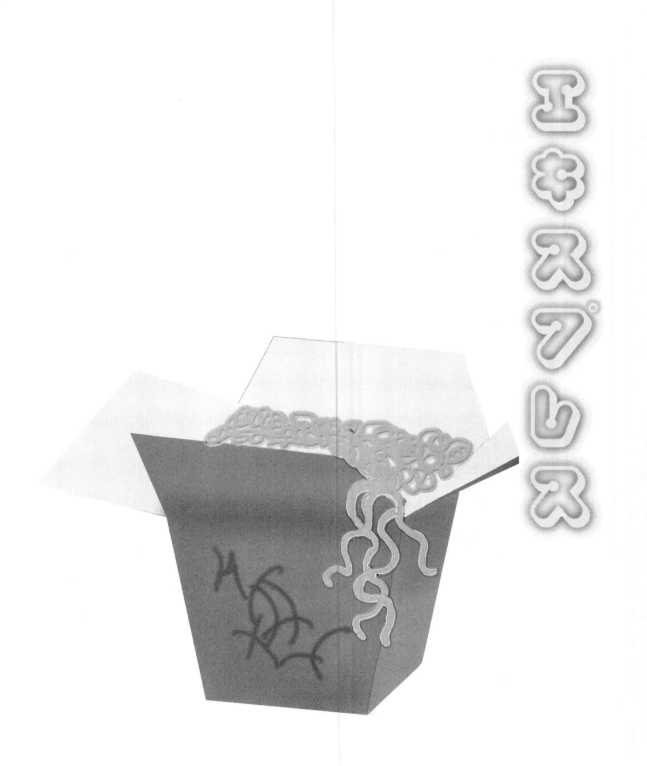

エキスプレス

Chapter 12
Using Sound in Flash

What's in this chapter:

- **Streamed** sound vs. **event-based** sound

- **Importing** sounds, and the sound formats that are available

- **Sound properties** – export, compression, and publishing settings

- **Editing** sound

- Using streamed and event-based sound in movies and buttons

Types of sound

Sound is one of the most critical aspects of modern multimedia presentations. Sound adds that secondary level of interactivity that people have come to expect when exploring content on the web, especially on Macromedia Flash sites.

So let's assume we've decided that we want to put some sound into our Flash MX movie. Where do we begin? What do we do? What factors do we have to consider? Well, in this chapter we'll answer all of these questions, and more. First, it's important to know that in Flash, sound can be delivered in one of two ways: **streamed** or **event-based**. The differences between these two methods are subtle, but important.

Streamed

Streamed sound can be played as soon as it starts to download – as soon as the first batch of sound data is received, it essentially downloads and plays *simultaneously*.

Consider a scenario in which we have a 5-minute song in a SWF – that SWF movie could be in the neighborhood of 1 or 2 megabytes in size! On a typical connection, this can take a few minutes to download. Would we want to make users wait before they heard a note of music? No, of course not! Clearly, any long pauses while the user is waiting for sound to match the graphics would kill the experience.

To combat this problem, Flash starts to play streamed sounds as soon as it has downloaded enough information to begin reproducing the opening bars of the song. As the song continues to download, Flash will play it back at a steady rate in parallel, with the rest of the song *streaming* into place.

In order to make sure that the movie doesn't race ahead, Flash ties the timeline, which contains the streamed sound, to the streamed sound itself. In simple terms, this means that a cymbal hit which falls on frame 115 in a movie will *always* fall on frame 115. Flash will skip frames of animation if it has to, in order to keep the sound synchronized with the timeline animation.

The nice thing about this is that if we move the playhead along the timeline with the mouse, we'll hear the song being 'scrubbed' – played back wherever the cursor is. This is somewhat analogous to fast forwarding and rewinding a VCR which plays the audio as you search. With streamed sound, we can safely line up animated events with specific areas on the streamed sound, and Flash will ensure that these always remain lined up.

Indeed, with streamed sound you can visualize your main timeline as a videotape, and the sound as an actual soundtrack on that tape. If you tell the timeline to stop anywhere, then the sound will halt, too.

Streamed sounds require some overhead because of the real-time dedication they require from the processor, and the on-the-fly decoding – they're usually compressed, streamed MP3 files. Accordingly, the main application of streamed sounds is to create a soundtrack or voiceover – we'll look at some specific examples of streaming sound in the latter half of this chapter, after we've covered all of the basics.

Event-based

Event-based sounds are triggered on a 'need-to-play' basis, and the sound must be fully downloaded before it will play.

Event-based sounds are not tied to the timeline, so once you tell an event sound to play (assuming it has completed downloading), Flash will send it off to the computer's sound system, and basically forget about it. Even if the main timeline were to stop playing, the sound would continue to play. In this way, event-based sounds are not tied to the timeline like streamed sounds are.

The nice thing about event sounds is that they can be used and reused without any more downloading or streaming being required. For instance, if we have two sound events on a timeline that trigger the same sound – perhaps a response to a particular on-screen action, like a balloon popping or a car driving by – Flash will just reuse the same single sound.

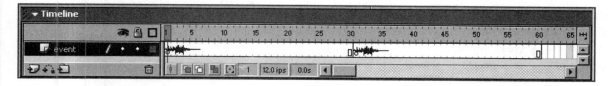

The advantage of this is, of course, in saving file size. The sound must be downloaded only *once*, and then it can be used and reused as many times as we want. If we download several event sounds, ready and waiting to be called upon, we can create an entire lively atmosphere with hundreds of non-timeline dependent sounds. This cookie-cutter approach to sound allows us great variation in our soundtrack, with minimal overhead.

 An event sound must be fully loaded before it will play, therefore it is not recommended that long sounds like songs and voiceovers be used as event sounds. Remember, the user will have to sit and wait while the entire sound is loaded before it will play, and by then the event may have long passed! So it's best to keep these elements as short, discrete sounds which respond to events. Event sounds are ideal for small, quick sounds like button clicks and rollovers – we'll take a detailed look at how we use event-based sounds towards the end of this chapter.

Format issues

Flash allows us to create our sounds – and import them into Flash – in one of four different formats. In a new FLA file, go to **File > Import**...

This will bring up the Import dialog box – use the dropdown menu to see the different sound formats that are available:

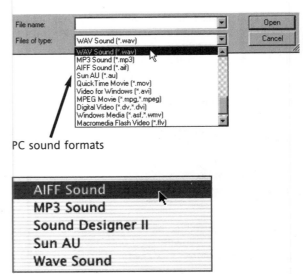

PC sound formats

- **WAV** – The most common event-based sound for small sounds on a Windows-based development system. WAV files are often uncompressed and can therefore lead to very bulky files. For this reason, WAV are best used as small event sounds.

- **MP3** – The most popular format for music and streamed sounds. MP3 has been made popular by the upsurge in online music sharing and trading on the Internet. It's also a very efficiently compressed file format, making sound files up to a hundred times smaller than their original size, usually with no noticeable difference in the sound quality.

Mac sound formats

- **AIFF** – Similar to WAV files, but used on a Mac-based development system.

- **Sun AU** – File format used by Sun systems (like Java).

- **Wave Sound** (Mac) – Mac options counterpart of WAV files.

- **Sound Designer II** (Mac) – A proprietary sound package.

Keep in mind that Flash is not an audio creation program. All sounds and music will have to be created in another program, like Acid, Cubase, Pro-tools, Sound Forge, or any other audio production system that fits your requirements. You can, of course, just use the sound recording application that comes with your operating system!

Importing sound files

Assuming that you've already created your award-winning sounds, you now want to import them into Flash. How do you set about doing this?

Open up the Import dialog box again (Ctrl+R/⌘+R) and, at the bottom of the window, choose All Sound Formats from the dropdown:

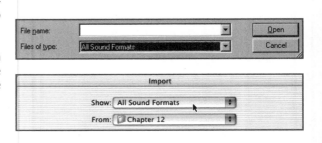

Next, using the folder navigation box, navigate to the directory where your sound is located:

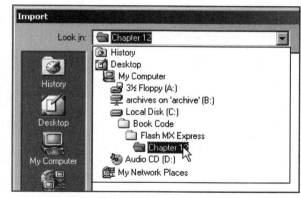

From the list of audio files in your folder, choose the one you wish to import, then click on the Open button:

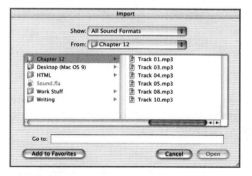

That's it! The audio file is now imported, and can be used in our movie. To check this, take a quick look in your Library (F11) and note that your sound has indeed been imported directly into the Library.

Sound properties

 Once you have your sound files imported, there are several things you can do with them. For instance, you can: change their compression settings and listen to the result; update the sounds if the source sound files have been changed; or choose a completely new source file for a sound.

For starters, open up the `sound_properties1.fla` from this book's source code download files and have a look at the sound in the Library:

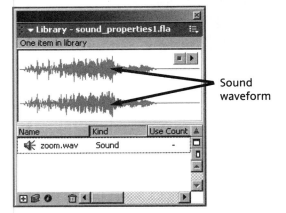

Click on `zoom.wav` to reveal the graphical representation of the **waveform** of this sound file:

Sound waveform

Now click on the Properties button in the library window – this is the little 'Information' icon on the bottom-left of the window:

Properties...

The Sound Properties window will appear. This window is divided into two sections. The top half is the 'sound information' section, which gives the filename and image of the waveform. We can also see the date and time that the file was created, the sound format of the original file (in this case, 44kHz, stereo, and 16 bit), the length of the sound (0.5 seconds), and the size of the original WAV file (82.7 kB).

The bottom half is where we configure the compression settings for exporting to the final SWF file – these settings are worthy of some discussion in their own right.

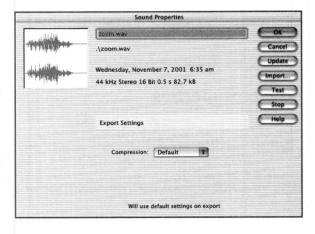

Compression settings

Decisions on compression depend largely on how the sounds will be used, the desired sound quality, and the characteristics of the original sound. When we pull down the Compression drop-down menu in the Sound Properties window, we see the following options in the screenshot:

Default will use the sound compression settings that are specified in the Publish Settings dialog from the file menu – more on this shortly. For now, let's look at the other four options.

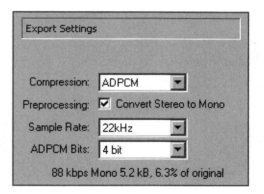

ADPCM

ADPCM stands for Adaptive Pulse Code Modulation. This format is best suited for event sounds as it is less compressed in the SWF than MP3 is, but it has a higher quality.

There are three settings with the ADPCM export format:

- **Preprocessing** – This is simply a check box which tells Flash whether to convert the sound from 2-channel stereo to 1-channel mono before exporting. The main advantage of this is that mono sounds are 50% the file size of stereo sounds. However, sometimes stereo is a very important part of a sound in conveying spatial perception. We must use our judgment and decide what is most important – stereo quality sound, or small file size.

- **Sample Rate** – Depending on the sound itself, sounds that are lower in pitch (a boom, a bassline) can be accurately represented with a lower sample rate. The lower the sample rate, the smaller the file size. However, sounds that have higher frequencies in them, like glass breaking, will require a higher sample rate to preserve the higher frequencies.

  It's worth noting that each option uses approximately twice as much file size as the next lowest option. So 22kHz produces a file twice as large as 11kHz, and so on. Note that 44kHz is the best sounding quality as it includes the largest range of frequencies.

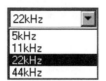

Sample rate options

● **ADPCM Bits** – The effect that this has on sound is not as easy to conceptualize – it doesn't so much affect the range of the sound, but the 'quality'. We can choose from 2 bits to 5 bits. In general, the lower the bits setting, the more 'static' we will hear in the sound.

Depending on how much is 'going on' in the sound, the static may not be heard, so it may be OK to use a lower bit count. However, a smooth sound, like a plucked guitar string, is very pure and uniform, so a lower bit count would be heard as a crackling static. It's best to experiment with this setting until it sounds just right.

MP3

To study this option, open up `sound_properties2.fla`, where you'll see that we've already imported an MP3 file into the library:

Open up the Sound Properties window again and, in order to see the full compression export options, unselect the Use imported MP3 quality check box:

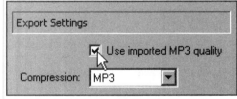

You'll then see all of the export settings:

The MP3 format is much better suited for longer, streamed sounds because its compression is more efficient over a longer period of time. In fact, it's not suited to short sounds because the overhead required to play an MP3 sound outweighs the advantage gained from the mere 1 or 2kB in file size saved.

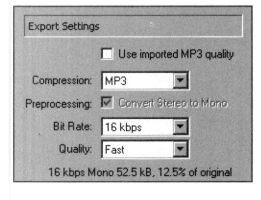

There are also three settings with the MP3 format:

- **Preprocessing** – This is essentially the same as with ADPCM compression. It allows you to determine whether or not stereo information will be preserved. The difference in this case is that this setting won't actually change the export size. Rather, it will simply decrease the quality of each channel (left and right). Notice also that if you choose a bit rate (see below) of 16kbps or less, stereo is not even an option.

- **Bit Rate** – This is the amount of data that is flying by in a fixed period of time. Measured in kilobits per second (kbps), it indicates the 'detail quality' in the sound. The higher the bit rate, the more 'information' Flash can convey about the sound in a fixed period of time, and therefore the better the sound quality.

  A simple analogy would be to compare the bit rate to the speed at which a person speaks – an auctioneer, for example, has a lot of information to get across to a crowd of eager buyers in as quick a time as possible. You might say that an auctioneer's 'bit rate' is a lot higher than someone in a checkout line making small talk about the weather.

  However, there is always a compromise – the higher the bit rate (and therefore quality), the larger the file size.

  Notice that the range is quite large. Again, it's best to experiment with different settings to judge the right balance of file size economy and sound quality.

- **Quality** – This is more of a convenience choice than anything; it uses a more or less efficient algorithm to export the sound based on your choice.

  For the most part, while you are developing your Flash movie, you should select the Fast option – this will build your SWF as quickly as possible. When it comes time to export the final SWF file, change this option to Best. Depending upon the length of your sound, this setting can make a substantial difference.

> **Tip**
> *Make sure you never choose an export bit rate that is higher than an import bit rate – that would clearly be meaningless.*

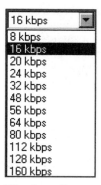

Bit rate options

Quality settings

Raw

Raw export format uses *no* compression on the sound file and is therefore the best quality export possible. But, obviously, it also creates the largest sized files. Raw export simply conveys all the sound information in its most detailed, uncompressed quality. The advantage of the raw format is that it requires virtually no overhead to play because it is not decompressing the sound file. However, the file size can be huge.

In this example, the export file size is 4.6 MB – over 10 times the size of the source sound file! This is the price we pay for zero playback overhead.

This format has only two options:

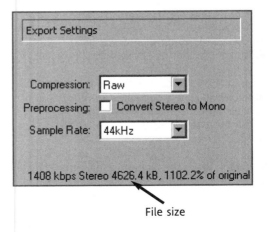

File size

- **Preprocessing** – As we've seen already, this is where we cut the file size in half, by converting 2-channel stereo sounds into mono, 1-channel sounds. The obvious disadvantage here is the loss of stereo effects, and the clear benefit is a 50% decrease in file size from stereo to mono.

- **Sample Rate** – Much like ADPCM, sample rate determines the dynamic range of the sound pitch. So lower sample rates will lose a lot of higher frequency sounds, but will be smaller in file size. Although high frequency sample rates will conserve higher frequency sounds, they will be much larger.

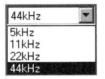

Sample rates

Speech

Speech is a special format, which uses optimized compression that preserves the information in the range of human speech.

The preprocessing automatically converts the speech sound into mono, as speech is technically a mono sound source, so the only real option available to us is the **Sample Rate**. In fact, it's very much like the ADPCM and Raw formats. In speech, the sample rate determines how much quality will be preserved in the speech sounds. For example, higher pitched sounds like 's' and 't' will be best preserved with a higher sample rate. As usual, the sample rates are 5kHz, 11kHz, 22kHz, and 44kHz.

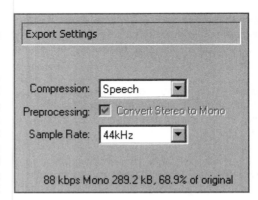

Publishing settings

One more thing must be pointed out. There are global sound compression settings contained within Flash MX. Go to **File > Publish Settings...** (or press CTRL+SHIFT+F12/OPTION+SHIFT+F12) and click on the Flash tab of the Publish Settings dialog box:

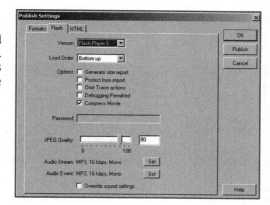

Notice the Audio Stream and Audio Event export settings at the bottom of the window. The main thing to pay attention to here is the Override sound settings button – this will allow you to *override* the quality of all exported sounds, regardless of their settings in the Sound Properties window. Clicking on the Set button next to each type will open up Sound Settings windows, very much like the ones we have discussed above, from which you can alter the sound properties and compression type.

Clearly, there are numerous options for sound compression and export settings. Choosing correctly is something of an art form at first, but it becomes easier and clearer with each new project.

Editing sounds

Let's take a look at how to edit our sounds using the Property inspector and the sound edit mode of Flash MX. Open up sound_edit.fla. This FLA has two sounds in its Library:

Note also that frame 1 of the main timeline displays what appears to be a sound waveform – this shows that an instance of zoom.wav has been dragged from the Library and dropped onto the stage:

Click on Frame 1, and make sure the Property inspector is open (CTRL+F3/⌘+F3). Take a look at the frame properties here:

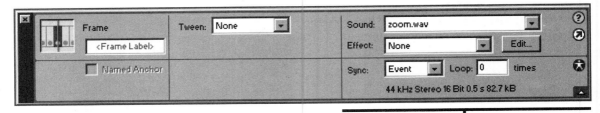

Sound properties

The sound panel is at the right hand side of the Property inspector – it's used to determine the sound information for that particular frame. The main things we're concerned with here are the **Sound**, **Sync**, and **Effect** drop-down menus, so let's look at these options individually.

Sound

Click on zoom.wav in the drop-down menu – you'll see this list:

This is a list of all the sounds that have been imported into this FLA, namely jazz.mp3 and zoom.wav. You can also choose to have no sound in this frame by selecting None. You can use this menu to specify which sound will be played as this frame's **sound event**.

Sync

Notice that Sync is set to Event. Click on the drop-down menu to see the other options:

Sync options

As we mentioned early on in this chapter, the two most important sound types in Flash MX are Event and Stream – we'll look at these options in detail shortly.

Effect

Finally, we have the Effect drop-down. You can use these options to make the sounds a little more dynamic and interesting. You can:

Effect options

● Play the entire sound in the left or right speaker only.

● Fade left to right or right to left – throughout the entire length of the sound, Flash will pan the sound from the extreme left or right, to the extreme opposite side.

- Fade in and fade out – the sound will rise from dead silence to 100% volume, or vice versa. Fade out will begin near the end of the sound file, while fade in will reach 100% volume shortly after the beginning of the sound.

- Customize the exact details of our volume settings. With the Custom option we use the Edit Envelope to set the characteristics of our sounds – we'll cover this in the next section.

Try playing around with these options using the sound files within `sound_edit.fla` – you'll soon learn which options are best suited for different situations.

Edit mode

Click on the Edit... button of the Property inspector:

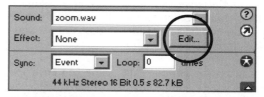

The Edit Envelope window will appear. The Edit Envelope window presents two waveforms – the top waveform represents the left channel, and the bottom waveform the right. Notice the small white square in the top left corner – as we shall soon see, this is rather important.

In this example, the effect is set to None; set it to Fade In and see what happens.

There's now a line with two square handles spanning both channels of the waveform. This is known as the **envelope**, and it represents the volume of the sound at a given moment in time. When the envelope is at the very bottom of the waveforms (as it is on the left edge), the volume is at 0%, and when the envelope is at the very top of the waveforms, then the volume is at 100%. As we can see, the envelope transitions evenly from 0% to 100%, on both the left and the right channels, representing the 'fade in'.

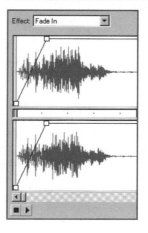

267

Now change the Effect in the drop-down menu to Fade Out and see how this contrasts to the previous image:

In this case, the waveform volume begins to fade out towards the end, and reaches 0% at the very end.

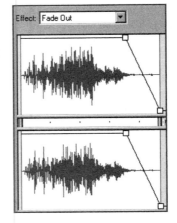

Let's see what else we can do in the edit envelope – return the menu selection to Fade In, and hit the play button in the bottom left of the window to hear your sound fade in:

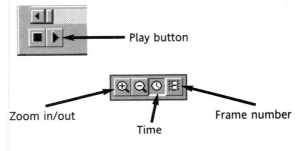

Play button

Additionally, on the bottom right of the Edit Envelope window, you'll see a row of four icons. With these icons you can (from left to right) zoom in/out, and change the x-axis displayed for the waveform to Time or Frame number:

Zoom in/out   Time   Frame number

If you click on the envelope at any point you can insert a new square control handle. Try it out – insert a new handle to the right of the second handle on the upper (left ear) waveform.

Notice that the option in the Effect menu automatically changes to Custom because we are effectively customizing our own envelope. Furthermore, even though we've only added a new handle in the upper waveform, Flash has automatically updated the lower one to reflect the changes, too.

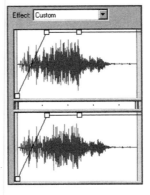

Drag the rightmost handle in the top waveform to the bottom of the box.

You've edited the left and the right channels independently – they will fade in together, but then the left channel will fade away to 0% volume while the right channel will continue to play at 100%. The effect is a fade in, and then the sound will appear to veer to the right. Click on the play button again to hear it in action (or check out sound_envelope.fla to hear the finished effect).

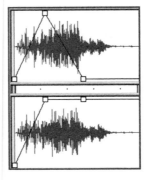

Try playing with different envelopes to create cool effects. An envelope can have up to eight handles on it:

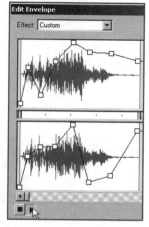

Max. control handles = 8

Cropping sound

 If you want to isolate a certain section of sound, you can use the cropping tool in the Edit Envelope window. There are two solid bars in between the two waveforms – these are actually handles that can be dragged left and right:

Draggable cropping bars

 If we drag the bars inwards, we crop the sound to a specific section (see also sound_crop.fla):

> **Tip**
> To change the height of any layer, simply right-click/CTRL-click on the layer name, select Properties, and increase the Layer Height option.

This is extremely useful if you want to isolate a particular word or a line of speech in a sound effect, but don't want to have to import an entirely new sound file just for that line. Now, when that sound is played in the movie, it will only play the section between the two cropping bars (the white section in the previous image). The waveform graphic in the timeline also appears shorter to reflect the cropping:

Note that in this view we've elongated the frame view by 200% – this gives us a much clearer view of frames with any sound clips attached.

Using sounds

Now that we've covered the basics of how to import, compress, and edit sounds, we'll round off this chapter by getting our hands dirty with some real-world examples using streamed and event-based sounds.

Streaming sound

Open up `stream1.fla`, and test the movie:

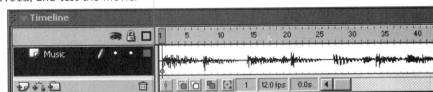

You'll hear some simple 16-bar jazz that has been imported from the file `jazz.mp3`. Click on frame 1 of the main timeline and look at the right-hand side of the Property inspector:

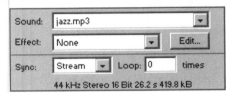

The Sync is set to Stream – so the movie, when loaded from a web site, will begin to play the sound as it streams. We won't have to wait for it to download completely first.

Drag the playhead horizontally across the timeline. Notice that you can hear the music playing as you do so. This is an advantage of streaming sound – we can hear it as we go, and use it to sync up the sound with the video.

Now open up `stream2.fla` – this is essentially the same as `stream1.fla`, except that we now have an animated bouncing ball, which is lined up with the streaming sound:

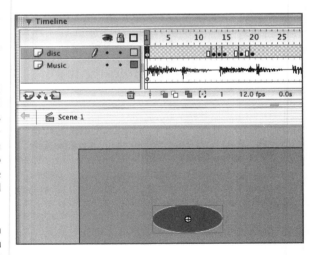

On the key hits in the jazz music (saxophone notes and trumpet blasts, for instance) the red ball jumps around the screen because of the strategically placed keyframes and tweens. When we test the movie (CTRL+ENTER/⌘+ ENTER) we see the effect in action – the ball bounces in time to the music. Remember, if the music cannot keep up with the animation, then Flash will force the animation to skip frames in order to keep the sound playback steady.

Another potential use is for a typographic presentation in which the words on the screen are synched with a narration of the same text, for users who don't have sound on their computers, and for the hearing- or sight-impaired.

Event sounds

The other side of the sound spectrum in Flash is using event-based sounds. The event sound is great for small sounds, triggered by *events*. Let's take a look at creating an event sound.

Load `event1.fla`, click on frame 1, and look at the Property inspector:

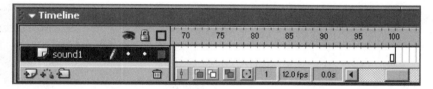

Here, the event sound is set to Sync as an Event. Try testing the movie – you'll hear the sound playing over and over again. Why is it looping? Well, because the movie is ten frames long, and when it reaches frame 10, it loops back to frame 1 again, where it re-encounters the event sound.

Event sound selection

Now insert some blank frames (F5) to make the movie 100 frames long (or just open up `event2.fla`):

Test the movie again – you can hear that the sound doesn't repeat as often – you'll hear the zoom sound every eight seconds or so because of all the blank 'filler' frames.

Again, click on frame 1 of the event sound, and look down at the frame properties panel. Note that the Loop entry box, next to the Sync box, is set to `0`:

Set this box to loop ten times, and press ENTER. Notice that the main timeline immediately looks different; the sound event has now changed visually so that it loops ten times:

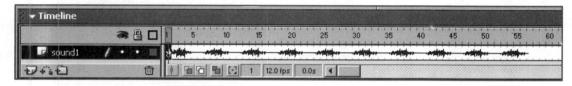

Test your updated version of this movie (or open up `event3.fla` where we've made the changes for you) – the sound repeats ten times in a row. This is useful for creating long background loops in which, for example, a background crowd sound repeats forever. To make a sound repeat effectively 'forever', simply type `9999` in the loop box.

Button Sounds

Open up `event_button1.fla` and notice that there's a button on the main stage:

Test the movie and see what happens when you press the button – a sound effect will play. This is very simple to accomplish with an event sound, which occurs on the *down* frame of a button.

Double-click on the button so that you are editing the button itself:

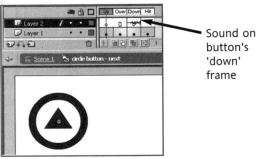

Sound on button's 'down' frame

On frame 3 of Layer 2 (labeled as Down for a button, as usual), we can see a waveform. Clicking on that frame and looking in the Property inspector reveals that it's our trusty zoom sound:

This is exactly like our main timeline sound event, except that this time it's within the frame of a button.

Now try adding sound to the Over frame of the button, in the same manner – insert a keyframe into frame 2 of Layer 2 (F6), then drag an instance of the `zoom.wav` sound onto that frame:

Sounds on two different button frames

As usual, the waveform of that sound appears in the timeline. Remember that the sound must be an Event sound rather than a Stream sound. Next, use the Edit Envelope (as discussed earlier) to make this instance of the sound a little different from the instance attached to the Down state.

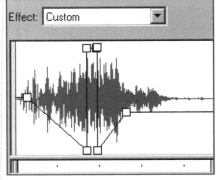

Test out your new button, or take a look at `event_button2.fla` – now the button makes a 'squeak' when our mouse cursor rolls over it, and then a 'zoom' when we click on it! Adding sounds to the various states of buttons (up, over, and down) allows us to create lively, interactive buttons that will really keep users interested.

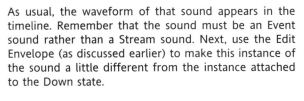

Summary

In this chapter we've learned all about sound in Flash MX; we've seen:

- The difference between **streamed** and **event-based** sounds, and how to effectively use both forms in their most appropriate settings

- How to **import sounds**, and what **file formats** we can use

- How to set up sounds with the appropriate **export and compression settings**

- **Editing sounds** to create different effects
  - How to stream sounds in a movie and **sync animation to the sound**

- How to add event sounds to a movie and a button

Armed with this knowledge, we can now create anything from sound-enhanced buttons to completely synced animation with sound.

Next

Exporting and publishing our Flash movies for all to see.

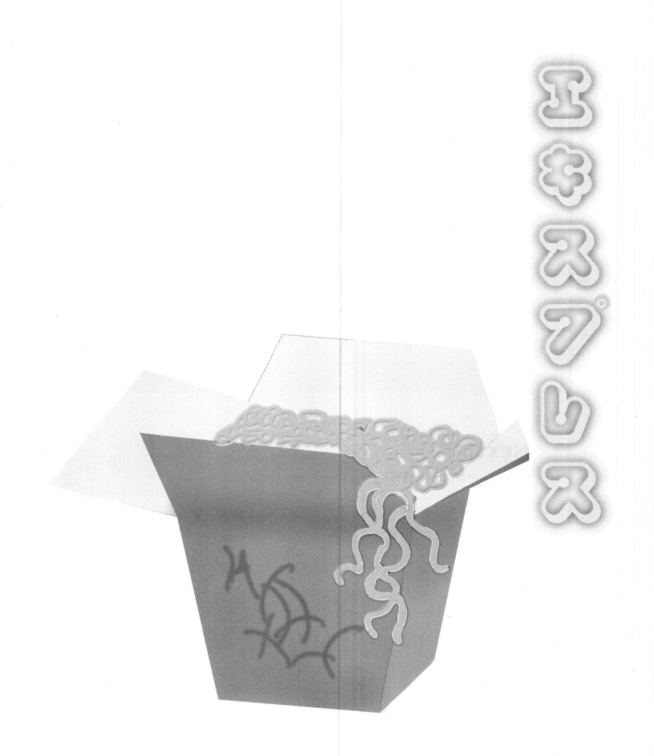

Chapter 13
Publishing
Flash Movies

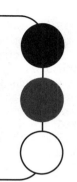

What's in this chapter:

● **Testing** movies

● **Exporting** movies in various formats: SWF, AVI, animated GIF, WAV, JPEG sequence

● **Publishing** movies

Exporting Flash content

One of the most important features that Macromedia Flash MX has to offer is the ability to output files in many different formats apart from the standard SWF. Although we typically use Flash to create complete web sites or animations that are then compiled into SWF files, Flash can output our movies in a number of other ways including popular image formats such as GIF and JPEG, movie formats like MOV and AVI, and sound formats such as WAV. This is just the tip of the iceberg of course! But before we delve into some of the finer details, let's cover some of the basics.

Test Movie

When we have a completed Flash movie and we want to see it in action, we usually use the Test Movie feature. With this technique all buttons and movie clips are activated and we can execute any ActionScript; we must use Test Movie to see any animation that's contained within movie clips, or to hear any event sounds, or to cause any code on frames and buttons to be executed.

Test Movie can be triggered in a couple of ways:

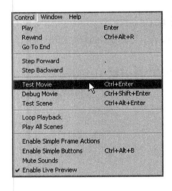

1. From the menu: go to **Control > Test Movie**

2. Using the keyboard shortcut: press CTRL+ENTER (⌘+ENTER on a Mac)

On testing your movie, the Flash MX panels will disappear, and it will begin playing from Frame 1. When we use Test Movie, certain aspects of our test are determined by the publish settings – so let's look at these settings. Select **File > Publish Settings...**

The Publish Settings box will appear:

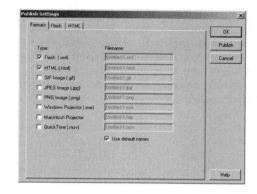

There's a list of file types under the Formats tab; we can export a movie in any or all of these formats when that movie is finally published – we'll look at these later in this chapter. With Test Movie, however, the only file type that's created and exported is the Flash SWF file. We'll get to the rest of the options in a short while, but first, let's look at the Flash tab, just to the right of the Formats tab:

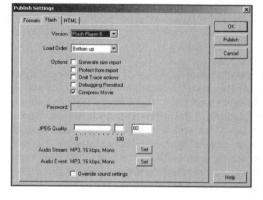

Any settings chosen in the Flash Publish Settings window will be applied to all movies created with the Test Movie command. Let's look at these settings a little more closely.

Version

Under the Version drop-down box, there's a list of Flash player versions starting at Flash Player 1, right up to Flash Player 6:

Flash Player version options

Here's a good way to see the limitations in each player version; select Flash Player 5 and click OK. Now open up your Actions panel (F9), and click on the Index icon on the left-hand side – this lists all of the actions and commands that are available in Flash, as shown overleaf.

> **Tip**
> *If you use some advanced ActionScript functions (see **Chapter 10**) or certain types of components (see **Chapter 14**) in a movie, you have to choose the correct version to export to – earlier versions of the Player don't support some of the more advanced features in MX.*

Notice that, because we've chosen to publish in the Flash 5 player, all of the newer Flash MX commands that *weren't* available in the older Flash 5 player are highlighted, indicating that we shouldn't use them if we want Flash 5 Player users to view our movie. This can be a real bonus for ensuring that your movies are 'backward compatible'.

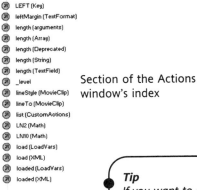

Section of the Actions window's index

Load order

This determines the order in which Flash will load the layers of your movie's first frame. This can affect the way things are displayed for the viewer:

Load order options

For example; if there's a black box on the highest layer covering all the assets beneath it (perhaps, for some reason, we don't want them to be visible until the entire movie is loaded), then we would choose Top Down from this box. This will ensure that the black box is loaded and drawn first. Anything beneath it will therefore not be seen because the black box is already displayed. We can be confident that none of the other content will be seen until we want it to be.

Options

Here we have a column of check boxes relating to some specific options:

- **Generate size report** – Generates a text file containing detailed information about the file size usage of different aspects of our movie. With the size report, we can determine what parts of our movie need to be trimmed to reduce its overall file size.

- **Protect from import** – Prevents people from importing our SWF files into their own blank FLA files and using our graphics.

- **Omit Trace actions** – This forces Flash to ignore any ActionScript `trace` commands that we have left in our movie after debugging.

- **Debugging Permitted** – Turns on or off the debugging mode in our final SWF file (this is a

> **Tip**
> If you want to ensure that your movie is viewable by the maximum number of users, think carefully about which Player version you publish to, and when. The further out we get from Flash MX's launch, the greater the global penetration of the Flash Player 6 should be. Macromedia publish their latest statistics on Player penetration levels on their site – currently to be found at:
> `http://www.macromedia.com /software/flashplayer/`

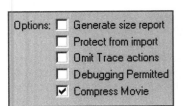

> **Tip**
> Trace commands help us debug the ActionScript in our movies – there's more on `trace` in the next chapter.

rather advanced topic, and therefore beyond the scope of this book).

- **Compress Movie** – Uses a form of compression, similar to the compression used in ZIP files, to make the size of the SWF file significantly smaller. This option is only available with the Flash 6 player, and it is checked by default in Flash MX.

Password

If a password is entered here, then the password will be required at runtime in order for the SWF to be debugged (if Debugging Permitted was chosen):

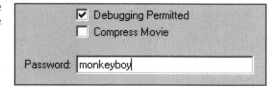

JPEG quality

This setting determines the default compression level of any bitmap images we have in our final exported movie. This can have a dramatic difference on the final file size, but it can also reduce the visual quality of our images – it takes some playing with to find the optimum balance.

Audio compression

These options determine the default audio compression settings for both streamed and event-based sounds (working with sound in Flash MX was covered in detail in the previous chapter).

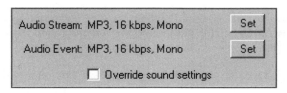

Selecting the 'Override sound settings' option will force Flash to use the settings specified here, despite any individual settings that may have been defined in the Sound Properties window via the movie Library itself (see **Chapter 12**).

Using Test Movie

Enough theory, let's try it out! Open up test_my_movie.fla – the first thing you'll notice is that there's some text in the middle of the stage:

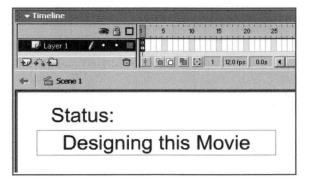

The words 'Designing this Movie' are inside a special type of text box that can be changed at runtime using ActionScript. Notice that on frame 1 of Layer 1, there's a tiny 'a' in the frame, reminding us that there's some ActionScript in this frame.

Make sure that this text is selected, and take a look at your Property inspector:

As you can see, this text box has an instance name `textdisp` – we can use this name as a 'label' to remotely call on the text box and get it to do things. In this case, we'll use it to simply change the text at runtime. But remember, ActionScript doesn't do anything until we test (or publish) our movie, so press CTRL+ENTER/⌘+ENTER right now. All the panels will disappear, as expected, and our stage will look like this:

Status:
Testing This Movie

The contents of our `textdisp` text box have indeed changed! Let's see what the code used to achieve this actually looks like – close your player down to return to the design environment, then open up your Actions panel (F9):

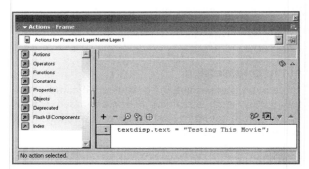

You'll find the relevant ActionScript in the scripting pane on the right-hand side of the Actions panel. For this movie, we've used the following code:

```
textdisp.text = "Testing This Movie";
```

This translates to "Make the text in the text box called `textdisp` read `Testing This Movie`". Pretty simple, huh! But if the code isn't immediately understandable, don't worry too much about what it does – after all, this is just a demonstration of how Test Movie works.

 Test Movie is the method used 90% of the time to view our Flash movies. When a developer is building a Flash game, for example, they will most likely use Test Movie every few minutes to check how small changes fit in to the look of the movie. In contrast, the Publish command (which we'll cover shortly) is usually only used to view the finished product.

Export Movie

Export Movie is another important feature of Flash. We can use this command to turn our FLA movies into one of many different types of files. At this point, we can take our FLA and turn it into a Quicktime MOV, or a Windows AVI file, and instantly our Flash animation can be used in any sort of production for video, DVD, film, TV, and so on. Or we could export just the soundtrack of our FLA as a large WAV file, and then take that WAV and publish it on a CD, or convert it to an MP3 file and put it on a web site. The variations are pretty much limitless!

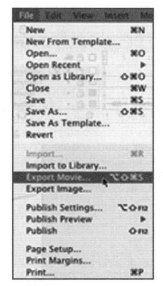

Before we look at specific formats, let's first look at how to get to the Export Movie option. Open any movie in Flash MX and go to **File > Export Movie...** (or press Ctrl+Alt+Shift+S/Option+Shift+⌘+S if you have a good memory and rather nimble fingers!).

The Export Movie dialog box will then appear. Before hitting the Save button, choose the format you want to export as (more on this shortly) from the 'Save as type' (PC) or 'Format' (Mac) drop-down menu, and enter the name of your file in the appropriate file name box:

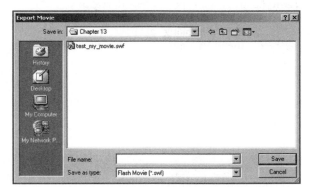

As we'll soon see, Export Movie is the command that we use to take our FLA movies and turn them into one of many different formats for various purposes, including:

- Film and television

- Website banner advertisements

- Soundtrack production

- Anything else that our imaginations can think of!

Using Export

For the purpose of demonstrating the Export Movie command, we're going to use the file `export_my_movie.fla`:

Open it up – it consists simply of a paper airplane, which flies from left to right across the screen with the accompanying sound of machinery. At frame 27, we've made it appear that a camera takes a picture of the plane – there's a camera shutter sound, and the screen goes black for two frames. Run it now by performing a Test Movie (CTRL+ENTER/⌘+ENTER) – we'll be using this FLA when we look at the different export formats in the next section, so keep it open for the moment.

Export formats

Movies in Flash can be exported in a number of formats – look at the 'Save as type' (PC) or 'Format' (Mac) drop-down menus in the Export Movie dialog box:

Before looking at how we can generate them, let's define the main formats.

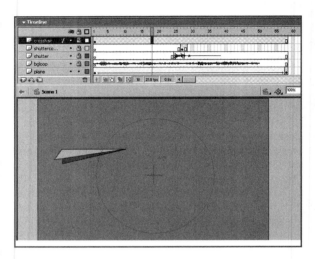

PC export format options   Mac export format options

● **Flash Movie (SWF)** – Our good friend the SWF file, identical to the file generated when you test or publish your movie.

● **FutureSplash Player (SPL)** – An old – and rarely used – format used by Flash's previous product identity (before it was acquired by Macromedia).

● **Windows AVI (AVI)** – Used to create video AVI files in Windows operating systems. The AVI format has many export options, and is typically used to allow complex Flash animations with many vectors to be exported as a simplified bitmapped movie. If a Flash movie is running a little slow in Flash, then exporting to AVI usually allows the movie to run at the desired frame rate perfectly.

● **QuickTime (MOV)** – Similar to AVI, except it creates vector-based movies playable on the QuickTime system. The use of vector graphics means the file size will be smaller, but it may not play back faster than Flash itself can play the movie.

● **Animated GIF (GIF)** – Creates a GIF image that contains as many frames as there are frames in the FLA. The animated GIF, however, was not designed for large movies, so a large FLA with many frames may produce a huge file size.

● **WAV Audio (WAV)** – Only the audio portion of the FLA movie is exported.

The remaining formats are sequences – rather than exporting a single self-contained file, they export a series of files to your hard drive:

● **EMF Sequence** – Creates a series of Enhanced Metafiles, a vector-based standard format.

● **WMF Sequence** – Creates a series of Windows Metafiles. Similar to EMF, but used by the Windows operating system.

● **EPS 3.0 Sequence** – Creates a series of Encapsulated PostScript files, often used by illustration programs and postscript printers.

● **Adobe Illustrator Sequence** – Creates a series of Adobe Illustrator (AI) files. These are vector based.

When we choose to export the movie as any of these file formats, Flash will automatically append the correct extension (e.g. `.wav`, `.gif`, `.avi`, etc.) and, in the case of a sequence, Flash will automatically create a four-digit number after the File name (which we specify) to reflect the order that the images occur in the SWF.

In the following subsections we'll take a more detailed look at the key formats: SWF, AVI, Animated GIF, WAV, and JPEG sequence.

SWF

Exporting your movie as a SWF file is identical to the type of export that occurs when you hit CTRL+ENTER/⌘+ENTER to test your movie. It does, however, give us a few additional options:

● We can name the SWF file anything we want every time we export the movie. Test Movie is set up to give the SWF file the same kind of name every time – unless we go into Publish Settings to change this default setting.

● We can choose the export settings each time because we'll be presented with the Export Flash Player window (see below) every time we invoke Export Movie.

● **DXF Sequence** – Creates a series of Autocad DXF files.

● **BMP Sequence** – Creates a series of BMP bitmap image files.

● **GIF Sequence** – Creates a series of GIF bitmap image files.

● **JPEG Sequence** – Creates a series of JPEG bitmap image files.

● **PNG Sequence** – Creates a series of PNG bitmap image files.

But remember – when you export as a SWF file, your movie doesn't run immediately, as it does with Test Movie; instead, you need to go into that folder and open it up after exporting it.

 With `export_my_movie.fla` still open, go to **File > Export Movie** – choose the SWF file format and call the file `airplane`. Once you click Save, you'll be presented with the Export Flash Player window:

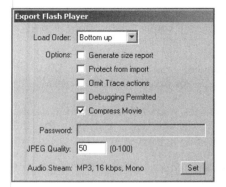

This is identical to the Flash SWF Publish Settings that we covered at the beginning of this chapter. We choose our settings and our Flash version, then press OK. Once that's done, Flash will create `airplane.swf`, which can be viewed outside of the Flash MX development environment in the stand-alone Flash Player (you just need to double-click on the SWF file in the folder – if you've got the Flash player on your machine, it'll play):

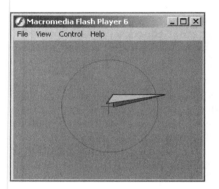

AVI/QuickTime video

Selecting these formats (on the PC and Mac respectively in this example) will turn our Flash movie into a video file. This means that the file will be larger, but it will be smoother and guaranteed to lock to a specific frame rate. This can also then be published on DVD, used in television, streamed from a web site, and a whole lot more.

On a PC, export the `export_my_movie.fla` as a Windows AVI file called `airplaneMovie`:

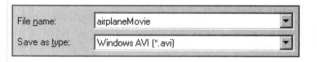

On a Mac, export this movie as a QuickTime video:

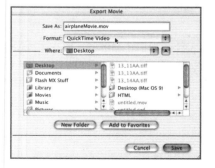

Once you press Save, the following windows appear:

Here, we can set some key options of the video file:

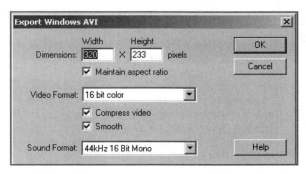

- **Dimensions** – We can set the desired output dimensions, in pixels; we're not bound by the dimensions of our FLA movie (which, in this case is 550 x 400). The higher the resolution, the larger the file size, but the better the picture detail. Experiment with what suits your needs.

- **Maintain aspect ratio** – If checked, the width or height will always adjust itself to match the ratio of the original FLA's dimensions.

- **Video Format** (PC)/**Format** (Mac) – In this drop-down menu, we will see a list of color resolutions at which we can output our video file. Higher bit color depths will produce richer images, but again larger files. Since vector images consist of vector colors and gradients, the level of color detail in the source FLA file can be very high, yet with very little file size expense. Not so with video files. Only use the bit depth required to accurately convey the necessary colors.

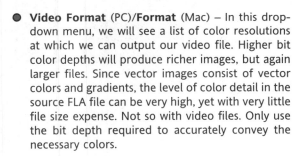

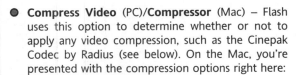

- **Compress Video** (PC)/**Compressor** (Mac) – Flash uses this option to determine whether or not to apply any video compression, such as the Cinepak Codec by Radius (see below). On the Mac, you're presented with the compression options right here:

- **Smooth** – Determines whether or not Flash will apply an anti-alias smoothing to the images or not. Without this, images may appear jagged and rough at the edges.

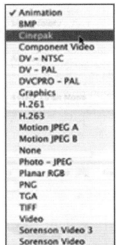

Mac video
Compression options

> **Tip**
> *Video compression is a bit of a black art, and choosing the right format isn't always easy. Accordingly, we'll return to this topic towards the end of this chapter.*

● **Sound Format** – Specifies the quality and type of sound that is exported with our video file. Since sound is embedded within video files, this is an important option and has a large bearing on the file size. Our options are sample rate of 5, 11, 22 or 44 kHz, bit depth of 8 bit or 16 bit, and channel in stereo or mono. All combinations are listed in the drop-down menu. The best sound, which is CD quality sound, is 44kHz 16 Bit stereo. The lowest option is 'Disable', which does not export sound with our video file.

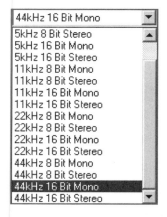

On the PC, once we've done setting our options and we hit OK (with Compress video selected), we'll be presented with the Video Compression settings dialog box:

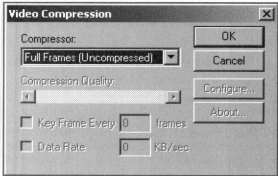

Under the Compressor drop-down box, depending upon what compression codecs are installed on your system, you'll see a list like this:

Cinepak Codec by Radius
Intel Indeo(R) Video R3.2
Microsoft RLE
Microsoft Video 1
Microsoft H.263 Video Codec
Microsoft H.261 Video Codec
Intel 4:2:0 Video V2.50
Indeo® video 5.10
Full Frames (Uncompressed)

To explain all of these options would soon get highly technical (and perhaps a little dull!), so it's recommended that you stick to the Cinepak Codec by Radius, Microsoft Video 1, or Full Frames (Uncompressed) for the moment. In fact, you'll find that many of the options won't even work unless your system has a license to export using that particular format. They're presented there in the list because the computer has the ability to decompress them, but it doesn't necessarily have the permission to *write* them.

So, pick a compressor – here, we've chosen Cinepak Codec by Radius:

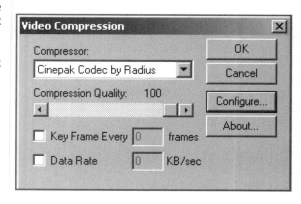

Next, click OK. While the AVI compiles, you'll see this:

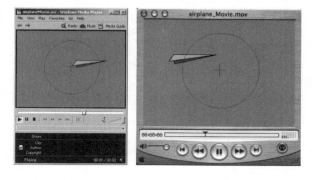

When it's done, our AVI/QuickTime file will be sitting in the designated folder ready to be played with your favorite media player:

QuickTime Export Issues

 Flash MX can export to a Quick Time movie from an FLA, but the precise nature of an FLA's content can affect how interactive the exported QuickTime movie can be. Some types of FLA content cause QuickTime problems, and you need to be aware of some of these wrinkles if you're going to output Flash movies to QuickTime; we'll be looking at some of the most important issues in this section.

Generally speaking, it's always best to try and view your finished output on as many different machines/operating systems as you can, and using as many different browsers as possible. If you don't have the resources to do this, then you can always publish the content on the web and seek feedback/advice from newsgroups or message boards. If you want to publish as widely as possible in different formats, then extensive testing, problem solving, and workarounds are needed if you want everyone to view what you've developed in a satisfactory way. Always ask yourself, "Do I really need to publish it in all these formats and, if I do, what features could I do without, and is there a way I can get round the problem by trying something else?"

Flash Player Version Considerations

At the time of writing, QuickTime doesn't support the Flash 6 player, so you should choose the Flash 5 player option (in the Publish Settings dialog) before you export from MX (Flash MX publishes out to QuickTime 4). If you try and publish out in Flash 6 player format, you'll get this message:

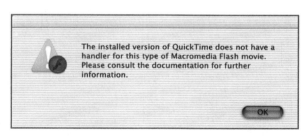

Hidden buttons

If you're publishing a Flash movie that has a hidden button (i.e. one that doesn't light up or change on rollover) linked to a URL, you'll have to publish with the Controller option (in the QuickTime tab of the Publish Settings dialog) set to Standard:

This enables the movie to display the hand cursor on rollover in stand-alone QuickTime Player mode.

Controller option setting for hidden buttons

ActionScript in Frame 1

You cannot put an ActionScript (stop); command in the first frame of any movie you're exporting to QuickTime – the movie will just play, ignoring the code in the opening frame. The workaround to this is to duplicate the first frame of the movie and put the stop(); action in the second frame. Open up apollo_dock.fla (in this book's download code folder) to see how this works:

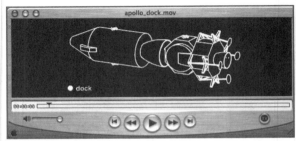

Thanks to Rod Cleasby and RCAD Multimedia (http://www.bizlink-uk.com/rod) for the original source images that this FLA was derived from.

Frame 1 is just a copy of frame 2 in the frame by frame animation, and the stop(); command is on frame 2:

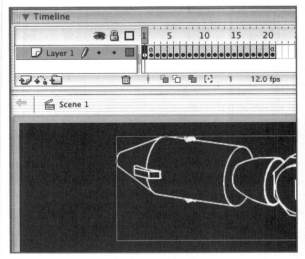

Frame 1 is a duplicate of frame 2,
but without the ActionScript

Truncated QuickTime controller

When you publish into an HTML file using the Controller *standard* option, you might find that the controller bar in the HTML page is slightly truncated:

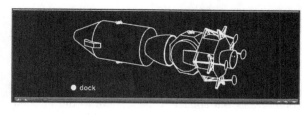

The different Publish commands don't always seem to accommodate this feature on export, and you may have to tweak the HTML source file to see it fully.

If you know a little HTML you can alter the height settings easily – go into your HTML page's source file and find the two places where the code shows the window height (different sizes for different types of browser and plug-in code):

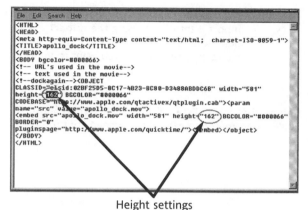

Height settings

Change that value to a slightly larger one (measured in pixels), and then resave it. In this case, the value was changed to 178. You should then be able to see all of your QuickTime controller bar – if not, keep tweaking the height value up or down until you can:

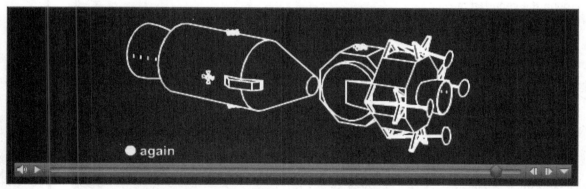

Controller bar is now fully visible

Masks

You can't use a standard mask layer to mask imported QuickTime content in an FLA. A workaround for this is to make a layer *above* the imported QuickTime movie and add some drawn objects that will act as a mask. This pseudo-mask will be exported with the rest of the content and will appear to be a mask in the finished product.

 If you already have a MOV video file you can import it into Flash using the **Import > File** menu option. You'll see this dialog when you've selected the file you want to import:

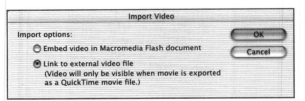

Choose the Link to External Video File option and then you'll be prompted to extend the timeline of the Movie:

Choose 'Yes' (so that your FLA timeline matches the length of the MOV clip), then drag your sample movie to the top right corner. Now go to **Modify > Document** and hit the Contents button to clean up the white space around the imported movie:

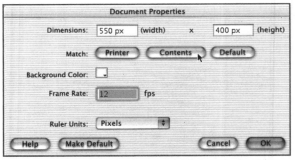

Now create a new layer called Mask but **do not turn it into a mask layer**; you won't be able to test the movie until you've exported it, so don't try and see how it looks at present. Lock the Mask layer and draw out a filled rectangle over obscuring the QuickTime movie underneath it completely. Draw one (or a series) of shapes on this rectangle and then highlight them and cut them out:

Now turn the whole shape on the Mask layer into a movie clip symbol.

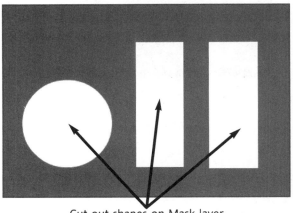

Cut out shapes on Mask layer

Next – and this is the most important step – go to **File > Publish settings** and check the Flash, HTML, and QuickTime boxes:

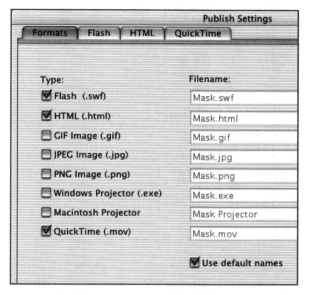

Now go to the Flash Tab and choose Flash Player 6, but **uncheck** the Compress Movie option:

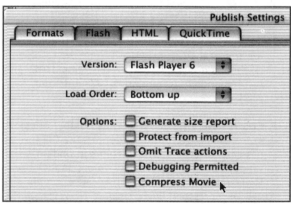

Now click on the HTML tab and choose the QuickTime option from the drop-down. Lastly go to the QuickTime tab and uncheck the Flatten (Make self-contained) option:

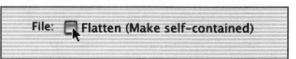

Then hit the Publish button. Put the HTML file, the SWF file, and the original QuickTime MOV file all in the same directory, open up the HTML file, and you'll see that you have a mask:

As you can see, workarounds need a little thinking through. If you were to create a mask in the traditional way it would not work and what's more it would disrupt the playback of the QuickTime movie.

Animated GIF

One of the most ubiquitous formats for graphics on the web is the ever-popular GIF. Moreover, advertising is common on today's Internet, with Flash ads in particular gaining popularity. However, at present, the most common method for online advertising is probably the animated GIF. This is simply a multi-framed GIF image that plays back animated in most web browsers – let's create one!

You know the routine by now – select **File > Export Movie...** with `export_my_movie.fla` open. This time choose Animated GIF as the type, and call it `airplaneAd`. Click Save, and the GIF options dialog box will appear:

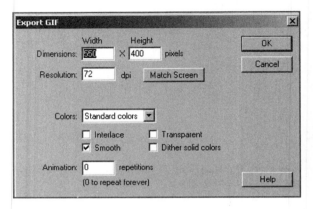

As usual, there are several options that you can set:

- **Dimensions** – This is the size of the GIF image. Usually set to a standard size for banner ads (468x60, for example) or simply set to match the FLA movie (it is set to this by default).

- **Resolution** – This can also be used to determine the size of the GIF image, as setting the resolution is reflected in the dimensions. Standard, and recommended, resolution is 72 dots per inch (dpi).

- **Colors** – Here we determine the number of colors in the GIF image (the color depth). The GIF format has a 'color ceiling' of 256 colors in one image. A simple FLA with only a few colors should use a lower number in this setting because the file size will be correspondingly smaller. However, if the FLA has many complex colors, then a higher setting must obviously be used. The other option is Standard colors, which forces the GIF to use the standard 216-color browser-safe palette.

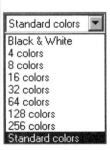

- **Interlace** – This should *not* be set for animated GIFs; it allows a GIF to be displayed incrementally as it downloads. This is, for the most part, a leftover from a time when a 28kB GIF image would take 30 or 40 seconds to download!

- **Transparent** – This tells the GIF image to treat any parts of the image where there's no drawn content as *background*. For example, the sky, in `export_my_movie.fla`; in this movie, the sky gets its color from the stage background – it's not a drawn element. If you choose the Transparent

Transparent animated GIF background

option, the browser color will show here instead, while the plane and the other drawn elements display as usual.

● **Smooth** – This allows Flash to perform some anti-aliasing (or more simply 'un-digitizing') and color blending on color edges to make the graphics appear smoother and less rigid or 'stair-cased'.

● **Dither solid colors** – Generally, gradients are simulated in 256 colors by applying a dither to them. If, for example, we have an original vector gradient that looks something like this:

The Dither solid colors option allows Flash to simulate a greater number of colors (and therefore save file space) because it can reproduce colors by mixing pixels of two different colors into one 'solid area'. So, with dither applied, the above gradient would be exported as a GIF like this:

● **Animation repetitions** – Setting this value causes the GIF to loop however many times you specify. It will animate, then start again as many times as are specified here. If we leave 0 in the box, then the GIF loops forever.

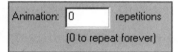

Finally, click OK, and the GIF file will be created. If we view the GIF in a web browser window, we'll see it animate. Note that it does not, however, have any sound – the GIF format doesn't support sound.

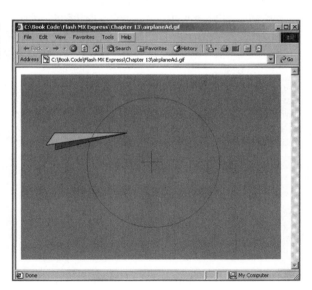

WAV

When we export our movie using the WAV format on a PC, all that's generated is an audio WAV file from the audio portion of our movie. In some respects, this is the direct opposite of the exporting to an animated GIF, which only exports images.

This time, export the FLA `export_my_movie.fla` as a WAV Audio file and call it `airplaneAudio`. When you click Save you'll be presented with one simple option box:

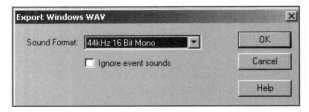

Our options are as follows:

- **Sound Format** – This determines the quality of the outputted sound file, which directly affects the file size. The highest quality is 44kHz 16 Bit stereo, which is CD quality. We'd never choose the top option, Disable, because it would cause Flash to create a completely empty sound file (dumb option, huh?).

- **Ignore event sounds** – This allows us to specify that Flash only exports sounds that we have set to Stream (see **Chapter 12**); if this box is checked, event sounds will not be included in the final WAV file.

Export as WAV means that we can use Flash to create a complete soundtrack, or 'sound effects' track that can be used in another program. Or, if you're an animator and you want to create an animation and then export the video and audio separately, you can do so easily.

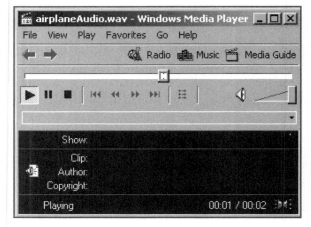

JPEG sequence

As we mentioned earlier, exporting a JPEG sequence creates a series of JPEG images – one per frame of its parent FLA movie. Go ahead and export `export_my_movie.fla` as a JPEG Sequence, name it `airplane_jpegs` and press Save. The following box will appear:

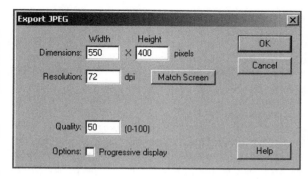

This is similar to GIF exporting, and the options reflect that:

- Set the **dimensions** and **resolution** as desired – generally, Match Screen is the best bet, but as the FLA is a vector image source we might want to choose a very high resolution, so that the JPEG quality will be smooth and crisp. This is ideal if we need to export an animated cartoon for transfer to film where the pixel resolution needs to be very high.

- **Quality** – This is used to determine the quality (and file size) of the JPEG images. The higher the quality, the larger the files (the highest quality setting being 100%).

- **Progressive Display** – This is used to set the JPEGs up for progressive display, similar to the Interlace option we saw with exporting animated GIFs. The images display as they're downloading, but it's recommended that you don't use this option as not all programs support progressive JPEG images.

Click OK, and the numbered JPEG sequence will be generated:

Publish Movie

We have yet another portal through which we can export our movies: the Publish command. With this command we can publish as many of the previously discussed export types, but there are also a few key new ones including HTML, and Windows and Macintosh Projector (more on these below).

When we visit a Flash web site, all Flash content we see is being displayed to us via a 'plug-in' in the browser. For the most part, the SWF files are not being displayed directly in the browser; rather, they're 'embedded' in an HTML page using some nice HTML code. By using the Publish command, Flash can create any HTML files that we might need. In fact, there are actually several HTML

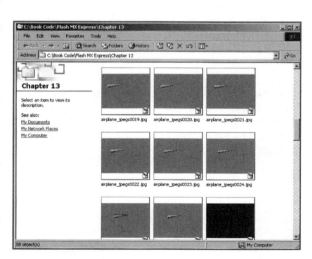

export methods that we can choose from, depending on our target browser and setup.

It's possible to let someone view a SWF file we've made without them needing to have the Flash plug-in or player installed on their computer at all. This is accomplished using a 'projector'. A projector is simply the stand-alone SWF player combined with our SWF file itself, all wrapped into one neat package. The projector is an executable file, which the user simply has to double-click on to see our movie. The other nice thing about projector publishing is that we can publish both PC and Mac formats of projector, no matter what system we are using to develop – a Windows developer can release their work in a format that PC *and* Mac users can enjoy.

To Publish a movie, you simply select **File > Publish**, or hit Shift+F12/Option+Shift+F12:

Tip
Outputting to a Projector file is achieved using the Publish Setting dialog – see below.

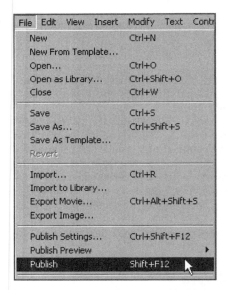

However, before we do that, we should return to the Publish Settings dialog box for a closer examination. We looked at this at the beginning of this chapter while studying Test Movie. Let's recap – go to **File > Publish Settings**...

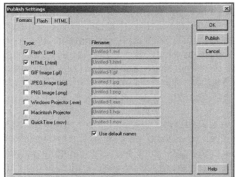

Notice the list of eight check boxes on the left, indicating all the available publishing formats. When we select a format, a new tab will appear at the top of the page suggesting that there are more options for each format. Only the Windows and Macintosh Projector formats do *not* have further options to specify. For example, if we select *all* of the check boxes, we see this:

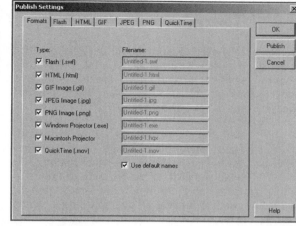

Notice that Flash uses the name of our FLA file (in this case, it's the default name, Untitled-1) as a base for creating the file names for each of our chosen export file types. If we want, we can de-select the option Use default names, and enter file names of our own that will always be used, regardless of the name of our FLA file. For instance, we could rename as shown in the screenshot.

Notice that each publishing file type uses a unique, descriptive name. This option is entirely up to the designer. However, as we'll soon see, *some* file names are important. The GIF file name, for example, is embedded in the HTML file when the HTML file is exported to include an alternate GIF to cater for when the user doesn't have the Flash player installed.

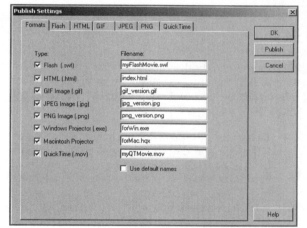

Flash, HTML, GIF, JPEG, PNG, and QuickTime are the standard publishing formats. The Flash format (the SWF file) was covered at the beginning of this chapter, so let's now look at the all-important HTML format.

The HTML file

Alongside the SWF file, this is perhaps the most important export file you'll come across – the HTML file is often used as the vehicle that carries an embedded SWF file; when you publish to an HTML file, Flash embeds the SWF in the HTML file and automatically creates all the necessary HTML code for you. There are many options, and each one dramatically affects the overall look of the final site. Click on the HTML tab in the Publish Settings window:

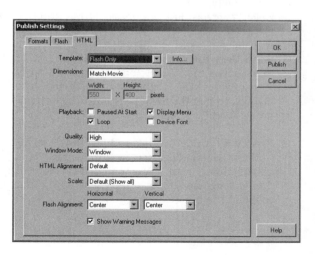

For information only, here's a view of what the actual HTML code looks like:

We don't really need to worry about this level of detail at this stage, since we can set all our HTML preferences from the Publish Settings window. However, you might want to look at the HTML in detail when you start tweaking sites of your own...

With the Flash HTML file we can export our Flash movies into robust (and tweaked) Flash-enabled pages. The other options, GIF, JPEG, and PNG, all export the Flash movie as bitmap graphics (more on these soon), which are most commonly used to provide an alternate image should the SWF file fail to load.

Let's look at the HTML options in detail.

Template

This is a pretty critical setting. Flash has many different templates it can use to output a particular style of HTML file – different templates serve different purposes:

- **Detect for...** – The first four choices will create an HTML file that detects the user's plug-in version. In case the user does not have that minimum version of the Flash player installed, an alternate image will be presented. These auto-detect versions use Javascript, which will be built into the HTML file and will perform the version check for us.

- **Flash Only** – Exports the simplest HTML file, which contains just the basic HTML code to embed the SWF file.

- **Flash Only for Pocket PC 2002** – Creates HTML that displays the SWF file on a Pocket PC display. It configures the alignment, positioning, and margins so that the SWF file is optimally viewable on a Pocket PC screen.

- **Flash with AICC Tracking and SCORM Tracking** – These use special code to enable tracking in conjunction with Macromedia's Learning Components (an advanced topic, and beyond the scope of this book).

HTML template options

- **Flash with FSCommand** – Exports the HTML file with support for FSCommand and Javascript (this is also an advanced option, only of use when using FSCommand ActionScript functions).

- **Flash with Named Anchors** – This HTML file version allows users to bookmark, and move backwards and forwards between individual pages in the SWF file using the Back and Forward buttons of a browser. Anchors are exported when frames are given labels via the Property inspector (see **Chapter 5**), and then the Named Anchor option is selected beneath the label name:

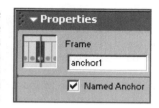

- **Image Map** – Exports the HTML file to contain *not* the SWF file, but rather the selected bitmap image format (GIF, JPEG, PNG). If no bitmap publishing file format is selected, a warning will be given.

- **QuickTime** – Creates an HTML file with the code that supports a QuickTime movie to be embedded in it. Correspondingly, we must also have selected the QuickTime file format before publication.

Dimensions

This determines the dimensions at which the SWF file will be embedded in the HTML movie. There are three options:

- **Match movie** – This will embed the SWF at the resolution it was created with. By default, it's 550 x 400.

- **Pixels** – When selected, the actual dimensions of the embedded movie can be specified. How these dimensions are translated to the screen is dependent on the Scale option (see below).

- **Percentage** – When selected, the movie is scaled as a percentage of the actual screen size. As the browser is resized, so too is the movie.

Playback

There are four options under the Playback section:

- **Paused At Start** – Selecting this will force the SWF to be stopped on frame 1 when the page is loaded into the viewer's browser/player. This can be useful in allowing the site to load fully before proceeding.

● **Display Menu** – This option determines whether or not the right-click/CTRL-click menu will appear when the site is running. The right-click menu provides users with options like Zoom In, Zoom Out, Rewind, Forward, and so on:

Disabling this option will ensure that the only things which appear in the right-click/CTRL-click menu are Settings and About Flash Player.

● **Loop** – Selecting this will tell the movie to loop back to the beginning once it reaches the final frame.

● **Device Font** – This is for Windows systems only. If the user's machine doesn't have a specific font installed that the SWF file is trying to use, then selecting this option will make the SWF use a smooth, antialiased font instead. This will help ensure that every user gets the visual experience you want them to have.

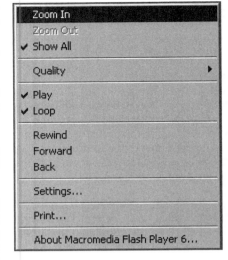

Quality

This determines the default display quality of the movie when it is running in the browser. The options are:

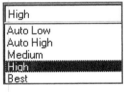

Choosing different values will yield different results in performance and appearance. If a Flash movie is running slowly, then try choosing a lower quality. The major difference is the amount of anti-aliasing, or smoothing.

The effect of the Quality setting varies greatly from project to project, so playing with it to determine the optimal setting is a necessity. Selecting the Auto Low/Auto High options forces Flash to do some diagnostics on the user's computer first, determining whether or not their computer can handle high quality. With Auto Low, for instance, it defaults to low quality, but if Flash determines that their computer can handle it, it switches the quality to high. With Auto High, it's the opposite: the quality starts off high, but if Flash detects that the computer is having problems, then the quality is dropped to Low to compensate.

Compare the Best quality

And the Low quality

Note the more ragged edges of the low quality in comparison to the best quality

Window mode

The Window mode is used to determine how the SWF will appear over the background. The options in Window mode are applicable to Internet Explorer 4.0 and above:

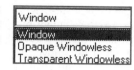

- **Window** – This is the default, and is how most SWF files normally appear: in their own dedicated rectangular window on the web page.

- **Opaque Windowless** – This sets the SWF above any other elements on the web page. Text and backgrounds will disappear behind the SWF movie, but the SWF hides them. We can see this, for example, if we simply change the background color of the exported HTML page, and notice that we can still see the background of the SWF in the browser window:

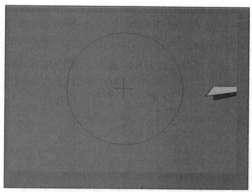

- **Transparent Windowless** – This sets the SWF above other elements on the web page, but also makes all areas of the SWF where the background is showing through transparent. The effect is fully animated graphics over the top of a web page. If we change the background color of the HTML page again to demonstrate this, the background of our SWF is now invisible:

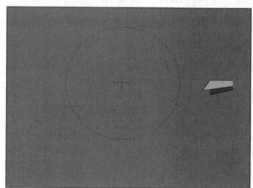

HTML Alignment

Determines the alignment of the Flash movie within the HTML window. If set to Default, then the SWF is centered in the browser window, otherwise we can choose from the following options to make the SWF file aligned with a particular edge:

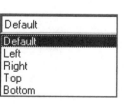

Scale

This determines how Flash will draw the movie within the specified boundaries of the embedded SWF. The options are:

● **Default (Show all)** – This option ensures that the SWF file will maintain its aspect (width-to-height) ratio, which brings us back to the Dimensions setting. If we specified dimensions that are other than the dimensions we designed our movie at, then we may see areas from beyond the edge of the stage appearing in our web page – usually not the desired effect!

● **No border** – This option scales the movie to fill the area specified in the Dimensions setting, while maintaining the aspect ratio of the original movie (no distortion). It will crop the movie if required.

● **Exact fit** – This forces the SWF to fill the entire stage, right to the edges of the embedded movie. This means that if we embedded our 550x400 movie to be 200x400 pixels embedded, our movie would appear squashed horizontally:

● **No scale** – This will crop the movie to ensure that it stays at 100% the size it was designed at. If the embedded movie dimensions are less than the size of the original FLA, then the SWF will be cropped in the window:

Flash Alignment

In a situation where the SWF is going to be cropped due to Scale and Dimensions settings, then setting the Flash Alignment will allow us to specify where the cropped Flash movie's position will default to within its own window.

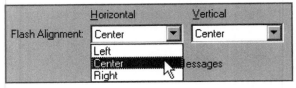

In the cropped image of the three objects above, the Flash alignment is set to center, both horizontally and vertically. In the same situation, if we choose a horizontal alignment of Left, we'd see the left side of the SWF, as opposed to the center:

Show Warning Messages

Selecting this option will force Flash to display any relevant warning messages when publishing a movie. For example, if we specify an HTML template that requires an alternate GIF image to be provided, and we fail to specify the image to use (we haven't checked the GIF publish option), then Flash will warn us:

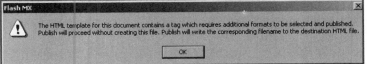

This has nothing to do with a runtime setting in the HTML file. It's simply a convenience setting for us when we're publishing our movies.

Summary

We've learned a lot about the way Flash exports its movies, and the different options that are available to us:

- Test Movie and the associated SWF settings

- Export Movie and the various export formats

- Publish and the options available for movie publication

- The HTML file, and its associated pre-publish settings

Next

The next chapter is the final chapter of this book – we'll be taking a look at some of the more advanced features that you can look forward to encountering on your future travels with Flash MX.

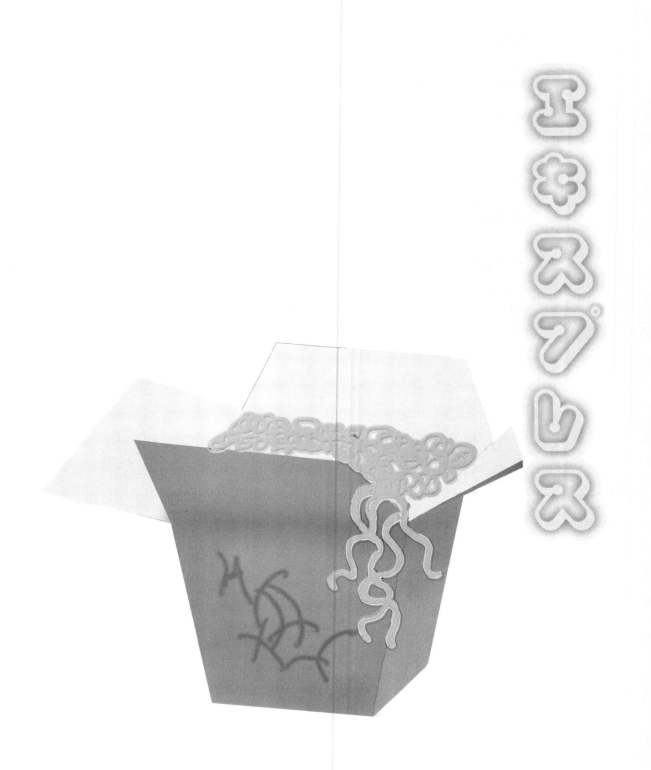

エキスプレス

Chapter 14
The Next Steps

What's in this chapter:

- Components

- Extending your use of ActionScript to modify
  movie clip properties

- Mouse interactions

- Importing video

- Dynamically loading JPEGs and MP3s

Where do you go next?

 So far in this book you've learned how to create animations, symbols, and standard web site elements like buttons and graphics, how to use simple ActionScript, and how to export it all in a working SWF. So what's left? Well, what makes Flash so powerful and so popular is the fact that it's a complete development system that allows you to build not only web sites and animations, but full applications as well.

In this chapter we're going to round off the book by looking at these final steps – we'll study several diverse yet bite-sized topics that will extend everything we've covered so far. After this final chapter, you'll be able to breathe life into your creations and turn the inanimate into the truly interactive!

Components

 Flash MX presents you with a wonderful feature in the shape of **User Interface (UI) Components**. Before Flash MX came along, creating the standard building blocks of websites like check boxes, radio buttons, and scrollbars, required some intricate ActionScript magic. But now, in MX, it's pretty much as easy as 'drag and drop'!

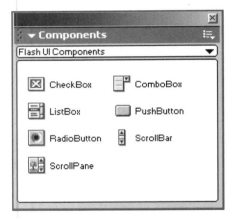

Flash MX offers several built-in UI components – open up your Components panel by selecting **Window > Components** (CTRL+F7/⌘+F7) to take a look at them:

You see these generic components all the time when you're surfing around the web or using software packages – they're standard parts of the Windows and Macintosh operating systems. Creating interactive Flash websites with components can be very cool – not only will they improve your workflow and design time, but you'll also be able to make your web sites and designs a lot more dynamic and interactive.

The great thing about UI components is that they're 'smart'. What does that mean? It means that you need only perform a minimal amount of work to make them behave properly on their own. Unfortunately, fully understanding components is something that would require a little more depth than one chapter can allow. So instead, as a kind of teaser, we'll look at two of most easily applicable components: the **Scrollbar** and the **PushButton**.

ScrollBar

As its name suggests, the ScrollBar component simply gives us the ability to scroll through content, be it text, images, or whatever. That may sound vague, but that's the point: you can use the ScrollBar for any scrolling purpose you desire. The simplest, and most straightforward use of the ScrollBar is to create a scrollable text field, so let's do just that.

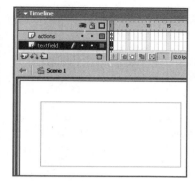

Open `scrollbar.fla` from this chapter's source code directory and look at the stage:

There are two layers in this FLA: one is named actions (note the tell-tale 'a' in frame 1 of this layer – we'll examine this shortly) and the other is named textfield. The only object on the stage is a simple text field, created using the standard Text tool from the toolbar:

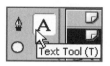

Click on this text field, and look at its properties in the Property inspector (CTRL+F3):

Although we studied text and text properties in Chapter 3, this particular text field is interesting because it's set up to display **Dynamic Text**, meaning that the text can be accessed at runtime; in other words, when the movie is playing we can use ActionScript to add or change the text displayed within the text field. We'll soon see why this is crucial to our example. The important properties that you need to set now are:

● **Instance Name** – theStory

● **Line Type** – Multiline

● **Show border around text** – selected

Now that you've set the text field so that it's dynamic and multilined, and has the instance name theStory, test the movie (CTRL+ENTER/⌘+ENTER). In the middle of the screen, you should see this:

> This is an example of text within a text field which would be required to scroll. The text itself goes beyond the borders of the text field. Most users don't want to have to select the text in order to scroll down, so a scrollbar would be helpful.

Where did the text come from? Well, as will soon become clear, this sample text is being placed in the text field at runtime using some simple ActionScript code. Click on the text with your cursor, and then try using your up and down keys to scroll the text – not very practical, huh? That's why we want a ScrollBar!

First, let's look at the code that made adding this text possible. Close down the Flash Player window and return to the FLA in the editing environment. Select frame 1 of the actions layer and open the Actions panel by pressing F9. Now go into Expert Mode by selecting it from the menu in the top-right corner, or just hit CTRL+SHIFT+E/SHIFT+⌘+E:

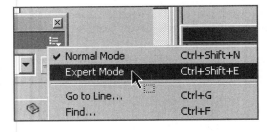

Maximize the scripting pane of the Actions panel by pressing the little 'shutter' switch, as shown here:

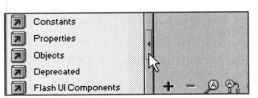

Finally, look at the actual code:

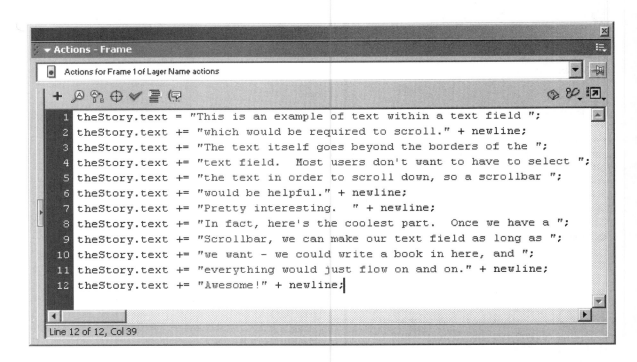

```
 1  theStory.text = "This is an example of text within a text field ";
 2  theStory.text += "which would be required to scroll." + newline;
 3  theStory.text += "The text itself goes beyond the borders of the ";
 4  theStory.text += "text field.  Most users don't want to have to select ";
 5  theStory.text += "the text in order to scroll down, so a scrollbar ";
 6  theStory.text += "would be helpful." + newline;
 7  theStory.text += "Pretty interesting.  " + newline;
 8  theStory.text += "In fact, here's the coolest part.  Once we have a ";
 9  theStory.text += "Scrollbar, we can make our text field as long as ";
10  theStory.text += "we want - we could write a book in here, and ";
11  theStory.text += "everything would just flow on and on." + newline;
12  theStory.text += "Awesome!" + newline;
```

OK, the code in this frame is telling Flash to insert the sample text (the text shown in blue in the script window) into the text field that has the instance name theStory. You might think that it seems a little jumbled, but that's because it's a multiline string of text.

Generally speaking, to assign text to any text field, we simply write something like this:

```
textFieldInstanceName.text = "Any text in quotes";
```

And, to add more text to a multiline text field:

```
textFieldInstanceName.text += "Any text added in quotes";
```

The important point to notice is that to add text, we use += instead of simply =. Also, in order to make Flash move the next line of text to a new line in the text field, we add the newline command to the end of our string. This is just like making Flash press RETURN.

So that's how you fill in the text field – fairly straightforward. What we want to do now is add a ScrollBar to the text field so that our users can scroll through all the text easily.

Close the Actions panel down, open the Components panel with CTRL+F7/⌘+F7, and locate the ScrollBar component. Click and drag the ScrollBar onto the stage and move it over the right edge of the text field:

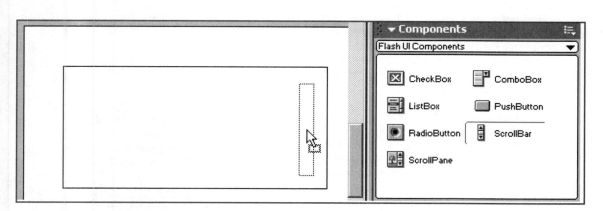

Release the mouse button, and the ScrollBar will appear and 'snap' to the chosen text field:

With the ScrollBar selected, look at the Property inspector:

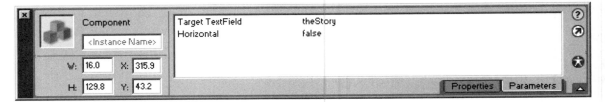

If your properties panel doesn't look like this, make sure that the Parameters tab (located in the lower right corner of the panel) is selected.

There are two parameters to modify in this component – Target TextField and Horizontal. Notice that Target TextField has automatically filled itself in with the instance name of our text field, theStory. Note that this Target TextField can be changed to any instance of a text field that we have in our movie. The other parameter, Horizontal, is a 'true' or 'false' flag that indicates whether or not Flash should display this ScrollBar horizontally – along the bottom of the text field. This is useful for wider text fields, rather than for taller ones. In our case, we'll stick with a vertical ScrollBar, so leave this setting as false.

Test this movie to see the ScrollBar in action:

Hey presto, the text field has a working ScrollBar. You can use this component anywhere on a website where you want to convey lots of dynamic information or, in a more advanced implementation, you could connect your web site to a database or external XML data feed – but that's for another book!

In fact, here's the coolest part. Once we have a Scrollbar, we can make our text field as long as we want - we could write a book in here, and everything would just flow on and on.
Awesome!

PushButton

The PushButton provides you with a very quick way to add an interactive button to a Flash movie; you can add a text label to this predefined button, and make it trigger any action that you desire when the user presses it. As you might expect, this functionality is all tied together with a little bit of ActionScript.

Let's use the PushButton component now – this exercise can be found, completed, in the source code files as `pushbutton.fla`. In a new FLA, open the Components panel once more and drag a PushButton onto the stage:

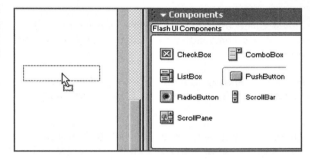

Next, with the button selected on the stage, open up the Property inspector and select the Parameters tab:

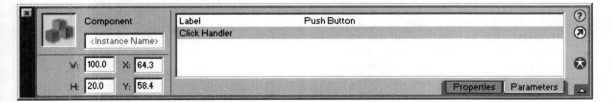

Click on the Label field, and type `My Button`. Hit ENTER and the button should look like this:

In the second field, Click Handler, type `myButtonHandler`. The parameters should now look like this:

Now for some scripting – remembering your good design practice guidelines, name this layer button, and add a new layer called actions.

Click on frame 1 of this new layer and hit F9 to open the Actions panel. In Expert Mode again, enter the ActionScript shown here:

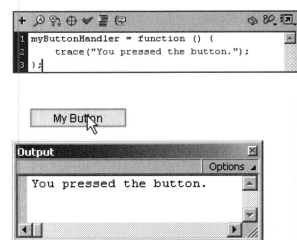

Before we learn how this works, go ahead and test the movie (CTRL+ENTER/⌘+ENTER). When you press the button, a window will pop up displaying a familiar message:

This is called the **Output window**, and it's opened by the trace command that's included in the ActionScript here:

```
myButtonHandler = function ( ) {
  trace("You pressed the button.");
};
```

Anything in between the quotes will be outputted to the Output window when that code is executed in Test Movie mode (trace has no effect in the published SWF). Its main use is to help you determine if certain code is being executed or not. By putting trace statements throughout longer sections of ActionScript, you can tell where errors may be occurring; the trace feature thus allows you to monitor ActionScript code flow and execution.

In this example we used trace to determine whether or not our button code worked – it did. We simply created a self-contained chunk of code called a **function** and attached it to a Click Handler called myButtonHandler. Functions are a rather large topic, deserving at least a whole chapter to themselves – but that's really a job for an ActionScript-specific book. However, in simple terms, a function is a segment of ActionScript code that will run whenever that named function is called from elsewhere in the movie. Anything between the two braces ({ and }) is considered to be the contents of that function. We'll use functions again later on in this chapter, but that's all we're going to say about them for now. The key point to remember from this example is that a button needs to be told the function name we want it to call and execute when it's pressed. The function name – myButtonHandler – is what we entered into the Click Handler parameter field name in the Property inspector earlier.

We use components whenever we want to add standard user interface technology to a Flash site or movie without having to spend our valuable time building them ourselves from scratch. From here, you should continue to explore components on your own, or graduate to a more advanced Flash book on UI design or application development. To make the best use of components, a deeper understanding of ActionScript is definitely required.

Taking your ActionScript further

ActionScript is a powerful language and it has some fundamental characteristics that are common to most programming languages. Before learning to apply our ActionScript to do useful automated tasks, let's look at two basic concepts common to most technologies: **variables** and **expressions**. Note that we'll be making use of the `trace` command here, so if you're not familiar with this it's worth having a glance at the example to get an understanding of what it can do.

Variables

A variable is best described as a container into which we can place anything we want. To actually put something into a variable, we'd simply make what's known as a **variable assignment**. For example:

```
a = 10;
```

Here, we're taking the value 10 and placing it in a variable called a. This means that anywhere in our following ActionScript , when we refer to the variable a, Flash will reference the value stored in the a variable – in this case, 10. If we then issue this code to Flash...

```
trace(a);
```

...Flash will display 10 in the Output window. Alternatively, we can place a 'string' of text in a variable, like this:

```
myString = "Hello world!";
```

Thus, when we run this:

```
trace(myString);
```

The Output will display Hello world! We can even perform arithmetic with variables:

```
1  a = 10;
2  b = 5;
3  c = a + b;
4  trace(c);
```

With this code, Flash will produce the following output:

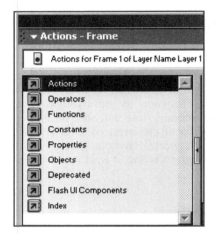

Of course, this is just the tip of the iceberg of the many things we can do with variables – a foundation ActionScript book would be the best bet for looking at variables in greater detail. For this chapter, we'll rely more on a 'learning by doing' philosophy. As we use variables, things will become much clearer.

Expressions

Expressions are what we use in ActionScript to make Flash actually perform tasks. As variables store information, expressions are used to 'do things' with those variables. The `trace` command, for example, is an expression. ActionScript has literally hundreds of expressions and commands that can be used to make Flash perform the core functionality of any interactive movie or website. We'll be covering some of these in the rest of this chapter, but for now have a browse in the library pane of the Actions panel (F9) to give yourself a taste of some of the common ActionScript expressions – the alphabetized Index is especially useful:

For example, find the entry for `trace` in the Index and double-click on it to enter it as an empty action (note that we're now back in Normal Mode of the Actions panel – choose whichever mode you're more comfortable with):

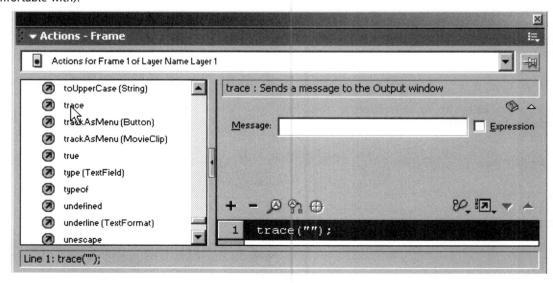

Now press the little Reference book icon in the top right of the Actions panel:

This button will bring up the Reference panel – you can also open it with CTRL+F1 (PC) SHIFT+F1 (Mac) – revealing lots of useful information about implementing the trace command:

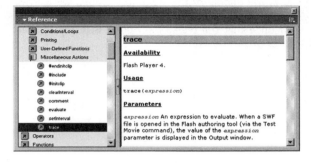

The Reference panel is an invaluable tool for both experts and novices when working with ActionScript.

Modifying movie clip properties with ActionScript

 Every movie clip object has several special variables built into it called **properties**. It's via a movie clip's properties that we're able to do the bulk of our scripted animation and interactive ActionScript programming. By separating parts of our ActionScript statements with 'dots' in the dot notation style (as discussed in Chapter 8), we can specify paths to specific objects and access the properties of any movie clip to read or modify them.

The most important properties of a movie clip are as follows:

- `_x` – The x (horizontal) position of the movie clip
- `_y` – The y (vertical) position of the movie clip
- `_xscale` – A percentage at which to scale the movie clip horizontally
- `_yscale` – A percentage at which to scale the movie clip vertically
- `_rotation` – An angle by which to rotate the movie clip
- `_alpha` – A percentage at which to set the alpha fade of the movie clip
- `_visible` – A property that's set to either `true` or `false` to determine whether or not the movie clip is visible

Let's now look at some examples of accessing these properties via ActionScript.

Position

Open up our template FLA file `mc_properties.fla` from this chapter's download package. You'll see that this movie consists of a simple filled rectangular movie clip in the middle of the stage (remember, we learned how to make movie clip symbols way back in **Chapter 4**). Notice that the registration point is in the top left corner of the `rectangle`:

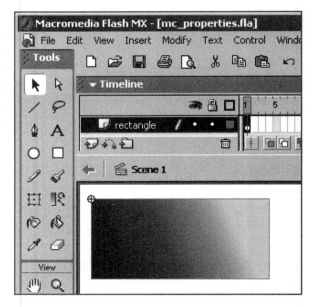

If you click on the `rectangle` and look in the Property inspector you can see that it has an instance name of `rectangle`:

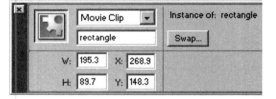

Indeed, if you look in the Library, you'll see the original movie clip symbol from which this instance came sitting there quite happily:

Notice that it's OK to have an instance that's got the same name as the original symbol. We cannot, however, have more than one instance of this movie clip named `rectangle`.

Next, create a new layer below the rectangle layer, called background, and draw a box in it that covers the full size of the stage. This is just for reference, so that when we test our movie, we can see the actual extent of the stage and ensure that our positioning code is working correctly. Lock this newest layer so that you don't end up accidentally moving the background:

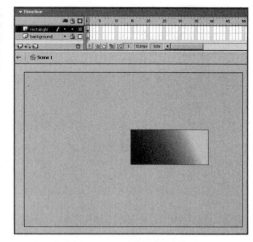

OK, let's now learn how to change the position of the movie clip using ActionScript alone–specifically, by changing the _x and _y properties of the rectangle instance. First, create another new layer called actions above all the others:

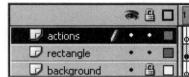

Next, click on frame 1 of the actions layer, press F9 to bring up the Actions panel, and activate Expert Mode with CTRL+SHIFT+E/SHIFT+⌘+E. Enter the following code:

```
rectangle._x = 0;
rectangle._y = 0;
```

Test the movie with CTRL+ENTER/⌘+ENTER and you should see this:

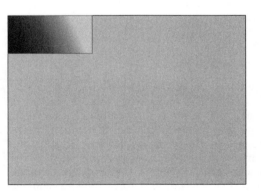

Your rectangle movie clip has moved to the upper left hand corner of the stage and aligned itself with the gray box because of the location of the registration point. This is position 0, 0 of the stage – the origin.

So how does the code work? Well, it relies on the use of the dot notation that we mentioned earlier: we're targeting the rectangle instance and addressing its _x and _y property variables specifically, so we use the syntax rectangle._x and rectangle._y. Note that as the ActionScript is attached to frame 1 of the main timeline, which means it's sitting in the root, we don't need to attach _root to the start of our code (as we sometimes do).

The screen is 550 x 400 pixels in size, so we can move the rectangle to any position within that range with ActionScript, and it will appear on screen. Try using some x, y numbers other than 0:

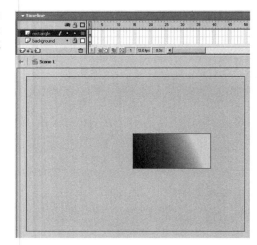

Let's now try some animated movement. Click on frame 1 of each layer, and one layer at a time, press F5 once to add a blank frame to each layer:

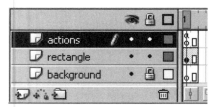

Notice that the movie is now two frames long. In order for us to repeatedly call ActionScript from the main timeline, a movie must be at least two frames long. If it's only one frame in length, then Flash will sit on that frame and not do anything.

Click on frame 1 of the actions layer again and press F9 to open the Actions panel. Change the ActionScript so that it looks like this:

```
rectangle._x++;
rectangle._y++;
```

Test the movie – the rectangle slowly moves down and to the right! What's happening here is that we're incrementing the _x and _y properties of the rectangle every time the frames loop. The ++ operator means 'increase by one'. So the script in frame 1 causes the symbol to move by one pixel in frame 2, then the timeline loops back to frame 1. The symbol is still in the same place that we moved it to in frame 2, and the frame 1 code now moves it even further as the playhead re-encounters the ActionScript that alters the x and y position properties. Because we're incrementing both the _x and the _y properties, the clip will move down and to the right in each loop through the frames. If you change the code to this:

```
rectangle._x--;
rectangle._y--;
```

...and then test the movie, the rectangle will instead move up and to the left. The `--` operator decrements the variable by 1. If we wanted to increment or decrement by a number other than 1, then we could do it like this:

```
rectangle._x+=5;
rectangle._y-=2;
```

In the previous example `_x` is increasing by 5 each frame and `_y` is decreasing by 2 each frame: `+=` means "increase by", while `-=` means "decrease by". In fact, if we try these values, the `rectangle` movie clip moves up and to the right somewhat more quickly, and at a shallow angle.

As you can see, there are a number of tricks you can do when using ActionScript to remotely change the position of the movie clips in your movies.

Scale

 Scaling is accomplished with ActionScript by modifying the `xscale` and the `yscale` properties.

Open up `mc_properties_scale.fla`, and notice that everything's the same as in our previous examples, except that the code is different. Look in the Actions panel after selecting frame 1 of the actions layer to see what the script looks like:

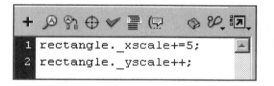

```
1 rectangle._xscale+=5;
2 rectangle._yscale++;
```

Here, we're simply increasing the `_xscale` by 5 pixels every frame, and incrementing the `_yscale` by 1 every frame. Try testing the movie – the rectangle expands with each new frame, growing horizontally 5 times faster than it does vertically:

Try running the movie with different numbers in the script. You could even try decrementing the `_xscale` or `_yscale`. When a scale is being decreased it will eventually reach 0, and if the scale goes to a negative number, then the shape will flip along that axis – neat stuff!

Rotation

Rotation of a movie clip is accomplished by modifying the rotation parameter with ActionScript. In `mc_properties.fla` (in the download package, as usual) we're modifying the rotation of the rectangle. The code attached to frame 1 is pretty simple, as usual, and looks like this:

```
rectangle._rotation++;
```

The rectangle will rotate around its registration point, which, in this case, is located in the upper left hand corner of the movie clip. Think of this as the movie clip's pivot – this is where an imaginary thumbtack is pushed through the shape. In this case, the `_rotation` property value is incrementing from 0 to 359 and, once it reaches 360, it's back to its original position at 0:

Alpha

The Alpha setting can be used to create some very cool transparency effects. We set the `_alpha` property to a number between 0 to 100, where 100 is 'completely opaque' and 0 is 'completely transparent'. Every number in between these extremes specifies a varying degree of opacity.

Look at `mc_properties.fla`. Again, it's just like all the others in basic construction, but the code is as follows:

```
rectangle._alpha--;
```

As the `_alpha` property approaches 0 the rectangle becomes invisible:

Cool!

Visibility

The `_visible` property is changed by setting it to `true` or `false`. When `_visible` is `true`, then the movie clip will be drawn by Flash, but when this property is set to `false`, the movie clip will not be drawn – it'll be completely invisible.

The ActionScript to hide the instance of the rectangle movie clip looks like this (see `mc_properties_vis.fla`):

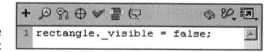

```
1 rectangle._visible = false;
```

Alternatively, you could use the following to make it visible again:

```
rectangle._visible = true;
```

The `true` and `false` keywords are special words in ActionScript known as **Boolean** values. A Boolean is a variable that has only these two states (sometimes also referred to as `on` or `off`, or `1` or `0`).

Modifying movie clip properties is perhaps one of the most commonly practiced uses of ActionScript. We use it whenever we want to create games, movies with dynamic animation, menus, characters, or anything else that we can dream up!

Mouse interaction

Flash allows us to use ActionScript to determine all the characteristics of our mouse cursor. It also allows us to turn off or on the default operating system cursor – we can replace the default cursor with a customized one of our own. Just a few lines of ActionScript is all it takes!

For starters, let's take a look at `custom_cursor.fla`. This is an example of a simple customized mouse cursor. It's called the 'molecule cursor' because the cursor becomes a spinning molecule, and it will follow the mouse around in your movie. The stage looks like this:

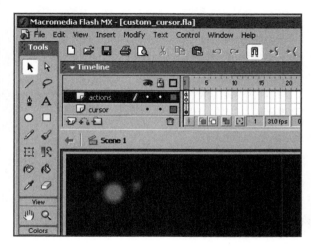

There are two layers, actions and cursor, and there's an instance of the cursor movie clip on the stage, which has an instance name of `myCursor`.

The cursor itself is simply three gradient-shaded circles. The blue circle is where the registration point of the movie clip is, and the other two smaller circles are on either side of the larger circle. This means that when the cursor rotates, the two red circles should appear to orbit the large circle:

Now, notice that on frame 1 of the actions layer that there's a small 'a'. As we've learned, this means that there is some code attached to that frame (which is on the root timeline).

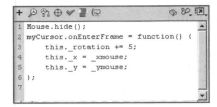

Click on this frame, and press F9 to open up the Actions window, where you'll see the following code:

```
Mouse.hide();
myCursor.onEnterFrame = function() {
    this._rotation += 5;
    this._x = _xmouse;
    this._y = _ymouse;
};
```

Before we try and understand this code, test the movie with CTRL+ENTER/⌘+ENTER. As we move the mouse cursor about, the molecule will fly around the screen:

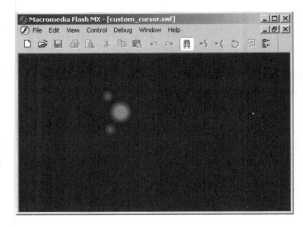

After seeing the effect in action, let's now see how the code works. Firstly, we have:

```
Mouse.hide();
```

This expression does one thing – it hides the default cursor, which is usually an arrow on most operating systems. Here's the next line of code:

```
myCursor.onEnterFrame = function() {
```

This means that any code between the braces ({ and }) is a function that will be run in every single frame (triggered by the `onEnterFrame` part), and it's attached to the `myCursor` instance of the `cursor` movie clip. Next up:

```
this._rotation += 5;
```

This means that in each frame we will be increasing the `_rotation` property of `myCursor` by 5 degrees. This will cause the cursor to rotate clockwise at a nice smooth pace – not too fast, and not too slow. We use the word `this` as a path definition in order for `myCursor` to talk to itself within its own function. If we didn't use `this`, then the code would be applied to the `_root` timeline by default, rather than `myCursor`, which is clearly not what we're after.

Then we finish the script with:

```
   this._x = _xmouse;
   this._y = _ymouse;
};
```

Here, we're setting the `_x` and `_y` properties of `myCursor` to the `_xmouse` and `_ymouse`, which are variables that are always set to the current position of the mouse cursor. By setting `myCursor`'s `_x` and `_y` position to these values, the cursor will always be following as we move the mouse around, even though the actual windows pointer is invisible. Finally, we finish the `onEnterFrame` function of `myCursor` with the closing brace.

This example demonstrates how easy it is to control and customize your mouse cursor. We've seen a fairly simple effect that can be really eye-catching, and is readily transferable to other designs.

Adding inertia to your cursor movement

In the previous example, as we moved the mouse around the molecule followed it along perfectly, no matter how fast the mouse moved. In the physical world, objects don't always move in this ideal manner – let's introduce some inertia to our molecule's movement to make it feel more lifelike.

Open up custom_cursor_inertia.fla – everything is the same as the previous example, except for the code attached to frame 1:

Try testing the movie to see what it does. Notice that as we move the mouse around the molecule seems to slide smoothly into place. We're doing a simple 'easing' equation to get the cursor into position. As before, we hide the mouse cursor and define an onEnterFrame function to run on every frame, associated with the myCursor instance. We're also rotating the molecule, as before. The inertia formula is new:

```
targx = _xmouse;
targy = _ymouse;
```

We're creating two variables, targx and targy, which stand for Target X and Target Y. The 'target' in this case is the point on the screen where we want the molecule to come to rest. It's the same location as the invisible mouse cursor, so the two variables' values are populated based on the current position of the mouse cursor derived from _xmouse and _ymouse. These properties are built into Flash, and are always available for us to use.

Next we have two more variables, curx and cury, which stand for the current x, y position:

```
curx = myx;
cury = myy;
```

We want to determine a percentage of distance (in this case, the .1 refers to 10%) between our target and our current position, and then move our movie clip by that amount. This is achieved with the following code:

```
myx += ((targx-curx)*.1);
myy += ((targy-cury)*.1);
```

```
 1  Mouse.hide();
 2  myCursor.onEnterFrame = function() {
 3      this._rotation += 5;
 4      targx = _xmouse;
 5      targy = _ymouse;
 6      curx = myx;
 7      cury = myy;
 8      myx += ((targx-curx)*.1);
 9      myy += ((targy-cury)*.1);
10      this._x = myx;
11      this._y = myy;
12  };
```

Finally, we're moving the movie clip's _x and _y coordinates to the position of myx and myy, and closing our function with the final brace:

```
    this._x = myx;
    this._y = myy;
};
```

This will have the effect of slowly moving the movie clip closer and closer to the actual mouse cursor position. If the mouse is moved, then the cursor will readjust its trajectory to head towards it. Try playing around with different values of the percentage figure (where we used the value .1, on lines 8 and 9 of the code) to create different effects.

We could use this effect in a web site with a cool pointer or cursor that is custom designed to fit the style of our website. Imagination is the only limit!

Video import

Flash MX has the ability to import several video file formats, and they can be used in our movies just like movie clips, bitmaps, or any other asset. You can view all of the different formats that Flash supports by going to **File > Import...** (CTRL+R/⌘+R) and looking in the drop-down menu of the Import window:

```
QuickTime Movie (*.mov)
Video for Windows (*.avi)
MPEG Movie (*.mpg,*.mpeg)
Digital Video (*.dv,*.dvi)
Windows Media (*.asf,*.wmv)
Macromedia Flash Video (*.flv)
```

Let's try importing some video content into a new FLA. Although there's a sample video included with the downloadable code for this chapter, sneaky.avi, you can use your own video file for this example — we're only really interested in learning the technique, after all.

Open a new FLA (CTRL+N⌘+N), and then press CTRL+R/⌘+R to bring up the Import dialog box. In the 'Files of type' dropdown, choose 'All Video Formats', and then browse to the appropriate folder where your video file is:

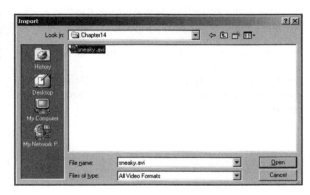

Select your video file, in our case it's sneaky.avi, and then click on the Open button. The Import Video Settings dialog box will then appear:

As usual, we have a number of import settings to contend with:

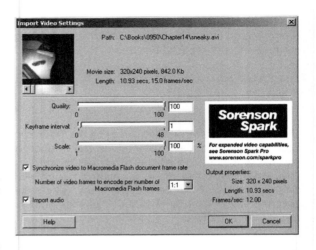

- **Quality** – Choose a quality level from 0 to 100. The higher the quality, the larger the final file size.

- **Keyframe interval** – A keyframe is a frame on which Flash stores some content, and it is crucial to animating your movies. The lower the keyframe interval, the greater the number of keyframes, and the larger the file size.

- **Scale** – Choose a scale from 0% to 100%. Use this to change the screen size of the video. Reduce this scale to make the file size smaller.

- **Synchronize video to Macromedia Flash document frame rate** – Select this to force the video to synchronize to the frame rate of the Flash movie (usually advisable).

- **Number of video frames to encode per number of Macromedia Flash frames** – This setting will cause the video to play fewer frames per Flash movie frame. The video will appear 'choppier', but not slower. It will still take the correct amount of time to complete, but it will create a strobe effect. The advantage of this, as usual, relates to file size: the fewer frames, the smaller the file size.

- **Import Audio** – Choose this option to import any audio track associated with the video file.

Press OK when you've decided your optimum settings – this generally involves a little playing around with values and testing – and the movie will be imported and encoded using the Sorensen Spark codec. Once imported, the video may not fit in the movie timeline. If this happens, then Flash will present you with a warning message and the option to expand the length of the timeline:

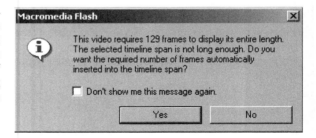

Choose Yes to change the timeline span; the video will be imported, and you'll find it sitting happily on the stage:

All you have to do is play your movie by pressing ENTER, or test it by pressing CTRL+ENTER/⌘+ENTER (note that if you want to hear the accompanying audio track then you have to use the Test Movie option).

Now that you've got your video inside Flash, take a look in the Library:

So, with the original video safely tucked away in the Library, we can drag out as many instances of it onto the stage as we want. We could create a video wall effect if we wanted – let's go crazy with videos!

Dynamic JPEGs and MP3s

 One of the nice features of Flash MX is the ability to load MP3 and JPEG files directly and dynamically with ActionScript. In the past, we would have had to convert all of our MP3 and JPEG files into SWF files first, and then load them into Flash using the loadMovie() command. Now though, we can use the loadMovie() command with JPEGs, and the Sound.loadSound action to load MP3 files 'in-flight'.

JPEGs

Open up `load_JPEG.fla` from the download package. In this sample file, we're opening a JPEG image of a cartoon cow (`cowpic.jpg`) that's stored in the same directory. You'll find both of these files in this chapter's source code download package, too. As you'll see, the FLA itself has nothing in it except for one line of ActionScript, attached to frame 1 of the main timeline. Click on that frame and press F9 to view the Actions panel. You'll see the following code:

```
_root.loadMovie("cowpic.jpg");
```

Test the movie with CTRL+ENTER/⌘+ENTER and, as if by magic, you'll see a cow appear:

What we're doing here is externally loading the JPEG into the root timeline at runtime. You could also attach this kind of action to a button or movie clip, or even to a dropdown list of items.

As the title of this section suggests, we can do exactly the same thing with a sound file.

MP3

If we want to add music to our Flash creations, all we need to do is use the `loadSound()` command to bring any MP3 music into our movies. Open up `load_MP3_1.fla`. Again, this is a fairly barren FLA file with nothing on the stage, and nothing in the Library (but there is something up my sleeve!) – select frame 1 and hit F9 to examine the code:

```
1  s = new Sound();
2  s.loadSound("jazz.mp3", false);
3  s.start(0, 2);
4
```

What we're doing is creating a new Sound object, imaginatively called s. In Flash, a Sound object acts as a 'container' for a sound. We can manipulate the object with ActionScript code. Next, we're loading the file `jazz.mp3` (from the same folder as this FLA) into that sound object.

It's important to note that the `loadSound()` expression requires two pieces of information:

- **The filename** – In this case, our sound file is called `jazz.mp3`.

- **Streaming:** `true` or `false` – If we specify `true`, then Flash will begin playing the sound immediately, even before it has completed loading (this is known as streaming the sound). If we say `false`, as we do in this example, Flash will wait for the sound to fully load up, and then we must tell it to start playing with the `start()` command.

The `start()` command also requires two parameters:

```
start(secondsOffset, loops)
```

- **secondsOffset** – How many seconds into the sound to begin playing. We could use this if we wanted to skip the first few seconds of the sound file.

- **loops** – Use this value to tell Flash how many times to play the sound file through. It will attempt to loop seamlessly, but sometimes MP3 files don't allow for a smooth loop, and you might hear a slight pause.

Test the movie, and you'll hear the jazz tune play through twice, and then stop.

The streamed version of this example can be found in `load_MP3_2.fla`. The only difference here is that the streaming flag is set to true (therefore we don't need the `start()` command). The actions on frame 1 look like this:

```
1 s = new Sound();
2 s.loadSound("jazz.mp3", true);
3
```

When you test this movie, the sound will begin playing and will only play through once. This is designed for longer songs, when you might want to stream the entire song as a backing track to your web site's intro page, and then stop.

Summary

In this chapter, we've explored the following techniques:

- Simple **components**: using the **Scrollbar** and the **PushButton**

- Simple scripting with **variables** and **expressions**

- Modifying the **properties** of movie clips with ActionScript

- Basic **mouse interactions**: drag and inertia

- **Video** import

- **Dynamically loading images and sound**

Armed with this introductory knowledge of ActionScript, and the associated tips and tricks that you've learned, you can start to explore the wonders of designing with ActionScript. Indeed, with scripting you can truly take your Flash movies to the next level, building them into complete applications, games, tools, websites, galleries, or anything else you can think of! It's over to you...

エスプレス

Index

The index is arranged hierarchically, in alphabetical order, with symbols preceding the letter A. Many second-level entries also occur as first-level entries. This is to ensure that users will find the information they require however they choose to search for it.

Notes

Notes

Notes

D E S I G N E R   T O   D E S I G N E R™

friends of ED writes books for you. Any suggestions, or ideas about how you want information given in your ideal book will be studied by our team.

Your comments are valued by friends of ED.

For technical support please contact support@friendsofed.com.

Freephone in USA: 800.873.9769
Fax: 312.893.8001

UK contact
Tel: 0121.258.8858
Fax: 0121.258.8868

Registration Code: | 09506C4M34B85Z01

Macromedia Flash MX Express – Registration Card

Name ....

Address ....

City ....State/Region ....

Country ....Postcode/Zip ....

E-mail ....

Profession: design student ☐ freelance designer ☐
part of an agency ☐ inhouse designer ☐
other (please specify) ....

Age: Under 20 ☐ 20-25 ☐ 25-30 ☐ 30-40 ☐ over 40 ☐

Do you use: mac ☐ pc ☐ both ☐

How did you hear about this book?.....................................

Book review (name)..

Advertisement (name) ....

Recommendation ....

Catalog ....

Other ....

Where did you buy this book? ....

Bookstore (name) ....City..........................

Computer Store (name)..

Mail Order...

Other..

How did you rate the overall content of this book?

Excellent ☐ Good ☐
Average ☐ Poor ☐

What applications/technologies do you intend to learn in the near future?...

....

What did you find most useful about this book? ....

....

What did you find the least useful about this book? ....

....

Please add any additional comments ....

....

What other subjects will you buy a computer book on soon?

....

....

What is the best computer book you have used this year?

....

....

Note: This information will only be used to keep you updated about new friends of ED titles and will not be used for any other purpose or passed to any other third party.

friendsof

D E S I G N E R   T O   D E S I G N E R™

NB. If you post the bounce back card below in the UK, please send it to:

friends of ED Ltd.,
30 Lincoln Road,
Olton,
Birmingham.
B27 6PA